BEYOND MY EXPECTATION

A Personal Chronicle

by GUY LYLE

The Scarecrow Press, Inc.
Metuchen, N.J., & London
1981

Library of Congress Cataloging in Publication Data

Lyle, Guy Redvers, 1907-
    Beyond my expectation.

    1. Lyle, Guy Redvers, 1907-   . 2. Librarians--
United States--Biography. 3. Librarians--Canada--
Biography. I. Title.
Z720.L94A32   020'.92'4 [B]   81-5071
ISBN 0-8108-1426-9   AACR2

Dedicated to my wife,
Margaret White Lyle,
and to our children and grandchildren

ACKNOWLEDGMENTS

I wish to acknowledge and thank the following for their kindness and assistance in the preparation of this book:

The Office of the Saskatchewan Archives (Saskatoon and Regina) for assistance in my studies of the Barr Colony over the years, including copies of several photographs reprinted herein.

Mr. V. Richards, Director of the Edmonton Public Library, for information about the Strathcona Public Library branch during the period covered by this book.

Ms. Gertrude C. Pomahac, Assistant Archivist, and the Office of the Archivist, University of Alberta, and its Photographic Department, for much helpful information and for copies of the photographs pertaining to the University contained in this book.

The Lauren Rogers Library and Museum, Laurel, Mississippi, for biographical data about Walter Watkins.

Bronson Y. Holsclaw and William F. Young of the Photographic Department of Emory University for photographs of the Woodruff Library and Lippincott award and for generous assistance freely given.

Mrs. Blythe Morley Brennan for kind permission to publish the letters of Christopher Morley to the author, contained herein.

Mrs. Ruth Liddle for permission to reprint letters by Albert Liddle to the author.

Mrs. Rita Healey for permission to quote from the late George Healey's address at the dedication of the Woodruff Library, Emory University.

Nina D. Myatt, Curator, Antiochiana, Olive Kettering Library, Antioch College, for permission to publish the photograph of the Horace Mann Library.

Jeann Greenway for typing the manuscript.

Ruth Walling for help in reading portions of the manuscript and proofreading as well as for many useful suggestions.

And finally to Kevin Guinagh for encouragement and comment and for a good part of the excitement in my life.

G. R. L.

CONTENTS

BEYOND MY EXPECTATION

"To recreate the past is always, in some
measure, to invent it."--Francis King

1: PROLOGUE: HOW IT ALL BEGAN

On Sunday, April 12, 1903, the SS "Lake Manitoba," a converted Boer War troop ship now bringing some two thousand
men, women, and children from the British Isles to Canada,
docked at St. John, New Brunswick, with one of the heaviest
loads ever seen on a vessel of its size. The far-famed "all-
British" colony, sired by an Anglican clergyman, the Rev.
Isaac M. Barr, was on its way to the Canadian northwest,
motivated by the desire for adventure, the pursuit of wealth,
and a hundred and sixty acres of free homesteading land. The
passengers had been through quite a battering on the voyage
over and were thankful to be safe on land once again. Life
belts were noticeably scarce on the "Lake Manitoba", as were
lifeboats and rafts. The ship was licensed to carry nine hundred passengers; it lay so low in the water at the time of em-
barkation that it was a miracle it did not swamp in the heavy
winter seas. Little thought had been given to either safety
or feeding the colonists properly during the voyage, perhaps
because, as one of their number slyly noted, there were two
clergymen aboard and it was expected that everyone would be
taken care of should Fate send the boat to the bottom of the
ocean. A few fortunate people with sufficient means secured
cabin space on the ship; they were described by a contemporary newspaper as "saloon" passengers. Among them were
two persons who later were to meet and marry and give birth
to two sons, my brother, Ken, and I.

My mother was twenty-six years old when she stepped
ashore at St. John, and she was accompanied by her first
husband, Drewry Nicholas Lynch, and their three children--
Molly, age five; Cecil, four; and Pat, three. Her name was

3

Marie Dolores Berta Lynch, and that fact is almost all I know of her family background. I was not nourished in my youth on the details of family ancestry. It was considered unmannerly to talk of one's self or family; no doubt part of the social hypocrisy of the day. I did learn later in life that my mother's parents were Frederick Miller and Marie Mayor, perhaps of German origin. She and her sister, Isa, received an excellent education, were fluent in French and German, and regularly attended concerts and plays in London. She was an accomplished pianist and, incredible as it may seem, brought her piano from England to the Barr colony site.

It was the custom in those days, I believe, to bestow some kind of nobility upon one's heritage, and perhaps because of this I harbored the impression that Mother's first husband, Drewry Nicholas Lynch, was a prosperous trader from the West Indies. I imagined him as exchanging grain and lumber for rum and molasses, but this of course was a childhood fancy. The British Colony venture had dire consequences for him. What a splendid prospect it must have seemed to him at first! A new land, a hundred and sixty acres of free land for raising food and wheat for making a fortune! After five months of slogging it out on a barren quarter section he could only report, "No wood, no suitable grass for cattle, no water except alkali water." With winter fast approaching he moved his family from their tent on the homestead to a log cabin in town. Bad luck pursued him. He encountered every conceivable hardship, and his health began to fail. A colonist who befriended the family noted in his diary, "Lynch going East for winter ... offers use of his cows and calves and oxen for us keeping them and building a stable." On November 30, six months after staking his claim at the Barr reservation, he moved his family to eastern Canada, where he died shortly thereafter. Marie Dolores Berta Lynch, too proud to return home and to dependence upon her family, brought the children back to the colony site to reestablish her title to the land. It was truly a heroic effort, the more so as she, like many of her friends among the Barr colonists, had absolutely no experience of fending for themselves under harsh, primitive conditions.

I often wonder how, in such circumstances, my father and mother met, and how he, a young, adventurous Boer War veteran, ever decided to take on the responsibility of marrying a widow, older and far better educated than himself, with three small children to raise and support. I think it must

4

have been a sort of pick-up at one of the socials in the log rectory-church. Mother was an inveterate church goer, and Father, whom I thought of as being political rather than religious minded, was reputed to have thought seriously of going into the Church as a young man. Parenthetically I might add that he opted for the army and at the end of the Boer War decided to seek his fortune in some faraway place like Canada, no doubt what his family had always wanted. Whatever the occasion of my parents meeting one another, I am sure that Mother was attracted by his service record and energetic temperament; he, perhaps, by her relative affluence (she received a small income from a source unknown to me), her courage, and her determination. Though not a beauty in any cover-girl sense, she possessed a kind of innocent charm, derived from the expression in her eyes. Even in her old age, when she had grown severe and was given to fault-finding, she still retained the look in her eyes that would make me or any man proud to have been one of her sons. However they happened to meet, a single-line entry in St. John's Church records for 1905 confirms their marriage vows. I have no photograph of the wedding ceremony, but I can see a young man of military bearing, smiling and looking appropriately uplifted, and Mother, perhaps because of the three young children trailing by her side, seemingly happy but retaining a slight reservation in the corner of her eye.

With this brief introduction I am about ready to begin my recollections of boyhood and youth, but before doing so I must go back to explain and follow the historic event that eventually brought my mother and father together and me into the world.

2: THE BARR COLONY

During the first decade of this century's westward expansion across the Canadian prairie no episode involving large numbers of people of one nationality and faith drew more attention or stirred more controversy than the "all-British" migration to the Northwest Territories in the spring of 1903. As already mentioned, my parents-to-be were members of this party. The self-styled founder and director of this scheme was the Rev. Isaac Montgomery Barr, who emerged at the age of fifty-three from a rather unspectacular clerical career in Canada and the United States to envisage a British colony enjoying its own land and bringing with it the cultural heritage of the mother country. He foresaw churches, schools, cooperative enterprises, libraries, railway transportation, prosperous farming, homes, and all the democratic possibilities of a new society.

Conditions in England after the Boer War were depressed. There was little hope of getting on in the world or even of finding a job. Early in February 1903 Harold Marfleet wrote to his sweetheart, Alice Warren, from St. Albans, Hertfordshire, England, where he was employed as a construction laborer at the Napsbury Asylum:

> Dear Alice:
> Just a line to let you know I am getting on allright hoping you are the same. I started on this job this week but it is not much of a job. You will be surprised to hear that me and Ted is going to Canada in seven weeks time to see if we can better ourselves for I don't think we can better ourselves

6

in England much as things are so bad now and so
many out of work. I shall be home in a week's
time and I will tell you all about it before I go.
Excuse more this time with best wishes to all.

> I Remain
> Your loving sweetheart
> Harry

Under such conditions as Harry describes what could people
lose from Barr's persuasive proposition? In any event, in
spite of the failure of many of his cooperative schemes Barr
showed a remarkable facility for persuading British middle-
class people of the incredible potentialities of homesteading
in the Canadian northwest. If on occasion his enthusiasm
was excessive, his bungling management deplorable, in the
larger sense the impact of his vision was both stupendous and
glorious. From a modest proposal he developed "the greatest emigration from England since the departure of William
Penn" into a major colonization enterprise that eventually
made a significant contribution to the Canadian northwest. He
was ably assisted in this venture by another clergyman, the
Rev. George Exton Lloyd, who was born in England but had
considerable experience in Canada and who elected at Barr's
invitation to serve as chaplain to the colonists. Through his
position as Organizing Secretary of the Colonial and Continental Church Society he spread the gospel of Canada-for-the-
British and the importance of Britishers taking up free land
in Canada before all the good stuff was lost to foreigners and
Americans from across the border. In a widely reprinted
letter, first appearing in the London "Times," September 20,
1903, he wrote:

> There is plenty of the choicest land to be had for
> next to nothing: Five years hence it may be in the
> hands of the aliens. Now is the time if English
> people are going at all.

My mother even went so far as to question Barr's
claim to be the leader of the colony. In the margin of one
of her books I find this comment:

> Barr did not start or even lead the colony. Ex
> Lloyd established an office in Fenchurch St., Lon-
> don, for exactly the purpose of keeping Canada Brit-
> ish. Barr heard of it, joined Lloyd, collected the
> money and made off.

7

This view was held by most of the colonists in the early years of the enterprise. Even as late as 1963 an article about Barr appeared in a leading Canadian magazine entitled "The Clerical Con Man of the West." My mother's accusations against Barr, however, failed to give him credit for the conception of the plan for emigration, and there is no substantial evidence that Barr was dishonest. But there is no question that the Rev. Lloyd, for whom the main town in the colony was later named, was responsible in large part for its early leadership and survival after the colonists reached their destination.

The Barr colonists made up a diverse mixture. There were shopkeepers from London, farriers from Woolwich, hatmakers from Bermondsey, and tradespeople from Manchester and Sheffield. There were professional men and clerks, families with comfortable fortunes and others with less than fifty dollars when they arrived in Canada, ex-soldiers and sportsmen who, like the old Virginians, knew much about guns, horses, and dogs, but very little about farming. There were bankers, architects, butchers, carpenters, bookbinders, jewelers, printers, teachers, ironfounders, marblemasons, blacksmiths, hairdressers, and many other types. There was a prevalent myth in England that farming could be learned by anyone, especially by single young men whose families did not know what to do with them. But even if this were true, few of the colonists were well adapted to the harsh life of the pioneer in a region remote from organized life of any kind. The wonder is that they survived at all. In their favor they possessed a common British background and a wide diversity of skills and talent. The "all-British" idea so widely trumpeted by their leaders was not an unmixed blessing. The colonists would have done much better in the beginning if they had not been so green and all green together without experienced farmers to advise them about the conditions and requirements of prairie life. Instead they had to learn the hard way, mostly by trial and error.

St. John was their disembarkation port after an eleven-day ocean crossing that some of the settlers described as "serene" and others as "sordid." One housewife and her family were unable to secure cabin space and were assigned bunks in booths leading off the dining room. Here is what she had to say about their quarters:

There were 28 people sleeping in our quarters,

men, women, and children. Seven upper and seven
lower berths on either side of a narrow passageway.
No sanitary accommodations whatsoever, and no privacy, so we had to sleep in our clothes.

The complaints about sanitary conditions, food, drink, and
lack of privacy were widespread. The men in the hold, a
space reserved for the horses and mules when the "Lake Manitoba" was a troop ship, suffered the most. They were confined in the bow for sleeping and eating and were constantly
seasick from the up-and-down movement of the ship. A di-
arist's entry for April 3, 1903, reads:

> When dinner time came around today I felt as though
> I could eat something so I went down into our hole
> and captured some corned beef & potato and took it
> up & eat it on deck. I simply could not stand our
> hold with its smell of soap, sawdust, the foot & half
> of bilgewater at the bottom that has been washing
> too & fro with a swish all night.

After what must have been a grueling sea voyage for
many the colonists landed at St. John on Easter Sunday, April
12, 1903. Church services in St. John were just ending, the
bells were ringing, and many of the local townspeople came
by to see the colonial party about which they had heard and
read a great deal:

> Hundreds of people were waiting outside the Govern-
> ment sheds to see us pass. St. John is a very
> cosmopolitan city, for many races were represented
> in the concourse of people--Canadians, Americans,
> Indians, negroes, Jews, half-castes, and many Chi-
> nese, but everybody was well-dressed, and seemed
> prosperous, in fact quite equal to the middle class-
> es in England. The Chinamen wore their pigtails
> hanging down, some inside their coats, others wear-
> ing them outside.

Owing to the enormous amount of luggage the disembarkation was slow business, and the scene in the government
freight shed was chaotic. It was practically impossible to
move around amongst the piles of luggage where the passengers were searching for their belongings. The confusion in
handling the baggage delayed the departure of the colonists by
train for the next stage of their journey, but it gave some of

them an opportunity to look about the town and to purchase a supply of food for the twenty-four-hundred-mile trip ahead of them. When the trains finally got under way, the colonists were dismayed to find that in many respects their traveling conditions were not much better than they were on board ship. There were four trains, and each hauled ten or more coaches; each coach held sixty passengers, with accommodations for heating and cooking on one small stove at the end of each car. One settler complained that these utilities were of very little use because they were usually surrounded by a crowd of fighting women, each trying to boil water or cook something for the children. Another spoke bluntly of the limited services: "No sleeping accommodations, and as to lavatory arrangements, they were simply a disgrace to civilization, and in this misery we were boxed up to spend a week." It was not all tedium for the youngsters or for those without family responsibility. When the train stopped for firewood, they would seize the opportunity to rush out and stretch their legs. At every station of any size along the route passengers would get off to buy something to eat and to replenish their food supplies. Ex-soldiers routinely fired their revolvers from the open windows of the train en route at gophers and rabbits, leading one colonist to observe, "One might have thought we were going to invade Canada instead of entering it peacefully."

Saskatoon--an Indian name for a berry growing on bushes along streams and the river running through the town--was as far west as the railway line ran for the colonists. Some say the arrival of the Barr colonists was the commercial beginning of Saskatoon, and there is much evidence to support the view, but from the standpoint of the colonists it was still two hundred miles short of their reservation. When the first of the four trains carrying the colonists pulled in on the morning of April 17, there was not much to look at:

> Saskatoon is merely a collection of stores and hotels, many partly built--some 50 or 60 altogether--mostly new since last fall when the town consisted of 6 or 7 houses. The storekeepers--mostly quite recently arrived--were doing a roaring trade as fast as they could unpack their goods.

The Rev. George Exton Lloyd, a firm believer in total abstinence, viewed with suspicion the only two hotels in the town: "There were two drinking places, one at each end of this line of stores, and as they provided some scanty sort of accommodation, they were called hotels."

Camped out in tents on the edge of town, the colonists needed everything by way of transportation and provisions for the two-hundred-mile trek by wagon to the settlement reservation. The weather was severe, and supplies rose to famine prices. One reporter described the camp as a "white canvas city," an effect strengthened by snow on the ground and huge chunks of ice breaking up on the Saskatchewan River. Pictures show the "white canvas city" resembling the huge army camps of World War I. Reality was lent to this impression by the presence of quite a number of khaki-clad ex-soldiers whose experiences in the South African veldt were not destined to be their last in empire building. They had many ingenious devices for bettering the colonists' condition. They built sod-made fireplaces, and in this and other ways their actions were soon imitated all over the camp. Water was obtained by cutting out lumps of ice, three feet thick, from the Saskatchewan River running through the town. Sanitary arrangements were few and far between. For the women, children, and many older people who were obliged to spend weeks at the campsite getting ready for the trek ahead, the experience was a nightmare. Few if any had been exposed to extreme cold and the primitive conditions of the encampment. Barr's plan for transport had collapsed--a system to convey the colonists and their belongings to the reservation, a cooperative store to supply all the necessities at a fair price, which was disorganized at Saskatoon and caved in completely at the reservation site, and jobs for those who did not have enough money to begin homesteading immediately upon arrival.

There is something tragic as well as ennobling about pioneering: men so ignorant of the handling of their horses and oxen that they drove them to their deaths, women who had never in their lives been transported in anything more rugged than a trolley car having to ride high on the top of baggage in a covered wagon, and young children crying and suffering from the cold. The Barr colony reservation lay some two hundred miles westward and could only be reached by following a meandering trail stretching far to the horizon, experiencing daily the fickle climate of a Saskatchewan spring, crossing countless sloughs with treacherous alkali mud-bottoms, undertaking the drudgery of loading and reloading heavy farm implements and baggage whenever a wagon became stuck in a slough, and sometimes having to fight prairie fires to save themselves and their belongings from being wiped out. A colonist who came through the hard way and yet in good spirits wrote home to his father in London:

We have had a rather rough journey all through,
especially while trekking.... I got a covered Waggon & a yoke of oxen, a plough and all necessary
goods & started off on our weary tramp of 200
miles. The road was just a worn track winding
across the prairie, over hill and dale and through
deep ravines and running streams, through bogs
and sloughs, and mirey places, in which at times
our waggon was stuck up to the axles. The road
just after the snow and ice had gone was awful, and
we had some of the most lively experiences....
The hills over which we had to go were very bad
also, in places. One I shall never forget. We had
to chain both back wheels & whilst I led the oxen,
there was a man on each side of the waggon with
a long pole sprogging the front wheels.... Harold
and I walked every step of the 200 miles, which
took us three weeks to do. We had to shelter 4
days through a heavy snow storm and another 3
days because of rain. Of course when I say shelter I mean just putting up our tents and stopping on
the prairie.

There were moments of excitement and delight that brought
relief. There was the spring greeting of the beautiful flute-
like song of the western meadowlark. The air was cool and
invigorating during the day. In the Indian reservations through
which they passed the settlers saw for the first time things
they knew only through pictures before--patched wigwams made
from the skins of animals, their tops colored brown from the
smoke of open fires in the center of the tents. And for those
who brought firearms there was the excitement of bagging a
prairie chicken, a mallard, or a rabbit to replenish their food
supply.

On the last lap of the journey to the reservation site--
known in the diaries as Camp Headquarters--there was the
additional hazard of prairie fires. Travelworn, their clothes
wet through from heavy thunder showers, and without com-
forts of any kind, the settlers were by this time weary and
depressed. The collapse of Barr's plans, suspicion regarding what they might find when they got to the site, and the
never-ending drudgery of the trek had subdued their sense of
adventure. Then to top it all came the excitement and real
danger of the prairie fires. One young man, whose turn it
was to cook while his companions stretched out for a short

12

nap under the trees, had just gotten together a pile of firewood and was beginning to mix his bread dough when he became aware of the smell and density of an approaching fire:

> Meanwhile the smoke from the prairie fire gradually
> became more dense, when suddenly I became con-
> scious of a loud crackling sound not far away. Off
> I went in the direction of the noise, but had barely
> got a hundred yards when I was obliged to turn back
> on account of the terrific heat and blinding smoke.
> Quickly rousing my slumbering companions, we de-
> cided to find a way if we could to escape the peril,
> and all went off in different directions. Shouts of
> "Fire here!" "Fire here!" came from all points
> and we were hemmed in a circle of fire caused by
> changing wind. Hurriedly holding a consultation we
> decided to do the only thing possible to avoid being
> burnt, and that was to "back fire" the woods, that
> is, fire it on our side with the wind.... As soon
> as this was burnt we drew our teams and waggons
> on to the newly-cleared patch, and looking saw the
> coming fire about fifteen yards in our rear.

Others were less fortunate and lost all their supplies and
transportation. Appalled by the barren desolation of the
burned-over areas through which his party was trekking,
another colonist observed that "the whole country for miles
round was burnt off and not a tree or blade of grass to be
seen, just a black smouldering turf left."

Camp Headquarters turned out to be a point on the
prairie located about a mile north of the present town of
Lloydminster, situated on the fourth meridian, which today
marks the boundary between Alberta and Saskatchewan. When
the settlers reached Camp Headquarters, the region was known
as the Northwest Territories, and the first mail to reach them
was addressed to "The Britannia Colony, Northwest Territories." In the afternoon of early May 1903 the Lynch family
and the party that they had joined up with on the trail got
their first view of Camp Headquarters stretching far in the
distance on a flat tableland, the tents of earlier arrivals
showing prominently against a background of blackened, burned-
over prairie. With a trace of Swiftian irony one of them remarked: "Now having the sky above us, the Rocky Mountains
not many hundred miles off, and a good big slough full of
frogs close by to drink out of, everything is at last all right."

Through their long and arduous journey to the Camp Headquarters the colonists had discovered something of the immense distances in Canada, but now for the first time they confronted realistically their virtual isolation from established towns and farms from which they could get advice and help. Food was scarce, and supplies for the cooperative store, which had been promised, had not yet arrived. The nearest town of any size was Edmonton, two hundred miles west. Battleford, through which the colonists had just passed, was approximately a hundred and fifty miles east, and the nearest railway connection was at least two hundred miles away.

There were other problems. The settlers were anxious to locate their quarter-sections of homesteading land immediately, to begin putting up shelters, and to plant gardens and crops in time for harvesting before the early winter weather set in. The failure of Barr's transport system and the partial collapse of the cooperative stores in Saskatoon had cost them dearly in money and time. Now, having reached what was euphemistically dubbed "the promised land," they found that in many instances the old survey marks for identifying their sections had been obliterated by fire, making it difficult if not impossible to locate their sections. The land guides and surveyors promised by the Canadian government were slow in coming, and there was also some confusion about homestead entries. This problem evolved around the question as to whether Barr had the sole authority to assign the homesteads or whether the colonists had the right to locate where they pleased within the land and regulations prescribed for the reservation. Some of the settlers accepted their allocations from Barr; others, after looking around for themselves, refused the section allocated to them and demanded one of their own choice. These and other matters brought to a head a growing storm of criticism against Barr, whom the colonists blamed for all their misfortunes since leaving England. The suspicion grew that he was dishonest; certainly he was autocratic. Threats were allegedly made against his life, and the headquarters camp became the scene of angry demonstrations. Following the return of Barr to Battleford from the headquarters camp around the middle of May the colonists called a meeting to discuss what might be done to save the colony from collapsing completely. It was obvious that a majority of those present had lost faith in Barr's leadership, and by unanimous resolution they voted to oust him and to elect the Rev. George Exton Lloyd as the new leader of the colony. Lloyd accepted only after they agreed to elect a committee of twelve of their number to serve with him. The Battleford resolution, as it was called, was then brought to and adopted at gatherings of colonists along the trail and at Camp Headquarters. The Rev. Isaac M. Barr was obliged to accept the terms of the new leadership and departed the colony for good early in June, drawing from the Saskatoon "Phenix" the comment that the settlers could now sing with heart and voice, "Britons never will be slaves."

After the new leadership took over the affairs of the colony improved. Battleford's "Saskatchewan Herald," previously quite critical of the colony's progress, reported:

> Affairs in the New British Colony are now making forward in a very satisfactory way. A marked change had come over the whole of the 20 townships which now constitute "The Colony." Where a few days ago one would drive for miles without seeing a sign of man only to find a large body of very undecided people camped at headquarters, now but few are to be seen around the headquarters' stores-- tents, waggons, and breakings showing all over the plains. A post office has been established in the Store Tent and mail is being received.... Altogether the outlook is very promising and the whole colony is settling right down to business.

Although it may have been premature to suggest that everything was sunshine, the colony was in every way becoming a more habitable and homelike region. It involved great personal hardship and courage, and this is poignantly portrayed in one settler's account of the first Dominion Day's celebration:

> July, 1903. Wed. 1st. Dominion Day. Finished clearing off turf for house in the morning--then changed into flannels & went into Camp, where the first social function of the Colony was held, consisting of sports--horse and foot races and a football match in afternoon and concert in evening. There was quite a crowd of people there looking quite smart & gay in flannels & summer dresses-- a pleasant change. Renewed one or two boat acquaintanceships. Got a bunch of letters. An air of importance was given to the scene by the pres-

15

ence of our detachment of RNW mounted police--an inspector and two constables--who kept the course in a very businesslike manner--hustling the crowd about with their horses as if we were packed in the Strand instead of a handful of people in the middle of thousands of acres of almost uninhabited land. A heavy storm came in the afternoon for $\frac{1}{2}$ an hour and I didn't stay for the concert but returned to my solitary supper and bed.

Credit for progress belonged not alone to the inspiration of new leadership--the Rev. George Exton Lloyd's reputation has weathered well--but also to the grit and determination of the settlers themselves and to the increasing concern and volume of help provided by the Canadian government. News of the growing stability of the colony spread and an influx of Canadian and American business and farming interests had much to do with its future success. In addition to the post office and police detachment mentioned in the "Herald" article the colonists soon had telegraph connections with the outside world, lumber was floated down the Saskatchewan River from Edmonton for building purposes, and supplies were "freighted" in from Battleford and Saskatoon by teams of horses or oxen. A large merchandising store was near enough completed by the first Christmas to be used for Christmas and New Year festivities by the entire community, a log rectory doubling as church and living quarters for the Lloyd family was erected, and by the following year the colonists were able to bring in their own produce from farming to Camp Headquarters to trade for their everyday needs. Within a year and a half after the colonists first arrived the village of Lloydminster was incorporated on land donated by the Canadian government as a center for the farming and trading interests of the colony. Although the village was named in honor of the Rev. George Exton Lloyd, the members of the "all-British" colony continued to refer to themselves as Barr colonists and have done so to this day.

3: WHEN I COME UPON THE SCENE

I was born on October 30, 1907, in the town of Lloydminster,
Saskatchewan, four years after my parents arrived as Barr
colonists; the year in which Elinor Glyn wrote the novel
"Three Weeks," whose commercial success deserves to rank
it as the mother of sex novels; and seven years before a cat-
astrophic world war was to blast Edwardian ease beyond recognition. These events must have had some effect in shaping
my future life and character. As the novelist Graham Greene
once adroitly put it, "Everything one was to become must
have been there, for better or worse." I've been away from
my birthplace for over half a century, but I've never gotten
over it. I know that my interest in books and sex, and my
love of the outdoors, and my fears, such as forked lightning,
being late for an appointment, and midnight burglars, all
stem from those days.

        For reasons that I am unable to explain I fell into er-
ror at an early age regarding my birthdate and the origin of
my middle name. On numerous occasions I have put into
print that my birthday fell on October 31, and to this day my
wife and children still give me presents on Halloween. I discovered the mistake at the outset of World War II, when at-
tempting to secure a commission from Washington. The officer with whom I corresponded requested a birth certificate.
When I wrote my mother about this, she couldn't understand
why the United States government wanted a copy of my birth
certificate. She seemed to regard the request as an invasion
of privacy. She may have been stalling, of course, as might
be expected of a mother who had already lost her oldest son
in World War I. Finally, after weeks of writing back and

forth, I received a transcript of the birth certificate from the Department of Health in Regina. I was startled to learn that I was one day older than I thought I was. I was born on October 30 and not October 31. Unfortunately the effort and paperwork involved in getting the transcript turned out to be wasted. Washington decided that it could do without me. All that work and all my friends' recommendations for nothing. Why fight to fight? Well, for one thing, I thought at the time that the Draft Board was probably breathing down my neck, and I had a family to support. But I proved to be wrong about this also. I guess the Draft Board figured that with three children I'd make a better father than a private, especially since I got along with my wife. After that I gave up the struggle and reconciled myself to the humbler role of paying for the war.

Now about my middle name, Redvers, or rather how I came to be given this rather unusual name. I had always been led to believe that I inherited the name from a "man of distinction," a Boer War hero named General Redvers. This gave me such an aristocratic thrill that I stuck with it during my youth and was not loath to explain its origin if called upon to do so--erroneously, as it turned out. Later on in life I began to have ambivalent feelings about the Boer War, and for this reason and for sanity's sake I confined my signature to the initial "R," period. When I discovered the error in the date of my birth, I thought it high time to check on the authenticity of General Redvers, and so I consulted a half-dozen histories of the Boer War, without finding a trace of a Redvers--not even a colonel, a major, or a captain. And then quite by accident, while running aimlessly through the pages of the "Columbia Encyclopedia," I happened on the name Sir Redvers Henry Buller. The name rang a bell. I have gone back as far as I can, and my early memory tells me that this name was frequently mentioned in our house and that this is the man for whom I am named. He had an extensive military career, in China and in campaigns against the Kafirs, the Zulus, the Mahdists, and was one of the most maligned British commanders in the Boer War. Recent research has upgraded him, revealing him as a good general who learned from his defeats. I guess that I should have more respect for my middle name than an initial. But I don't. At least I'm getting somewhere in straightening out the facts of my life.

Before flying backward into further instances of personal and family memory I should like to say a word about the town where I was born. It began starkly but it grew vigorously. It was incorporated as a village under the provisions of an ordinance of the Canadian Northwest Territories in 1903, and, as already noted, it was named Lloydminster in honor of its Anglican minister, the Rev. George Exton Lloyd. A year later with pride and satisfaction the Rev. Lloyd wrote home to his church sponsor in London: "Thank God, here we had God's building first [the famous log rectory-church hauled down from the north and erected by Indians] and so far no drinking place." But unbeknown to him liquor was flowing from somewhere. At its March 11, 1904, meeting the village council fired its Notary Public for "acts of drunkenness and violation of social usage as between a married man and single woman."

In time Lloydminster grew up to become an incorporated town--the year I was born. When the two provinces of Saskatchewan and Alberta were carved out of the Northwest Territories in 1905, the boundary split the town into two, with the main street dividing the Saskatchewan half from the Alberta half. This proved to be a serious municipal drawback for many years. As in Noah's ark, there were two of everything--two separate municipalities, two governing councils, two schools, two fire brigades, and two of every other kind of municipal function and service. Not everything was a disadvantage, according to a local wag. Remember that main street ran down the center of town and divided the two provinces. "Rarely if ever," he remarked, "were both provinces under the pall of prohibition at the same time."

In the second year of the town a printing press arrived by scow down the river from Edmonton, and the "Lloydminster Times" made its maiden appearance on April 25, 1905. It was a shot heard 'round the world. From Paris Mother's sister added this note to her postcard for July 8, 1905: "J'ai lu le journal de Lloydminster avec le plus intéret." At the time of my birth the town possessed among other businesses two or three hardware and general stores; two delivery and feed stables (part of every pioneer town); Miss Posthuma's "Minster Restaurant," where first-class meals cost twenty-five cents; two practicing doctors (also the proprietors of the "Medical Hall" dispensing drugs, cigars, wines, etc.); five resident ministers; a visiting dentist; the Royal Northwest Mounted Police; and an undertaker. The population numbered twelve hundred souls.

19

I was probably born in Devonshire House, which is the name my parents gave to their home in Lloydminster. The occasion passed unnoticed by the press. Devonshire House was one of the largest residences, and certainly the most modern, in this small community. Situated on several acres of land, it had such sumptuous features as a large drawing room, library, dining room, indoor plumbing, hot-water heating, and log fireplaces in most of the principal rooms. I do not remember that the indoor plumbing was used except in the winter and when there were guests. At least we youngsters were encouraged to use the jaunty old john at the end of the currant-garden shrubbery. I spent many a happy hour there in the summer reading through the pages of Timothy Eaton's mail-order catalog, with its enchanting picture-starred pages of magic lanterns, fishing equipment, revolvers, tennis and soccer gear, and dozens of other fascinating things. A rhubarb bed adjoined the outdoor privy, and we were encouraged to chew on a stalk if we felt the need of a laxative. It had a bitter, tart taste.

The name Devonshire House may seem a bit pretentious for a home on the Saskatchewan prairie, but I'm sure it reflected nothing more than my parents' deep affection for the Old Country. My mother was an ardent Anglophile. At sea, returning from a visit to friends and relatives in Paris and London, she wrote to her husband's father:

> The weather is fine and they say the sea is calm. I have my doubts about that, but have made up my mind not to give in. I wish this boat was going in the opposite direction. I am afraid my holiday has not cured my homesickness.

Perhaps naming her home Devonshire House helped to recreate something of the atmosphere of life under pioneer conditions that she knew and loved in her beloved England, to which she knew she could seldom if ever return. I have known people who felt that way about Dixie when they were uncertain of returning. It is also quite possible that the house was named for my father's birthplace in the county of Devonshire. The custom of naming one's home after a family place name or given name was not uncommon in this transplanted English community. Alice Rendell, who wrote such interesting letters to her friends back in the Old Country during the first weeks and months the colony was getting established, named her new home on the prairie Doriscourt in honor of her eldest daughter.

20

The house stood by itself at one end of the town, deep in its own grounds amidst lawns, fruit trees, and vegetable gardens. There were circular and rectangular flower beds with a glowing abundance and variety of flowers. I remember best the mignonette for its elusive fragrance, the pansies for their kitten-like faces, and the poppies for their gay and brilliant colors. In early fall after the potato crop was harvested we youngsters who had helped with the planting, weeding, and harvesting piled up the old potato vines into forts set some twenty feet apart and engaged one another in furious battle. The ammunition was the residue of small potatoes left on the vines that were not worth picking for eating purposes. Stretching back of the garden and an adjoining lawn was a large pasture completely fenced, where hay and clover basked in the summer sun, and a large barn providing shelter for the time when our family had a cow and horses. There were no animals in my time, and the stalls had been removed to convert this space into a garage. The Sunday carriage still remained with its cloth cover. The front of the barn was open, with a roof overhead to serve as a shelter for sawing and storing logs for firewood in the early fall. The wood was poplar, cut with an axe from surrounding bluffs, hauled home by sleigh or wagon, and sawed into stove and fireplace lengths with a bucksaw. Next to the woodpile was a chicken house, warmly insulated against winter weather. It was one of my chores to feed and water the chickens and collect the eggs. I enjoyed this task and spent many an hour devising ways and means of keeping the water bowl filled with fresh water while at the same time observing the pecking order of life among nonhumans. From the rooster and hens I also learned some things about that phenomenon of life concerned with sex. In our ostensibly highly moral and respectable family there was no discussion of the reproductive function, although we were not discouraged from reading the sterilized and homogenized works of the Rev. Sylvanus Stall, one of the first to recognize the commercial possibilities of sex literature when interspersed with the evangelical message. I found his "What a Young Boy Ought to Know" in our family library about as enlightening as Peter Rabbit and the Seven Dwarfs. I wanted to become acquainted with "What a Young Woman Ought to Know" but was unable to locate it.

Every house had its barn with a loft for hay. The hayloft was a favorite haunt. It was a generous shield for the practice of our minor vices. A couple of rungs at the top of the vertical ladder were missing, but at that age we

21

were agile enough to hoist ourselves by a sharp upward jerk of the arms onto the upper floors without difficulty. Horatius, of Roman legend, could not have contrived better strategy for keeping the enemy at bay. For in a sense this hayloft was our refuge and security. Here my brother and I stored our homemade bows and arrows, spears, and shields and shared the glamour of improvised meals of canned pork and beans, bread and jam, and candy. There was a charm about these snacks that no regular meal could match.

A large window with heavy wooden shutters enabled us to view the outside world, to spy on a half-breed family living across the back road in a scarcely habitable shack, and to keep an eye out for the fate of hoboes who rode the tops of boxcars on the Canadian Northern. Less than a hundred yards from our lookout the railroad tracks ran through a large hollow that at certain times of the year was filled with water on both sides of the track embankment. Train detectives would stop the train in the middle of this pond if they spied hoboes riding the boxcar tops, and the unfortunate riders would then be obliged to jump off into the icy water and slip away in the bordering woods. When the train moved on again, they would emerge soaking wet, make themselves a log fire, and dry off.

Our spying on the half-breed family might suggest that there was a this and a that side of the tracks in this small town, and to some extent this was true in spite of the democratic Canadian spirit to which most were succumbing. Most townspeople were relatively poor by English standards, but the half-breeds and the Indians who came from their reservation once a year to collect a government bonus were savagely poor. Inevitably there was always a ragged procession of half-starved children among them. Occasionally there were unpleasant incidents, of which I recall two in our family. My stepbrother Pat had curly black hair that the Indians either did not like or were superstitious about. When he happened to stray over to their camp during one of their annual visits, they seized him and stuck his head in a pail of whitewash. He came home screaming and vomiting. On another occasion I was returning from the public water well where we got some of our water for drinking purposes. It was about the equivalent of a city block away from our house and the half-breed family shack at the back of our property line. I was carrying two buckets of water within a square framework constructed from lathes, which was designed to keep the buckets from slamming against my legs and spilling water. As I approached our house one of the half-breed boys slipped across the open field, greeted me by name with a friendly smile, and then without warning struck me in the eye with a hammerlike blow. Sparks flew like a Roman candle. Entrapped inside my water-carrying contraption and with a heavy bucket of water in each hand, I was in no position to defend myself or to take after him in pursuit. Truth to tell, the blow took all the fight out of me anyway, and I felt sick from the pain in my eye. I cannot think why he did it, but, to be perfectly fair, it may have been a fifty-fifty exchange for something we had done to him or to his brothers. There was no doubt a strain of anarchy in these half-breed boys. They could be both kind and cruel.

I left Devonshire House thirteen years after I was born, never to see it again. It was sold for taxes, I believe, and demolished in the late twenties, but it is the only place in Lloydminster that I really remember. In a sense Devonshire House and its immediate surroundings--the prairie, woods, sloughs, schoolhouse and playing grounds--still mean the Canada that is Canada to me. I can still see the triple-gabled front façade, with ornamental scroll beneath each gable, with windows grouped in pairs reflecting sunshine and shadows by day and forked lightning by night during violent thunderstorms. As a child this house was for me one of the seven wonders of the world, a monument to lovely spring days when the snow first melted, sparkling sloughs filling up in the hollows in the prairie, crows cawing the end of winter at last, and crocuses carpeting the fields to the far line of the sky. Soon silver catkins would hang from the pussy willows, wild strawberries would dot the banks, red lilies would roll gently in the wind, and gophers would emerge squealing their defiance at hawks circling in the blue sky above.

4: A SASKATCHEWAN UPBRINGING

There are not many things during my childhood that seem worthy of record, but since this is the only period of my life in which I have any remembrance of my father, I shall begin with him. I must confess in this regard that the more I seek to recapture the events of those days, the less confidence I have in my recollection.

Before me are two photographs that offer clues to the character of my father in those early years. The first shows an officer in the Canadian army, probably taken at the time of his enlistment during the first or second year of World War I. I inwardly genuflect before this portrait. It is the epitome of all that is romantic about a military hero--a handsome face, firm mouth and chin, intense purposeful eyes, trim figure, and a military bearing resplendent in an officer's uniform with side arms. One may conjecture from it that here is a man of considerable vigor and personal charm. The second is a postcard showing one side of Main Street, Lloydminster (circa 1910), the stores fronted by a raised-plank sidewalk and unpaved street. On this street father had opened a real estate office in a two-story building, dwarfing the post office next door. Between two windows on the second floor he had a huge sign the approximate width of the building, reading "Canadian Northern and Government Lots and Farms for Sale." On the first floor, next to a large display window, he described his manifold duties in even bolder type as "J. P. Lyle, Estates." A more modest sign on the corner of the building announced his interest in other assorted businesses, such as insurance and general agency services. This postcard suggests to me a strong, virile businessman in his

24

economic prime. Combine the personal charm of the first photograph with the aggressiveness of the postcard and it is not difficult to understand how father served sequentially on the town Council, became mayor, and was elected to the Legislative Assembly of the provincial government--all within the first decade of the town's and province's establishment.

I have few recollections of my father. One of his hobbies was hunting, and he was a crack shot. Sometimes I was his retriever; he usually procured his bag of prairie chicken, rabbit, and duck. Pulling alongside a country road, car top down and valves tapping away like mad, he would stand up and knock off a prairie chicken from the top of a wheat stack at thirty yards. It was even difficult to find the mark of the bullet. (Whenever we motored a few miles into the country, there was always the chance of getting stuck in a mudhole. Father would then take the wheel while the rest of us would get out behind and push, mostly spattering mud all over ourselves and finally having to go a mile or so for a team to pull us out.) I was never party to large-game hunting, but deer were frequently met within a mile or so of the town limits, and it was not surprising to find moose and elk in plenty along the Saskatchewan River to the north of town in winter. Coyote hunting was a favorite sport in the winter. Pelts were worth five dollars each, and in addition there was a provincial bounty per head. A friend of the family had two Irish wolfhounds that he had especially trained for coyote and wolf hunting. The trick, as I remember, was to catch the coyote in open country. If he could escape into the woods, he could more easily elude the hounds and possibly endanger their lives at the speed they were running. Butch was the faster and would spin the coyote until Blue Boy could come up and make the kill. In one unforgettable chase Blue Boy hit a tree head on and was killed.

As children we were encouraged to believe in Santa Claus. Father always made a breathtaking appearance each year on Christmas Eve, disguised, of course, as Santa. After supper we and children of family friends would gather together at our house and sit in an expectant circle around a great lighted Christmas tree in our drawing room. The tree was lighted by candles, and the adults took special precautions to see that none of the candles ever burned too low or caught on fire. We were told to be very still and listen, and soon we heard bells coming nearer and nearer. Finally the bells stopped, and out of the shadows came this mysterious man all dressed in red with a long white beard. Mother and some of the other ladies present were most solicitous in their welcome--they hoped the journey had not been too much for him. What remains in my memory most was not the presents that Santa distributed from his bag as much as my excitement in anticipation of his visit and the air of mystery surrounding it.

My father traveled extensively in eastern Canada and parts of the United States in those early years, whether in connection with his own business or his elected duties in town and province I do not know. I seldom saw him and consequently had no real relationship with him, but while he was absent he always kept in touch with the family by sending us postcards of natural scenery and famous buildings in cities where he was staying. Sometimes he would send each one of us a separate card, and I still have two or three of these he mailed from Ottawa and New York. I must have read them many times; they are badly soiled from handling. His comments were concise but warm and affectionate--in my case, simply "Guy, Love/Dad." When my brother Kenneth was six years old, he was given an opportunity to accompany our parents on a visit to the Old Country. Mother and Kenneth spent part of their vacation in Paris with the Poiriers; father revisited his home in Barnstaple, Devon, and then rejoined his family in Torquay before returning home. There was a general understanding, quid pro quo, that my turn would come later, which it did in 1913, when my parents took me with them when they went for a vacation to Victoria, B.C. For me a trip on the train to Vancouver across the Rockies was a trip to Wonderland itself. I dimly remember my excitement as the train snaked its way around snow-covered mountains and ice fields. I saw my first Rocky Mountain goats from the observation car. This time it was mother who wrote postcards to the other children at home. In one to Kenneth she wrote, "How are you, little boy? Guy is seeing some wonderful mountains and says you did not see the like on your trip." My brother and I had been given a choice in our parents' travel plans but clearly I felt that I had made the correct one.

Mother had the main care of our early education. She had had a fine education herself and was a good teacher. She added French and music to our curriculum. Tunes from "The Merry Widow," "The Chocolate Soldier," and the Gilbert and Sullivan operettas were popular at the time and helped to recreate many a lively evening, but the music I remember best from those childhood days are snippets from the great composers. Mother was a tough teacher. She insisted on giving each of us piano lessons, exacting hours of practice from Molly and Kenneth, who showed some evidence of talent, and insisting on teaching my brother and me our school lessons at home for the first three or four grades. Whatever advantage we derived from home learning, however, was greatly diminished by the physical and mental hazing we were subjected to by our teachers and fellow students during our initial years of public schooling. Partly in retaliation I stole pencil boxes on weekends, using the fire escapes for entrance and exit, and hid their contents under the back flaps of the school's outhouses.

I do not remember what grade I was assigned to when I entered public school, but I think it was grade four. The school was a brick-veneer building that opened its doors only a few months before I was born and, more importantly, was within easy walking distance from our home. I enjoyed the walk and knew every loose plank in the wooden sidewalk and every tree and stone on the way to school, as I knew every stone and gopher hole when I took a shortcut home across the playing field. But my elementary-school years were one long misery for me. If I had no favor from the teachers, who probably resented my first years of schooling at home, I might still have found it endurable, but it was more than that. I felt alien and alone among the other children, who had already formed their friends and clans, and, as anyone knows who has seen that remarkable play and movie "The Prime of Miss Jean Brodie," children can be inexplicably cruel to anyone who is in any way different from the group. I had not only entered school late but I had an unusual given name and a slightly British accent. Perhaps I was hard to handle. I remember that I was reprimanded several times for spitting on my slate and wiping it clean with my hand. Cracks on the knuckles were as easy to get as scratches in a blackberry patch. The emphasis was not on how well you did your homework but how long you spent doing it.

Fortunately there was one good and kindly teacher to whom I certainly owe something for anything I learned in those early years in school. She was young, pretty, and believed in praising you if you did anything well. She took time to talk with you and to get to know your problems. I loved her in an innocent, childish way. It was not until years later

27

that I had an opportunity to thank her. While microfilming
local records relating to the Barr Colony, I was in a small
millinery shop talking to one of the old-timers when in came
a lady who, I knew instantly, had something to do with my
past. She was Miss Irene Leckie, the proprietor informed
me, a former schoolteacher now retired. There was no need
to tell me more. Her name was all I needed. Her hair was
snow white, but she still had those fine blue eyes and a com-
plexion as pink and white as when she taught the fifth grade
thirty or more years before. I introduced myself and thanked
her for her encouragement and kindness to her young pupils.
I even told her of my childhood infatuation. She smiled a
Brodie smile and said she remembered me. Such are the
delicious pleasures of vanity that this was the happiest memory of my visit.

It was on account of childhood illness that I discovered the
pleasures of reading, although I am sure that our mother
must have read to us when we were very young. I do not
remember what she read, but fairy tales--frowned upon in
an earlier period but once more in favor in the first decade
of the century--were my preference, and I am sure that I
learned at her knee such classics as Mother Goose, Puss-in-
Boots, Little Claus and Big Claus, and many of the tales of
the greatest of all fairy-storytellers, Hans Christian Ander-
sen. In any event the first books I remember reading by
myself were volumes of the "Book of Knowledge, " where I
found my favorite fairy tales enchantingly illustrated in color.
By way of contrast I was also very much interested in articles on how to make things--the magic lantern was a fascinating discovery--and anything relating to magic. I trace my interest in novels largely to the fact that I survived the common
childhood diseases--pneumonia, measles, rheumatic fever,
diphtheria, scarlet fever--with long periods of convalescence
during which I spent many hours alone. Fortunately I had the
pick of an extensive library of boy's and girl's books--"Anne
of Green Gables" was a favorite--belonging to my brothers
and sister as well as my own. Two holding top honors were
the "Swiss Family Robinson, " which I read again and again
until I knew every detail, and the more realistic but delightful adventures of "Robinson Crusoe. " My copy of the former
had several color illustrations that still stick in my memory:
one of the house in the tree reminding me of a knight's castle, with the rope ladder serving as security like a draw-
bridge, and another of a snake in the act of swallowing one

of the children's pets. Even today I loathe the sight of a snake. "Robinson Crusoe" was a favorite of all of us. I read it more than once as I grew older. It satisfied my hunger for adventure even more than the "Swiss Family Robinson," probably because it was less Sunday-schoolish, though deeply religious, and seemed to me to deal more with the real world of things rather than the imaginary. Crusoe with his goatskin cap, his umbrella, and his calendar of notches, was a real man, a figure you just didn't wipe out of your mind quickly. His baskets, his earthenware pots, his field of barley, his little flock of goats, and his rescue and later instruction of Friday endeared him to me.

If sheer weight of numbers means anything, George Alfred Henty was the most popular author with my older brothers. Some forty of his works are still in print, evidence that he retains a large readership even today. We had at least a dozen of his novels on the shelves. I read and enjoyed them very much, but I skipped the heavy stuff. He seemed a bit stodgy to me because of his habit of interrupting a breathtaking narrative of rescue with a large chunk of historical exposition. I liked especially his stories of the exploits of daring Englishmen in foreign countries ("These fellows know they don't stand a chance against an Englishman's fists"). What magnificent titles they had: "Sturdy and Strong," "With Kitchener in the Soudan," and "For Name and Fame"! Two titles, "The Bravest of the Brave" and "The Reign of Terror," Christmas gifts of my father to Cecil, are both on my bookshelves today. Bound in beautiful primary colors that have not faded in sixty or more years, always the figure of some soldier or feat of arms imprinted on the spine and front cover, and full-page illustrations in black-and-white--no wonder they were irresistible! I dare not read them again today, but from time to time I pat them on the spine and make a low bow to their author and publisher.

The first Yankee to enter my childhood reading was Horatio Alger, whose theme for some one hundred and thirty novels was the embodiment of the thrifty virtues of the Puritan tradition without its piety. Alger was no Benjamin Franklin, for whom success meant leisure to read and write and make scientific experiments. His newsboys and bootblacks were out to make their fortune, at least to attain the respected image of the upper-middle-class American, and if they often succeeded by rough and ready means, it did not tarnish their reputation for fortitude and courage so far as we were

29

concerned. These boys knew their way about the great city.
They were city-wise. I envied them at the time. Later, as
a young man, some of the seamier sides of city life so vividly depicted by Alger in his favorite locale, New York City,
came back to haunt me.

I have mentioned previously that Devonshire House had
a separate library room, which, in addition to serving as my
father's den, held a treasure trove of books, many in multi-
volume sets with beautiful bindings and illustration, belonging
to my parents. I delved freely into this library but never
tackled the serious stuff. In the course of my reading there
I discovered Marie Corelli's "Thelma," which had something
to do with women of loose living, to use the contemporary
mode. I was strangely moved by Corelli's passionate out-
bursts; she gave her characters as much sentiment and melodrama as they deserved. Of course, in the end the good tri-
umphed and the bad withered, but there were a lot of other
things I didn't understand that interested me. During one of
my childhood illnesses I discovered in the library the works
of F. Marion Crawford, who wrote a number of novels about
Italian society. I read four or five of them, indeed, I think
I was beginning to fancy myself being found reading an adult
book, even though Crawford's extraordinary mixture of love,
hate, brigands, conspiracy, and poisonings scared the hell
out of me. There must have been many other books in that
library that I read or at least lingered over, but I do not remember them. Memory is a very fragile thing. You remember only fragments of many things, and fragments are not
sufficient to reconstruct the truth. I know that I was not particularly bookish and certainly not precocious as a child. I
read indiscriminately and occasionally, picking up anything
that interested me and reading quite a lot of things that I did
not understand.

Thinking over what gave me the most pleasure in my childhood, I should include the coming of spring, heralded by the
first crow "caw" and the song of the meadowlark. Bare
patches of earth sprang up everywhere; you could imagine the
earth slowly bursting its way through the snowlike silver puss-
ies clinging to the wands of the willows. Melting snow and
ice filled the gullies alongside the railroad tracks, so that it
was no great trick even for small boys to float out a railroad
tie or two for rafting. My brother and I would rope two of
these ties together--called sleepers by the railroad mainte-

nance crew--to form a raft that we would pole out to the rush-rimmed slough, now swollen in my imagination to the size of a giant lake by the spring thaw. The sun was luxuriously warm after the winter cold; frogs shrilled among the rushes, and beauty unfolded itself like sticky buds on the poplar trees. Here was nature in all its primeval beauty, its freshness and wildness unsullied. Ducks, rails, coots, and other marsh waterfowl rose with a great din and in general alarm as the raft pushed its way with a rustling sound through the waving grass. What a paradise that view presented! I have often recreated it in my half-dreams, knowing every channel through the tall grasses, every island clump of bush and shrub, and every point along the edge of the slough.

Another memory from childhood was our fairly rigorous discipline in matters of etiquette. Mother did her conscientious best to remedy our multifarious deficiencies in this regard, but it was my sister, Molly, who was my champion in manners and to whom I shall always be most grateful. She developed a telepathic communication between us that spared my friends and me many a fall from grace. She reminded me recently of one appallingly close shave with disaster. As children we were allowed, in turn, to bring one friend for supper on Friday evenings. When my turn came, I brought along a stranger to the rest of the family, one Alec Cumas, three-quarter Indian. The folks were a bit startled, but all went well until Mother, following a custom in the family, began saying Grace. Everyone's eyes were respectfully closed. Alec, no doubt thinking something queer was going on, cautiously took the napkin next to his plate, unfolded it, and completely covered his head. Fortunately, aided by mental telepathy from Molly, I caught sight of it and snatched it off his head before Mother noticed it, thus avoiding a harsh rebuke for bad manners.

From time to time my mother would take me to visit the McCallum ranch, some forty miles north of Lloydminster. I always eagerly anticipated this summer visit. Mr. McCallum, a Scot from Fifeshire county, was an absentminded, enchanting human being, generous, and blindly Anglophilic; his wife was a gentle, reserved lady whom I always remember as making wonderful suet puddings. They put me on a horse shortly after the first time I was there, and pretty soon I was herding the milk cows and bringing in the horses for their evening grain ration.

31

The ranch lay in a rich pasture and wood belt formed
by the confluence of the Red and the North Saskatchewan riv-
ers. The settlement in which it was located was called Tangleflags because the pioneer settlers were English, Irish,
Scottish, Norwegian, and American. On the high north bank
of the Saskatchewan they erected a tall flagpole. When mail
was delivered weekly from Lloydminster, the postman ran up
the flag, and anyone in the settlement seeing it wasted no
time in rowing across the river with the determined strokes
of an experienced oarsman. He had to lean on the oars because the current was very strong. The same signal served
visitors and others who had business to transact with the settlers. If the flag went unnoticed--and that, indeed, was the
situation on several occasions when I was there--the visitor
had the option of taking a circuitous route to the nearest fer-
ry crossing, adding some twenty miles to the trip.

The south bank of the river where the ranch was located was terraced. On the lower flat were large white and
black poplar and willow, while the highest terrace was largely open land with good prairie wool for grazing, broken here
and there by shallow sloughs and some trees. I don't remember much about the house except that it was built with
lumber and shingles, but behind it was a shack made of logs
with a sod roof, which was the first house the McCallums
lived in after they arrived. I suppose in a way they lived
the life of a Robinson Crusoe for the first year or so, confined to a log shack, enduring the hardships of the pioneer in
a severe climate, and making a living by hard, manual labor.
To be sure, prairie chicken and ducks were plentiful, and
there was always a great variety of wild fruit to fill the lard-
er--strawberries, raspberries, gooseberries, currants, cranberries, saskatoons, and cherries.

Among the delights I was looking forward to this summer were fishing and flushing the prairie chicken and rabbits
with McCallum's puppies, who were always eager to follow
the trails in the woods and fields. Back of the bunkhouse
was a wooden bridge stretched across a narrow, fast-flowing
creek. I would lie here on a summer afternoon and dream
of sailing with Captain Kidd while spying on a school of trout
feeding in the crystal-clear water pools below. To me it
was not a place to catch fish--the river was the place to
catch pike and pickerel, though I was not allowed to fish
there by myself--but rather to dream broader dreams and to
observe nature's freshness and wildness still unsullied. By

afternoon myriads of fluttering leaves from tender green pop-
lars made my spirits soar with sheer joy.   Robins called to
each other from the swaying treetops.   An occasional rabbit
would rush across from one thicket to another in a wild bur-
lesque of speed as if it were urgent to go--then sit still for
half a day--or so it seemed to me.   Roots and stones broke
the main force of the stream, creating rivulets and swirling
shoals.   Sometimes a leaf dropping from an overhanging
branch would frighten the trout, and they would jet away to
deeper pools only to reappear again if I remained patiently
and motionless.   The soothing stillness of the stream, the
flight of large and brightly colored butterflies back and forth
across the bridge, the beauty of the flowers that dotted the
banks, the reflections in the pools, and the occasional thump-
ing of frogs dropping off the banks into the water seemed only
to emphasize the underlying tranquility and mystery of my
surroundings.   Was I asleep or was I awake?   Was it all a
dream?   I believe that on those occasions I must have experienced what the poet so happily expressed:

"I for a time was lifted above earth
And possessed joys not promised by my birth."

One Tangleflags incident that remains as vivid today as
the day it occurred took place in my hometown.   Call it the
racetrack debacle!   Monty, our affectionate name for the head
of the McCallum ranch, was persuaded against his better
judgment to enter his three-year-old stallion, Rubydox, into
the children's race at the annual Lloydminster fair.   This
was one of the main attractions for many in the crowd who
attended the three-day fair.   I was among those who came to
cheer.   On the advice of his friends Monty selected a boy
named Byron to make the ride because he was light and a
very good rider.   The race was to be in three heats.   In the
first Rubydox appeared to be a bit slow at the start.   Apparently, looking for a mare in season, he was content to follow
the other horses ahead of him and ended up last.   In the second race he was placed on the outside because of his poor
showing in the first heat.   But this time he got off to a good
start and dominated the race until he spied some Indian ponies tethered outside the race course.   Rubydox made a three
o'clock turn off the course and ran straight for the ponies
through five strands of four-point barbed wire.   Byron came
off, of course, and had to be hospitalized for concussion.
With his active strength it was a wonder Rubydox got out of
the wire entanglement without being ripped wide open.   As it

was there were bad cuts on his front legs and shoulders, but fortunately the town veterinarian was able to save him. Monty was thoroughly shook up and had an enormous bill to pay for being persuaded against his better judgment to enter Rubydox in the race. My witnessing the tragedy was emotionally upsetting, and for months afterward I had a recurrent nightmare. In my dreams I was the one who rode Rubydox and caused the accident.

The first real sorrow in my life came when I had to leave Tangleflags after the short summer visit to return home. I kept turning over in my thoughts the things I would be doing if only I were back at the ranch--riding bareback to round up the cows, feeding the chickens and ducks, swimming in the creek, churning the butter, and listening to the stitching sound of the grasshoppers and the wind stirring through the poplar trees before falling asleep at night. For the first day or two after my return there seemed nothing to do at home and I felt a strange emptiness as though my life had been robbed of all solace. In my despair I would rush out into the currant garden and sob in a subdued, hopeless sort of way. And to this day I cannot return from visiting close friends and relatives away from home without experiencing a few moments of profound melancholy.

It was about this time that I started going to the movies. I remember it quite well because it was my first real introduction to old-fashion melodrama. I was accompanied by my sister, Molly, and we went regularly on Saturday afternoons. The main attraction was the serial, which at that time featured Pearl White in "The Perils of Pauline." And perils there certainly were. Who can forget the locomotive rounding the curve and bearing down on the heroine tied to the tracks, with the villain--always with a large black moustache and a twitching eye--hissing through his teeth. After the hero arrived in the nick of time to stave off disaster it was always my ambition to do heroic deeds; this was repeated at next week's episode. I suspect now that Pearl White's heroines were challenging the audience to do uplifting things. The other thing I remember most clearly was the stuffiness and odor in the moviehouse, which reminded me of our chicken house on a wet day. Molly assured me that the management squirted perfume in the air during the show. Even though these movies were pretty choppy, in more ways than one, they remain for me a pleasant memory of a pleasant time.

5: WARTIME TRAGEDY

Hot summer days were not the only pervasive element affect-
ing conditions in 1914.   Suddenly war clouds appeared on the
horizon.   News did not reach us until several days after it
had been printed in the eastern newspapers, and consequently
we were poorly posted on outside world events.   But by August the Kaiser had overrun Belgium, England had declared *Aug. 4*
war on Germany, and we knew that we were at war.   Re-
cruits still in civilian clothes were forming ranks and marching to the accompaniment of the town band playing "O Canada"
and "The Maple Leaf Forever."   People gathered in small
groups at the railway station and newspaper office to hear the
latest bulletins.   Volunteers came forward promptly, and the
mayor declared a holiday to give them an enthusiastic sendoff.
Practically everyone gathered at the station to hear the patriotic speeches, to shake the hand of each departing soldier,
and to wish him Godspeed.   Headlines in the local paper bla-
zoned the atrocities of the Germans in Belgium and the hero-
ics of the British navy and urged every Canadian to stand up
and be counted.   These denouncements and commendations
continued to appear for weeks until the Lloydminster annual
fair, an invasion of gypsies, and the final matches in the J.
P. Lyle Football Cup series blew war off the first page.

Because officers were in short supply, Boer War veterans, including my father, were in demand in the early days
of recruitment.   By the end of the second year of the war
Cecil also enlisted with the University battalion at Saskatoon
by adding a month or so to his age to meet the minimum requirement.   As for Pat, the youngest of the Lynch family, he
calculated that if the war lasted another five years, he would

also be eligible. As a matter of fact he succeeded in joining up, but when Mother heard about it, he was mustered out in a hurry. Both the Lynch boys were born in London. Their attitude toward the war was simply, "It's our country and we'll fight for it." Contrary to the patriotic sermons reported in the local paper, it is more than likely that many of the young men living and working on isolated homesteads in the Lloydminster area saw in war an escape from boredom and hard work under the most severe conditions, as well as an opportunity for comradeship, which they lacked on the farm.

I have only fragmentary recollections of the war years. After an initial period of training Cecil came home on leave and brought with him an army buddy. This boy and Molly became very good friends, and I have often wondered, but never dared ask, whether they were secretly engaged before his leave was up. At the time they were home I was very much into Meccano, the leading erector-set manufacturer of the day, and had accumulated a formidable set from parts received each year at Christmas. I wanted very much to build something a little more majestic than windmills and trucks, and it so happened that Meccano was sponsoring a national contest, which I decided to enter. Cecil and his friend volunteered to help and suggested that a long-range cannon mounted on a mobile carriage would be a suitable and relevant entry for the contest. They assisted, and, I suspect, largely took over the construction of such a model and gave it the care and attention to detail that one might expect from soldiers fresh from military training. Photographs of the model, views taken from all sides and angles, were then mailed in to the contest, with everyone at home agreeing that I had a likely winner. I learned much later that our entry had won a prize, whether first, second, or third, I do not recall. But whichever and whatever it was, I shall always associate the act of building it with my brother, Cecil. In my fragmentary but clear recollection of his presence and enthusiastic help on this occasion, I have built a small shrine in my memory to honor a kind, generous, and brave brother.

One morning the phone rang as I was finishing breakfast in the kitchen. Molly was the only other person present. She answered, and I thought she turned deathly pale and seemed quite dazed. She asked several times if the caller was sure of what he was saying and then insisted that he repeat the message while she wrote it down. When she hung up, I could see the fine shine of tears in her eyes. She re-

36

sponded to my questioning look by reading what she had copied down. With brutal brevity it stated the bare facts: "Regret to inform you that Private Cecil Lynch was killed in action, March 24, 1918." She then wept openly and hurried out of the room to break the news to Mother. I didn't know what to do, but suddenly, without consciously knowing where I was going, I went outside to the currant-bush garden, where I had always found solace during the first hour or two after my return from Tangleflags. Only this time I didn't weep, but I kept remembering the good times--when Cecil made us all proud as a player on the football team and scout leader, and how he saved me from a pummeling by some of the school bullies, and how enthusiastically he helped during his first leave with my entry into the Meccano contest. I supposed that he never knew that we had won a prize or how much I loved and would miss him.

A year before Cecil's death Father was wounded and, through the effect of gas poisoning, temporarily lost the power of speech. He convalesced in French and English hospitals, went in and out of service, and finally was mustered out after Armistice Day. Unlike some with physical or mental disabilities, he appeared to be in relatively good shape though bruised and ungeared for the old life back home. I now wonder why I was not told about his injuries in battle, or if I was informed, why it made so little impression upon me at the time. The simple truth of the matter is that I only recently learned (from one of the old "Lloydminster Times" papers) that he had been gassed. Had I known and understood what he had been through at that time I might have been far less critical of future events. For after Father returned home life was never the same in our family. For many the war was only a memory to be recalled once a year on November 11, Armistice Day; for our family it was an unspeakable disaster. Father found his business interests pre-empted by others, took to drinking heavily, and was frequently absent from home for long periods of time. His absences and the company he kept during the time he was away were never explained to Mother. She greatly resented his defection, and the suspicion to which it gave rise led to frequent bitter quarrels. I sensed the impending crisis without really understanding it. One night it reached a point of violence and unreality that I should like to forget but cannot. Father returned home very late, probably drunk as a fiddler, woke Mother out of a deep sleep, and nearly frightened her to death. She seemed like a trapped animal and rushed down the hall to our bedroom, sat on the edge of my bed, and wept uncontrollably. She clutched my blanket as though seeking protection and was obviously in a state of great tension. Yet when Father, now partially sobered up, declared that he was going to call our family doctor to give her something to calm her hysterics, she quieted down and made it clear that the best medicine for her was for him to clear out. I pretended to be fast asleep the entire time and do not remember how it ended, but it was one of the most painful and racking experiences of my lifetime.

"Children are not creatures of justice; they lay blame and praise about them as their needs demand," wrote the playwright Moss Hart. There is much truth in this epigram for me. Not long after the debacle I have just described Father left us, and I never saw him again. Our fortunes changed drastically. From what was then regarded as relative affluence we were now obliged to live in genteel poverty. I blamed Father for this as well as for deserting Mother and the family. Mother, too, was embittered by her experience, and no doubt this affected me. Most of all I blamed him for the bitterness and shame that he had brought on all of us. Here was a man who had been one of the town's leading citizens and was now a drunk. One does not expect one's father, who has served gallantly in two wars, to be an alcoholic and a failure. I felt so keenly about this that when we moved away from Lloydminster to Edmonton I took refuge in a lie when asked about my father. I responded that he died in the war. I repeated the falsehood many times until I think I actually came to believe it.

When I was supporting myself as a graduate student at Columbia University, I received a number of wretchedly written appeals from his friends. While I knew that they were not in his handwriting, I assumed that he approved of sending them. They were often so illegible and untaught that I hastily burned them. On more than one occasion, much to my mortification, they had already been opened by University personnel, perhaps to determine their proper recipient when the envelope address was unreadable. How and where my father discovered where and what I was doing in the United States I have never known, but it struck me as tragically ironic that he should be begging help from one who had been obliged to make his own way without the aid of the paternal purse.

As I look back on the circumstances that led to the breakup of our family, I am now quite sure that Father was a war casualty, and for good reasons. It is undeniable that the war interrupted his career in business and in politics and made it difficult if not impossible for him to pick up again at the end of the war where he had left off. He seemed to have lost his momentum and to have fallen into a kind of inertia. In the second place I realize now that as one of those officers who early in the war was called upon to shape up thousands of young volunteers at great speed in the military mold he must have been aware that they were ill-prepared for the hell of trench war. The casualities were enormous. That must have weighed heavily on his conscience. Moreover, he himself was wounded when the Germans used gas warfare for the first time, and he experienced at first hand the horror, brutalization, and loss of sensitivity that trench warfare brought. Speaking about the effect of this war on the men who had a career underway before 1914, the novelist John Galsworthy wrote, "There is something gained in them but there's something gone from them.... A kind of unreality must needs cling about their lives henceforth." Many of the young men who volunteered in the early months of the war did so to escape the boredom of farm and village life. I am certain that this was not my father's reason for joining, but as a returning hero who had experienced the bottom of things in no-man's-land he may not have been able to cope with the normal activity of home and business life after what one writer has aptly described as "the uncertainties and drama of war." I suspect that alcohol and camaraderie with other veterans may have helped him to forget his troubles, but they also hastened his debasement.

Some thirty years after our father had left us my brother Kenneth told me that he was living with a woman in British Columbia. I believe he said she was a nurse and he spoke well of her. Apparently Father expressed a wish to him that he might see and talk with me again, but I refused. My antipathy ran deep. It had caused me to live almost half my life concealing the truth because my ego could not accept the facts. Father died shortly afterward. I still feel ambivalent about him, but I now realize more than ever before that his real enemy was war and that it not only obstructed a promising career but in the end ruined his life.

6: SCHOOL AND SPORTS

In June of 1921 the following advertisement appeared in the
weekly "Lloydminster Times":

DEVONSHIRE HOUSE

W. H. Thomas
The Royal George Dining Room
begs to announce that on
the 1st July next he will
open the
J. P. LYLE RESIDENCE
for the accommodation of those
requiring a private boarding
house.

After a futile attempt to sell the house as a hospital for the
town Mother rented it to Mr. Thomas and moved to Edmonton,
Alberta.

Although the population numbered only sixty thousand,
Edmonton seemed like a metropolis compared with our small
town. It covered a very large area, and there was a hustle
and bustle about it that gave the folks who lived there a sense
of unlimited growth still to come. Everything seemed to me
to be on a giant scale. The majestic North Saskatchewan
River, which we referred to as "the Saskatchewan," bisected
the city north and south, with the provincial Parliament Buildings, beautifully landscaped, commanding the north bluff and
the youthful University of Alberta occupying a dominant position on the edge of one of the highest banks of the south side.

And connecting the two the spectacular High Level Bridge, thirty-five hundred and fifty feet long and one hundred and fifty-two feet high, spanned the fast-flowing river for street-car, automobile, and pedestrian traffic. The trolley, riding high on the top level of the bridge, without guard rails of any kind, was to me a romantic and frightening sight.

Edmonton was established as a post of the Hudson Bay Company in 1795, when the Saskatchewan was the principal waterway for the Indian fur trade. At the time we moved there it was not only the capital of the province but the principal railway center in the northwest for traffic east and west and the natural distributing point for the Peace River and Mackenzie districts to the north. Perhaps it was an omen of better days for us when we began life in this booming city in the twenties, because Strathcona, as the south side of Edmonton was called, was named for a famous railroad builder and these were the days when railroads came into their own.

In such a setting Mother rented and later bought a house at 8311 106th Street, where she, Molly, Kenneth, and I lived together for the next six years until I broke the family circle, or what was left of it, by leaving home following graduation from the University. Our new residence was a rather shapeless two-story, wooden-frame building with so little insulation that in winter it was cold as a refrigerator. A third-story attic, entered through the only bathroom in the house-- what we would have called a garret at Devonshire House-- served as sleeping quarters for Kenneth and me. When the temperature fell below zero, we had a small coal-burning stove to supplement what little heat came from below. It worked well when the fire was built up and one was close to it, but by morning it was dead. Molly and Mother each had a bedroom on the second floor. The first floor consisted of a combined living and dining room, a kitchen, and a scullery. Dominating the living-room furniture was the piano Mother brought over on the SS "Lake Manitoba" and transported from Saskatoon by horse and wagon to the Barr colony site. At the rear of the house a narrow wooden walk led from the kitchen door to a small utility structure, which Mother later converted into an apartment for rental to University students. Across the street from the front of our new home were two large brick houses with lovely shade trees and lawns extending down to the sidewalk edge. If I remember correctly, one of these homes belonged to the Wymans, whose son later became president of the University, and the other to the Davies

41

family. I knew Percy Davies slightly during my first year at the University. He graduated that year, a man of the utmost charm and perspicacity, and one, I am sure, who would have much to do with the rising fortune of his city and province.

High school made very little impression upon me. I attended the first year of high school in Lloydminster, for which I received a certificate awarding me an average percentage of 75 "with honours." When we moved to Edmonton, I attended Strathcona High School, which was only a hop-step-and-jump from our house. The school looked baronial to me. It had two large playgrounds separated by the school building, and also a double offering of courses in certain fields, thereby affording me my first introduction to segregation. I was shy, but I never got any pleasure out of dividing the sexes.

My three years of Latin under Mr. Niddrie were wasted. Not that he was a poor teacher. I simply failed to realize the importance of his repetitious drill in Latin syntax to my understanding of the English language. And here, of course, I never met up with the Greek epics or the story of Aeneas or the country-squire poetry of Horace. The only teacher I remember with any degree of appreciation in high school was the Rev. Walter E. Edmonds, who taught history. I never knew he was a reverend at the time; we called him "Shorty." Occasionally he would stray from marching through centuries of English kings, wars, and victories to tell us something about our own country, particularly Rupert's Land and the Red River Settlement, from which he came. I enjoyed these lapses greatly, but I remember him best because at graduation I received an inscribed copy of a little book of his essays, entitled "In a College Library." I still possess the copy, but unfortunately the paper cover and inscription are missing. Some culture must have been pumped into me during high school days: at the time I entered the University I was enrolled as a second-year student, which permitted me to graduate in three years.

Mother believed that life meant work and duty rather than pleasure, but in spite of family chores, in and outside the house, I managed to spend a great deal of time on an empty lot next to the Carrigan home playing tennis and hockey. The Carrigan boys and their sister were natural athletes; one of the boys, I believe, some years later played professional hockey. Carrigan's empty lot, catercornered across from the Catholic church, served as a grass court for tennis in the summer. When the grass was worn away, it became a clay court of sorts. We used whitewash for line markings, which came off on the balls and had to be replaced frequently. When the winter season rolled around, the right combination of snowfall, noonday thaw, and hard freeze at night would produce a rough, corrugated sheet of ice over the entire tennis court. We would then bank the sides of the court with snow a foot or so high, frame the inside surface of the snow with boards, and flood the rough ice bed until the surface was as smooth as glass. From then on it was just a matter of keeping the ice cleared of snow and occasionally reflooding when the surface became too badly cut up during a hockey game. Hockey was a rough game even in those times though not brutally malicious as is often the case in professional hockey today. We youngsters wore heavy woolen stockings that came well above the knee and padded them with sections of newspapers to prevent leg bruises. There were few rules and no referee, but any player who made a practice of hitting, jabbing, or tripping with his stick was thrown out of the game and not welcomed back. A good hefty shoulder bunt was permissible, and the game continued with a remarkable mixture of checking, practicing rebounds, and ripping the net with a nicely executed pass from wing to center.

In January and February, particularly on moonlit nights, the cold was intense. On these occasions the hospitality of the Catholic fathers, who allowed us to put on our skates and leg guards in the small vestry back of the church, added immeasurably to our comfort. The vestry had a large coal-burning heater and long benches around the walls where we could put on our skates and leave our coats during the game. On rare occasions, if we were lucky, one of the fathers would join us around the heater to recreate some of the highlights of our games. I remember one father who had fascinating stories to tell of his adventures in northern missions. I do not recall ever hearing a word about sin and damnation, which was the principal fare when I attended church with my parents. Indeed, it struck me, contrary to Protestant opinion in the neighborhood, that the fathers were a remarkably pleasant bunch of fellows.

My first love in sports was tennis. I began playing at the tender age of twelve on a grass court on the school playground, whose surface was not unlike the rough of a modern golf course. I played with a slightly warped racket and a bucket of fuzzless balls. More than likely I played by my-

43

self. In those days team sports were the rule for adolescents, and tennis was considered somewhat effete for a youngster. By the time I reached college it was gaining in popularity among students, but the players who signed up for the Tennis Club were few indeed. The public regarded tennis as an aristocratic sport attended largely by high society at such decorous places as Wimbledon and Southampton. The Australians and the southern Californians revolutionized the game in the mid-thirties and forties and brought in talented young players in increasing numbers from all classes of people. The big boom in the seventies brought a demand for courts and a commercialization of the game that would have seemed incredible in my youth. Today tennis is mass entertainment.

It was not until we moved to Edmonton and I was fortunate enough to be able to play on the Carrigan court that I became totally committed to the game. I spent time each day on the court during the summer months. If one of the Carrigans was not free to play at the time, I badgered someone else. We volleyed long and ferociously from the back line, practiced backhand strokes and net play, lobbed and smashed from service and backcourt, and worked continuously to increase the force and accuracy of our serves. In recent years I have noticed that a great many young players who are serious about the game practice without interruption against a backboard. I preferred the competition and companionship of a partner. My feeling was that while one could improve the accuracy and consistency of one's stroke against a backboard, this was quite a different thing from returning the ball when moving rapidly about the court or when your opponent was smashing the ball back at you. In the tennis craze of today I get more than a little tired of the great emphasis placed on the necessity for having a coach, studying the flood of manuals on tennis practice, and the indispensability of enough equipment to outfit a basketball team. For me tennis is a game in which you should endeavor to do your own thing. No two individuals have the same talents, and the important thing is to capitalize on any latent ability you have. Someone has said that the first rule of the game should be to have fun playing it. I agree wholeheartedly. I would add a second rule, which is that you practice regularly and play with someone in your own class. When you reach a degree of self-confidence and proficiency in the basic plays, there will be plenty of time and opportunity to take on someone who is a little better than you are. None of this is to argue against the importance of the coach if a young player has natural

44

talent and a flair for the game. Quite the contrary. Whenever a young man or woman shows definite championship quality, the importance of the coach grows.

There were other sports we enjoyed during my high school days, but of these none compared with the thrill of bobsledding. Hurtling down the slope of a steep hill in a curving run amongst the deep timber has a sort of tenseness that needs busting. And a busting it often got when the sled went sailing over a snowbank on the curve. Many a newcomer to the sport offered a fervent prayer of thanks when the flats burst into view at the bottom of the slope. In comparison with today's custom-made job, at least as viewed on the Olympics television scene, the bobsled we used was a rather clumsy contraption, consisting of two coasting sleighs in tandem connected by a plank to hold as many passengers as desired. My brother and I decided one fall to make a bobsled to end all bobsleds, and we almost succeeded. We got a plank long enough to hold twenty riders, upholstered it with gunny sacks stuffed with straw, furnished crossbars for each rider to brace his feet, ran a string of battery-powered lights along each side of the plank, and attached an auto wheel to the rope-guiding mechanism. It was a thing of beauty when completed. I am told that George III liked walking, and that when he came to a bridge where children were playing he would ask, "What's the name of the bridge?" When he was told, he would reply, "Let's give three cheers for the bridge." I'm sure that good old George would have cheered his head off if he could have seen our bobsled.

On a gusty November evening a sizable line of fans gathered at the top of the embankment of the Saskatchewan ready to make the run on our maiden trial down suicide hill. We had previously banked snow almost treetop high on the most dangerous curves to help make the swing. The passengers on each bobsled were supposed to lean left or right simultaneously to help the steersman round the curve. The cold was intense; the excitement even more acute. A quarter-moon hung on a huge arc of starlit sky above, as cold and resolute as the frozen Saskatchewan below. The downhill run began with a few shallow dips, and the bobsled seemed to drag, but then it quickly gathered speed as it swept down the declivity, a drop of several hundred feet to the bottom of the slope. On the straightaway it plunged downward like an osprey making a strike, the shrill scream of the steel runners mixed with the whoops and yells of the riders. At the three-quarters mark, approaching the most dangerous curve, it looked as though we were about to set a record for speed when suddenly the bobsled hit a piece of fallen log, jumped like a kangaroo and came down like a brick, locking the steering mechanism. For a hair-raising second we tilted wildly, then struck the curve dead on center, plowed through the protective snowbank, and landed smack in the small timber bordering the run. Many of the riders tumbled or were brushed off on impact with the snowbank, but those who hung on protected their legs by squeezing them together on top of the plank as it ripped through a dozen small birch and pine before coming to a grinding halt. The front sleigh was demolished, every crossbar was clipped off, and the lighting and padding were torn loose. Fortunately the tandem plank had not splintered and only the steersman was hurt. He was doubled up in pain against the pine tree that brought us to a stop. He seemed to have had his wind knocked out more than anything else, and after a while we got him straightened out. My brother and I admitted that our creation was a disaster, but a fragment from an exchange among the riders as we trudged home was consoling: "It was a sensational ride. We split the wind like a butcher knife."

7: THE EVERGREEN AND GOLD

We frequently hear about the frivolous, gay, and roaring twenties, but as far as our family was concerned there was very little roar and even less frivolity and good cheer. It was a matter of survival. Mother obviously had some income and savings, but I was never privy to its source or amount. Molly was working at the Canadian Bank of Commerce and Kenneth at the Edmonton branch of the Credit Foncier corporation, and both boarded at home. I was the only noncontributor to the family's finances, and up until the time I graduated from high school I hadn't the foggiest idea of what I wanted to do or how I might help. Then two things happened rather unexpectedly that were to have a considerable bearing on my future career. I secured a part-time job, probably through my mother's efforts, at the Strathcona branch of the Edmonton Public Library, and I was accepted for admission to the University of Alberta as a second-year student. I had my doubts about college--not that I had any reservations about the difficulty of handling the course work, which I considered largely incidental to the social, athletic, and other extracurricular activities of students at the University, but the tuition costs seemed to be an impossible barrier. Also I had a rather disagreeable acne problem and was extremely sensitive about mixing with large numbers of my peers. Considering my determined neuroses about these matters, I probably saw the part-time library job as an excuse to stay clear of most extracurricular activities and provide a partial solution to the tuition expense.

Most likely there was never any question about what I wanted to do. I am sure my mother had decided all along that one of her children would receive a college education, and I was her last hope. In some respects she was an enigma to me. I am sure that she loved me, cherished ambitions concerning me, and never ceased to be interested in my welfare, but she seemed compelled to thwart every natural desire I had, and at times she criticized bitterly my actions, even in petty matters. She derided me for taking up pipe smoking, pointing out that I looked ridiculous standing on the street corner with a pipe in my mouth. She pooh-poohed my desire to study law, declaring that it was a deceitful vocation and that in any case I had little talent for verbal expression. If I employed a foreign phrase in speech or in writing, she was quick to puncture my pretensions. If I spent money on a date other than the minister's daughter, she was likely to regard me as improvident and wayward. As a result, instead of confiding to her my hopes and aspirations, vague though they were, I grew more and more secretive. In the summer months, for example, if I were at home, I would often camp out in the yard or on someone else's property in order to spare myself her disapproval or the necessity for misrepresenting my behavior. Mother's upbringing was part and parcel of the Edwardian environment, and anything that did not fit into her strict code of propriety, social class, or religious mold she was apt to regard as unsavory. I felt instinctively that she looked on my friendship with people who had not enjoyed our former advantages as evidence of a serious flaw in my character. Nevertheless, I had a deep affection for my mother, and later on, when I had left home but communicated with her regularly by letter, my affection deepened with respect.

The Alberta sky is never so blue nor the still, fleecy clouds so white, nor the autumn leaves so red and yellow, as on the opening day of college. This picture by Lovat Dickson, a graduate of the University and a successful London publisher, conveys something of the charm of the campus at the time I was a student there:

> There was something symbolic to me in the very site where the university stood, high on the bluffs above the swift-flowing North Saskatchewan River. It bore to the untidy straggling town below the eminence and remoteness that the Acropolis bears to Athens. I had no aesthete's eye. My life had been spent in mining camps where the coal-tip and the slagheap or the ugly-shaped chimneys of the refinery

48

or the mill-house were the prominent features of
the landscape. I was no judge of beauty, but these
plain rectangular brick buildings with windows cased
in stone, fronting onto a green quad which was
criss-crossed by board walks, to save the tender
grass in the summer, to surmount the snow in winter; all this seemed to me impressive. There was
not a tree in sight. Though no ancient chapel or
Gothic archway, no cloister where one might walk
in contemplation, marked this academic scene, as
they had some of those which I had read about in
books, yet I was thrilled by it. A brightness
seemed to me to fall from the air. The season
was at its sweetest; the sun shone mellowly, the
air was invigorating; I felt myself drawn irresistibly
into a large company of the élite, and experienced
such a surge of happiness as I had not known for
years.

The "plain rectangular buildings" described by Dickson consisted of the Arts and Medical buildings and three residence
halls, Pembina, Athabasca, and Assiniboia. Except for a
few wood-frame buildings that were used as temporary quarters for Agriculture and Engineering, and the University's af-
filiate, St. Stephen's College, that was it. Nothing like the
dazzling complex of today--sixty or more brick, glass, and
steel structures standing out against a splendid Albertan blue
sky. One thinks of the thousand ships that were launched on
the Hudson River around Manhattan during the celebration of
the bicentennial of the United States. But as everyone knows,
or should know, the emphasis in a university is not on buildings but on fundamental values and knowledge. At the time
the University of Alberta was a mere infant. It had just celebrated its seventeenth birthday, and from a student body of
forty-five in its first session, 1908-09, accommodated in
rented quarters, it had grown to approximately thirteen hundred and fifty students during my first year. The founder
and president of the University, Dr. H. M. Tory, was still
the administrative head, and many of the Deans who joined
with him in this pioneering effort were also there to ensure
consistency in policy and a superior education. Also there
were half a dozen faculty who in their respective fields would
have been difficult to duplicate anywhere on the continent. If
I recall correctly, two of them were drafted shortly after my
graduation for major positions at the University of Minnesota
and the University of California, Berkeley. Indeed, if the

instruction in the subjects in which I was primarily inter-
ested--Classics (in translation), French, History, and Philos-
ophy--has been improved in colleges today, I am not aware
of it. And I base this opinion on forty-two years of experience in colleges and universities in Canada and the United
States, and seven years of retirement to think it over.

Many of us were obliged to work our way through college, and we learned to budget our time as well as our resources. A constant watch for possible ways of meeting
emergencies helped to develop discipline. Also I am sure
that the fierce long winters contributed to the bursts of energy
needed to carry on a heavy load of study and work. Along
with my peers I had my eye on one major goal: early graduation in good standing.

My initial enthusiasm for college life was somewhat
dampened by initiation week, which, as a second-year student,
I had hoped to escape. No such luck! I had my head shaved
with all the freshmen and was required to wear a silly little
cap with the University colors--green and gold. At one point
in the initiation I was forced to walk a plank blindfolded, without knowledge of how far the drop was, and then my friendly
guardians, the sophomores, shoved me off the end. I am the
worst sort of coward, and although the drop was probably less
than three feet, it scared the daylights out of me. I detested
being shoved around and paddled, and showed my annoyance,
and this only brought on more punishment of an even more
humiliating nature. Had I chosen to accept the ordeal with
meekness or with a little humor I expect the hazing might not
have been such a nauseating experience. As it was I hated
every minute of it and vowed that when it came my turn to
humiliate the incoming freshmen, I would have nothing to do
with the initiation. And I am proud to be able to say that in
the reverse situation a year later, I kept my vow.

When alumni get together for a reunion, there will always be
talk about their old professors. There are a few good ones
in every college. A former instructor at Harvard, Dr. Ed-
mund Kemper Broadus, was regarded by many at the University as a superman professor. In appearance he was rather
donnish, sported a neatly clipped Vandyke beard, and possessed a pair of eyes that looked like stones. Here is how
Lovat Dickson, his friend and one of his favorite students,
describes him:

50

He was a little man with a large and rather fine
head which perpetually shook and trembled like a
flower on a long stalk.   He wore gold-rimmed spec-
tacles from behind which his eyes looked coldly.
He smoked without ceasing, when one cigarette was
nearly done stubbing it out with his brown wooden
holder, and replacing it with a new one.

Dr. Broadus's undergraduate course "From Bacon to Hardy"
was required of all students proceeding toward an Arts degree.   I looked forward to his class because I hoped to major
in English and had been given some encouragement in high
school to believe I could write.   Much to my surprise and
embarrassment I received a failing grade on my first theme.
I was terribly upset and humiliated.   I was shot down before
I had hardly got started.   Lovat Dickson claims that this was
a device Dr. Broadus used for ensnaring future prospects for
the field of English, but obviously it did not work in my case.
I was too shy and proud to ask for a conference with him.   I
simply slogged along quietly, hopeful that I would improve
enough to get at least a passing grade, which I did.   I have
no doubt that Dr. Broadus was a fine teacher and that he was
totally immersed in English literature, but for me at least he
lacked the human touch and courtesy to communicate it by
contagion.

According to rumor or legend, if you dropped into
Room 205 in the Arts building to make some affirmation, its
occupant, Dr. Edouard Sonet, professor of French in the Department of Modern Languages, would pretend to agree with
you and then respond, "Ah yes, but...." And then, as his
colleague, E. J. H. Greene, points out, "he would adduce
five reasons why your proposition would not hold water." A
witty, not at all humble Frenchman, Dr. Sonet was not without prejudice, but he loved "the interplay of ideas and inspired in his students a desire to match their ideas with his."
I never knew him intimately enough to match ideas with him
because I was too busy with outside work, but I regarded him
as an excellent teacher though one to be feared.   His sar-
casm was sharp, and he had a loud voice.   Some students
claimed that he could be heard down at the High Level Bridge
when lecturing.   That may have been a bit of exaggeration,
for the Bridge was half a mile away, but there was no lan-
guid elegance about his teaching technique.   He would pace
the floor, shouting, gesticulating, and directing a regular
drumfire of questions at some unfortunate student.   Before I

51

took his course I already knew something about gender, declensions, conjugations, and the like, and possessed some facility in translation, but I could not speak a word of French except for a few ordinary phrases that every schoolchild knows. So when Dr. Sonet began his classroom interrogation, all my interest and pride in what I knew was quickly dashed because I was unable to follow what he was saying. I sat tongue-tied as in a nightmare. For the first month or so it was awful and I felt helpless. My stumbling block was that I could not speak French or understand when spoken to without thinking in English. But after repeated practice in which nothing was spoken except French Dr. Sonet performed a miracle. I suddenly discovered that my native tongue no longer rose in my mind to blot out the connection between the sound of French words and the things and actions they stood for. Before the end of the year I could carry on a conversation, in the classroom at least, with a reasonable degree of fluency. In my second year of French Dr. Sonet introduced us to the literature of France, and by the end of my senior year I had developed some appreciation of the classic short stories and novels. However, I am sorry to say that I never achieved the equivalent of an "A" in any of Dr. Sonet's courses.

In my time at the University no one was more highly respected and admired than William Hardy Alexander, Professor of the Classics, a youthful and handsome gentleman of of forty-seven. From his lectures I got some comprehension of what real education is all about, some understanding of the classics, and some tentative assumptions about beliefs and motives that give character and direction to one's life. During my first year he was elected Honorary President of the graduating class. His advice to the departing seniors was typical of the man: "Be simple, be direct, be human. Try to keep your spirit free, have an eye out for the beauty of which the world is full, and know that life is a jewel of many facets." If to any degree I have obtained a small measure of self-determination and appreciation of nature and the arts, I owe it in part to his influence, his lectures on Greek culture, and to other scholars, such as Livingstone and Zimmern, to whom we were introduced in our supplementary readings.

Of one thing I feel fairly certain. My courses in the study of Hellenic civilization provided an alternative to the confusion and dissatisfaction in which I found myself at this

time as a result of my early religious training. I grew up
in the Protestant tradition in the local Anglican church, where
my family attended conscientiously and where I knew and liked
many of the kindly and honest folk who made up the congrega-
tion. On the negative side I seldom left the church after the
Sunday service without feeling that religion was a stern and
frightening thing, implying not joy but punishment. I also observed that anyone holding views contrary to the church was
looked upon as a questionable character. So it was not un-
natural that when I became acquainted with Dr. Alexander's
liberal religious beliefs and his aggressive warfare against
fundamentalist religion I was delighted to discover that ethical
excellence could be measured by some other standard than
tradition, dogma, custom, and instinct. And in the study of
Greek culture I found first and foremost a confidence in the
capacity of people to solve their own problems where critical
inquiry is allowed full freedom to operate. What the Greeks
sought was knowledge, not for materialistic purposes but for
its own sake and for the sake of the person who acquired it.
By knowing the truth one would also know the good. Thus a
critical intellectual inquiry could broaden into a moral quest.
This was the message I received from Dr. Alexander's lectures and the readings he prescribed.

The late Stephen Leacock, who wrote much genial wisdom concerning what a university is all about, said that if he
were founding a university he would first found a smoking
room, a dormitory, and a library. After that, he added, "if
I still had more money than I could use I would hire a professor and get some textbooks." Well, the founding fathers
of the University held a different point of view. Professors
and textbooks we had in abundance. A few of the former were
exceptional by all accounts, and there was no shortage of textbooks even though the students had to pay for them. On the
other hand my impression of the library was that it consisted
of a very modest book collection and one large reading room
in the Arts Building. A canny Scots librarian, Donald Ewing
Cameron, had good rapport with his faculty colleagues and
students and was reputed to be an inveterate bookman. Something of the style and character of the man is revealed in his
letter to the University president on learning that his repeated
efforts to secure financial support for a separate library building had been torpedoed in the budget hearings by the legislature. As reported by Bruce Peel in his historical sketch of
the University library system, Cameron wrote the president
after he had been given the bad news:

I do not find myself this morning quite as staunch a stoic as I tried to be yesterday, and feel somewhat as a man does who has been running around a bit without knowing that he has been shot.

In spite of Cameron's noble efforts I do not recall any occasion when I was required in my course work to use the library in a genuine way. The attitude of many students was probably reflected in a statement of the senior who observed just before graduation, "A few more times in and out, and then Goodbye Library!" A good place to study one's textbooks, no doubt, while sitting beside library books.

If the University was short on books, it had one of the largest cluster of clubs, societies, and committees of any university north of the border. Their names were legion--the Debating Society, Glee Club, Student Christian Movement, Varsity Five, Press Club, Student Parliament, Mandolin Club, and many more--all designed to generate enthusiasm for group thinking and activity. I am sure that all these organizations were worthy in their way; they promoted friendships, managerial skills, and techniques for developing a high profile. At the same time they stole a great deal of time away from acquiring knowledge, which is the fundamental reason for attending college. There's a line in one of Stephen Leacock's essays that exactly describes the dilemma: "Odd, isn't it.... You must go into life body first and drag your head in afterwards."

I was not a member of any club, perhaps in part because I lived at home and worked part-time, and perhaps because I was a bit of a loner and my native reserve may have been mistaken for aloofness. The only organization I might have joined was the Tennis Club, but I do not recall ever receiving an invitation. It is quite possible, however, that one became a member automatically if one participated in tennis practice and the tournament games. In my second year at the University I entered the varsity tennis tournament, won, and was awarded a "Second 'A' Class" letter by the Athletic Association. Obviously tennis was not held in high repute as a varsity sport; it was still a game for the few rather than the showy spectacle it is today. My opponent in the finals was a very personable chap, Tommie Cross, who had a masterly command of the net and the ability to put away high lobs from deep in the backcourt. He was clearly the favorite to win the tournament. Here's the student reporter's account of the game ("The Gateway," October 29, 1925):

54

The men's singles was the big event with thirty-two
entries. G. R. Lyle proved the dark horse of the
tournament, subduing such players as MacKenzie,
Newson, Saucier, Giffen and Cross in hard-fought
matches. His match with Cross in the finals was
exceptionally interesting, Cross taking the first set
6-2, lost the second 6-3 and had Lyle down in the
third 3-0. Then Lyle, by hard driving and covering
every inch of the court, took six games in a row to
win the championship.

No one was more surprised than I by the outcome of the
match. And no one was more gracious about accepting defeat
than Cross.

There comes a time in the life of all students when they need
relief from the daily grind of study and working their way
through college, month after month, year after year. One
day at the end of spring semester I had a stroke of luck. I
happened to see a note on a University bulletin board inviting
applications for summer employment as truck drivers, golf
caddies, and waitresses at the famous Jasper Park Lodge in
the Rockies some two hundred and fifty miles west of Edmonton. I applied immediately and got a job caddying for visitors
and tournament players. If I remember correctly, the modest
pay was fifty dollars a month with full board and tips extra.
A paying job was not my principal concern. I wanted to eat
well and live and work outdoors. I could never afford a holiday in the Rockies, but I longed for the life of a forester or
guide--at least for the summer.

I had dreamed about the place many times, but when I
got there, I know of no words to express how this dream
came true. I was overwhelmed by the vastness and wonder
of it all and the spectacular mountain sights that I had only
seen in paintings and photographs before. Even the mountain
and lake landscapes of the brilliant Canadian artist A. Y.
Jackson could not compare with the originals. There were
exciting views of jewellike lakes hemmed in by the mountains,
glimpses of large game animals in their native habitat--elk
and deer so well protected and so tame that they often appeared on the fairways--and perhaps most thrilling of all, the
opportunity to stand on a glacier thousands of feet thick,
knowing that the ice beneath was formed in prehistoric times.

The Lodge was located a mile or so away from the

town of Jasper on beautiful green Lac Beauvert. Even though
it was less than five years old when I was there, it was considered one of the finest resorts of its kind anywhere. Behind it towered pyramid mountains, and amid the encircling
peaks we could see dimly in the south Mt. Edith Cavell. The
luxurious main lodge and the surrounding cottages were all
built of native logs on boulder foundations. In their spectacular setting, with which they were in perfect harmony, they
provided a quality of outdoor life unlike anything I had ever
experienced before or since.

By Labor Day I was beginning to tire of toting heavy
golf bags up and down the steep sides of the mountain-girt
course, which was constructed for superhuman caddies as well
as championship golf. I had enjoyed enormous meals, felt
physically and mentally revived, and was ready to return home
to my studies and work at the public library. I suspect that
I was beginning to miss my books, the newspapers, the
Saturday-nighters who came to return library books while in
town for shopping (and always knew that the book shelver had
"another one" just like the one they'd had before), even my
solitary walks along the banks of the Saskatchewan, but most
of all the easygoing, weekend companionship of my two canoeing friends, Don Sandilands, the artist, and Jack Smiles, jack-
of-all-trades.

Don was a lanky redheaded Scot with a passionate dedication to canoeing, painting, and poetry. His mystical feeling
for nature is revealed in these exquisite lines from his poem
"1934-1935":

>   Parabola of life! O'er steppingstones of doubt,
>   Misunderstanding, contradiction, faith
>   In further seeing, broadens as it moves,
>   Embraces all men, new horizons shows.
>   We must not stop! We cannot for the bowl
>   Against us spins! We must keep pace and more,
>   Or perish! There is no end, but one
>   Immense, continuous Motion.... Infinite....

Jack had some glaring faults of a kind that would dis-
pose mothers to regard him as a corrupter of their sons'
morals. At times he would walk into a sporting-goods store
and come out with a couple of hunting knives or some other
expensive item hidden in his trousers. He drank quite a bit,
although I never saw him drunk. I was never sure whether

he was just plain cuckoo, delightfully so in many ways, or whether he felt so damn sure of himself that he just let his Id go. He ended up marrying a nice lass who frequently accompanied Don and his girl and myself on canoeing trips. When last I heard of him, long after I had left the city, he was peddling milk for one of the city dairies. His warm relationship with his mother was a never-ending delight to me. I often sat in their kitchen, sipping hot cocoa, while Jack and his mother gossiped and joshed one another in the most endearing way, seemingly quite oblivious of my presence. Finally Jack would rise from his hard, upright chair, give his mother a hug, and then shout at me: "Let's go, Sanitary Man. Mother wants to get rid of us." This is how I remember him.

Apart from my mother and sister and the staff of the library there were few women in my life. I was shy and awkward to be sure, but even so there was very little opportunity for an off-campus student to date a Wauneita (varsity squaw) because the boys in residence outnumbered the girls in Pembina two to one. There were numerous dark-haired women in my dreams who consoled me sexually, but about the only way to meet and enjoy the company of girls at the University was to attend the dances.

I was not keen on dancing until I met Kay, a secretary working and living across the river in Edmonton. She was a well-made girl, rather small and slender but anything but fragile. She had soft, wavy black hair and wide-set eyes. She fairly vibrated with vitality whenever the word dancing came into the conversation. We met occasionally at a dime-a-dance hall at the north end of the High Level Bridge. The more I saw of her dancing with other fellows the more ill at ease I felt about my lack of terspsichorean skill. I decided that my career depended upon doing something about it, so I began paying attention to the advertisements of the Sullivan Dancing Academy in the student newspaper. These folks promised to make you a Fred Astaire, unless you broke a leg; here's how their ad read:

THESE ARE THE THINGS YOU WILL BE ABLE
TO FOLLOW WITH EASE AND CONFIDENCE
   How to dance the waltz step
   How to dance the right waltz turn
   How to dance the left waltz turn
   How to dance the forward and back waltz step

How to dance the Fox Trot with many variations
How to dance the One Step with its different com-
binations
How to dance the right and left turn in the One Step
How to dance the forward Two Step
How to dance the backward Two Step
How to dance the right and left turn in the Two Step

The lessons actually went ill, but at least I managed to improve my facility as a waltzer and fox trotter while holding
my partner in the prescribed manner, which one local wit
described as "the syncopated embrace."

Dancing was popular at the University. There were
informal stag dances every Saturday night that were well attended, but unfortunately I had a library job that got in my
way. Although the student code frowned on taking outsiders
to the major social functions--one student was hauled before
the student honor board and banned for the rest of the year for
violating this provision--I never felt the slightest hesitation about
taking Kay to the Freshman and Sophomore Receptions, the
Undergraduate Dance, and the Junior Prom. Her dance program was booked long in advance of each affair--a practice
objected to by the student newspaper as promoting "cliqueish-
ness," but widely followed--and I always looked forward with
a mixture of pride and anticipatory delight to escorting her
and showing her off to my friends.

The music for these functions was supplied by the University Orchestra or the Varsity Five and sometimes both,
the former being especially popular for the supper dance and
the latter for the boys and girls in good shape who varied the
waltz and fox trot steps with the latest imports from Harlem's
Savoy Ballroom, the Charleston, the Lindy Hop, and the Shag.
The decorations for these dances were elaborate and elegant.
I vaguely remember one that had an Irish theme, in which the
ceiling of Athabasca Dining Hall was canopied with streamers
and shamrocks lit up by some kind of winking glow lights, the
walls covered with Irish shields, the orchestra stand supported
by huge golden Irish harps, and the rendezvous doors decorated in the manner of old Irish inns--behind one of which
was served Irish punch. Even the programs, in the form of
a harp, were Irish, and during the evening one of the girls
danced an Irish jig and sang the song "The Love of Molly
Maloney." The most popular dance tunes, as I remember
them, were "Collegiate," "Yes Sir, That's My Baby," "Sleepy

Time Gal," "Rio Rita," "Always," and "Moonlight and Roses."

The greatest drawback of these dances for me was that I spent all my money on tuxedoes and taxi fare so that I was obliged to walk home in the early hours of the morning. I invariably missed the last tram car. Crossing the High Level Bridge on a blustery winter night with the temperature below zero was an ordeal. The snow-covered river lay hundreds of feet below, silent and frozen solid. The Northern Lights ran up and down the horizon like moving streamers of ever-changing color. It was beautiful but a bit frightening. The cold was intense and the wind stung like a whip. By the time I arrived home I was half frozen, my ears and nose badly nipped in spite of frequent rubbing with snow during the three- or four-mile walk.

Another girl I dated, Hildegarde, worked in the city but lived in Strathcona, not too far from our home. Like Kay, she was as slender as a boy but attractive in quite a different way. She was tall whereas Kay was small. She wore her light brown hair short and had prominent cheek bones and the clear-skinned wholesome look of the outdoor Canadian girl. She loved to joke and laugh; I felt very comfortable with her. We walked, skated, and spelled out our fantasies together. She lived with her charming married sister, to whose home I was frequently invited for dinner. I felt free to drop in at any time. By the end of my senior year Hildegarde and I may have had a flicker of something going for each other, but after I left Edmonton it quickly burnt out. We exchanged letters for a time, but her letters grew fewer and fewer. And then they stopped.

8: APPRENTICE YEARS

There are three women who recur persistently to my memory when I think of my part-time job at the Strathcona Public Library, but perhaps I should first say something about the Library itself. Located two blocks north of the straggling main street of Strathcona, Edmonton South, the Library was a small but handsome two-story brick structure designed in what I thought was some form of modified gothic but which Vincent Richards, Director of the Edmonton Public Library, informs me is something quite different: "The architectural style is known as English Neo-Renaissance, of which there are a few examples still left in the city, including the Strathcona Library." Twin towers flanked the entrance to the building, which was approached by a short flight of steps and adorned with mullioned windows. The front entrance door was crowned by a rounded arch. There was a church across the street, and I forget what the other buildings were, but I remember quite distinctly that the Library offered a welcome variety to the uninspired architecture of the surrounding buildings.

The interior of the building was arranged in the library mode of the day, with the registration and circulation desk at the front, a children's room to the left, and a reference and reading room for adults to the right. Behind the circulation desk, extending to the rear for some twenty feet, was an open-stack book area with wide aisles where readers were permitted to select their own books. The stack was bordered on one side by a staff workroom and on the other by the Librarian's office. Since the latter led to the basement stairway, it afforded very little privacy. Indeed, I seldom remember seeing Miss McNee in her office. She was always busy assisting readers in the reference room or directing the staff. A large lounge area in the basement was used almost exclusively by checker players, from whom I earned many an extra dollar by keeping the place open after the library was closed. The basement also housed the furnace and a catchall storage room that looked as though it had been devastated by high explosives. There was a large auditorium and a small staff room on the second floor. I came to know every nook and cranny of that building during the three years I sweated nights and weekends there to earn my daily bread.

If my years at the University failed to implant an interest in books and reading, I discovered it at the Strathcona Public Library. In this small house of books you couldn't find the missing works of Tacitus or the Abracadabra of Polyphemus, but its shelves housed the largest collection of third-rate adventitious rubbish that it has ever been my pleasure to find brought together in one place. I read it all: Zane Grey, Harold Bindloss, Clarence Mulford, and the rest of the cowboy writers; E. Phillip Oppenheim's mystery thrillers, which he produced at the rate of three a year for over fifty years; F. Marion Crawford, whose criminal characters rivaled the Mafiosi in glamour; Ethel May Dell and Marie Corelli, ultra-romantics; Julia Moore, who Clemens once declared "had the touch that makes an intentionally humorous episode pathetic and an intentionally pathetic one funny"; Sax Rohmer, creator of the imperturbable Fu Manchu; Anthony Hope; and others. These were the masters to whom I owe my initiation into the world of print. And there were many others like me.

People by the score came to the library on Saturday nights--mothers dragging children after a day's shopping came to exchange their books, women gossiping with the staff across the circulation desk, and earnest, upward-striving men hoping to improve themselves on the job. Sooner or later most of them would make a beeline for the book stack and the boy pushing a cart full of books or replacing them on the shelves. They would whisper to him conspiratorially, "Have you anything good?" Being that boy, and having attained the summit of literary acumen, I proceeded to hand out one thriller after another: Sir Rider Haggard's "King Solomon's Mines" or the daring "She"; one of George Barr McCutcheon's "Graustarkian" romances; Zane Grey's "Riders of the Purple Sage," and so on ad infinitum. In so doing I discovered what education is all about: you start by reading what you enjoy reading. Later you learn to discriminate.

I do not recall that I had any special title at the library, and perhaps none would have fitted me. I had no specific area of responsibility. If I had finished putting up books that readers had returned or "reading" the shelves to see that books were in their proper places, I might be directed to repair books in the staff workroom or to file newspapers in the basement, or--if there was a great rush at the circulation desk--to help charge and discharge books. Staff members often asked me to get them midmorning snacks from the nearby Greek confectionery and ice cream parlor, or to pick up a suit at the cleaners. On my full day, Saturday, I might do all of these. No authority was attributed to my job except at closing time, but I derived no little prestige from my proximity to the staff and attendance at the University. I never took the job too seriously or thought of it as a profession. For me it was a financial assist in my studies and a step on the way to a career as yet invisible.

The Strathcona Public Library contributed a great deal to my education, and for this I am greatly indebted to Margaret McNee, the Librarian, and her two assistants, Edna Brushett and Miriam Inkpen. Miss McNee represented authority tinged with temperament; Edna, practical wisdom and old-fashioned propriety; and Miriam, an innocent flapper immersed in the lifestyle of her day.

Judging from the vigor of her makeup, Miss McNee was in her late forties. She was a graceful, well-tailored woman with bobbed black hair that shone with a soft radiance. She showed an interest in my studies at the University and impressed upon me that it was my duty to take advantage of the opportunities I was enjoying. She was strong on discipline. If I displeased her in any way, she might banish me to what I called the Black Hole of Calcutta. This place defied description. I had never seen such disorder before. It was a stuffy, windowless room in the basement next to the furnace, with discarded gift books strewn about and piles of dusty newspapers that I was supposed to arrange and tie up in orderly files. If Miss McNee was particularly pleased with me, I might be told that I could mend books in the staff workroom or replace the books that had been returned during the day. The former was my favorite, and if I do say so myself, I believe that I developed some skill in book repair during my stint in the library.

Edna Brushett was a tall, slender woman in her mid-thirties, intelligent and attractive, who reminded me very much of the idealized heroines found in Victorian novels. The women in these novels were certainly long on engagements, and Edna attested to this practice. For the three years I worked at the library her fiancé came by every evening at closing time to escort her home. Their wildest debauch was probably a visit to the local moviehouse.

Miriam was blond, petite, pretty, chic, and far more attractive sexually than anyone in her own class that I was likely to encounter. From the fringe of her short skirt to the base of her low neckline, I discovered that women are equally divided down the center. One day I accidentally spilled a large blob of library paste on her neck that dropped into the cleavage. She let out a yell, and I practically tore off the front of her blouse mopping up the spill. After that we could never again be formal with one another.

There were two men connected with the library during my time there: Charles Flack, temporary staff assistant (perhaps on loan from the main library in Edmonton when the Strathcona branch was shorthanded) and C. A. Russell, the janitor. Both men were veterans of World War I and had suffered severely at the front. Charlie was wounded at Passchendale and Russell at "Wipers," the Tommy's pronunciation of Ypres. I looked up to Charlie not only because of his war record and senior year at the University that I had just entered, but also because he was handsome, stylish, and highly respected by everyone. An unusually white face drew attention to his jet-black hair and moustache; his eyes were sharp behind glasses. He walked with a cane and a noticeable limp, the result of his war wounds. He was well informed about library practice, having taken courses in library science at the University of Wisconsin before enrolling in 1921 for an Arts degree at the University of Alberta.

C. A. Russell was short, chunky, and looked a bit vulgar, but he was a "right decent fellow," to quote one of his admirers. When he walked, he kind of rocked along using both arms as ballast. When he sat down, I often observed him looking sorrowfully at his gouty legs, which were a legacy from marching through sloughed-up mud and shell holes filled with putrid water. He was married to a pretty English lass and was a staunch supporter of the British Empire. They lived with their two children in a house back of the post office in a household as near to a pigsty as it is possible to

63

get. I spent a summer there camped out in their backyard and became good friends with the family. The children would sometimes bring a mug of strong, hot, mud-colored tea and jam puffs to my tent on Sunday morning.

Some twenty years or so after I left Edmonton I happened to be correcting student papers in my office at the University of Illinois, where I had a summer assignment, when in walked a figure from my past. It was Charles Flack. His hair and moustache had turned completely white, and at first I did not recognize him. He had heard that I was teaching at the University during the summer session and had dropped in to say hello. I believe he said that he was cataloging at a college in the Midwest. I do not remember how we celebrated the reunion but having the idol of my youth take the trouble to visit his former pageboy gave me an hour of the greatest pleasure, which I shall never forget.

9: BID FOR FREEDOM

After the tumult and shouting of Convocation dies one is pretty much left to oneself to take the open road--a phrase William Hardy Alexander coined long before Jack Kerouac made it popular. Among the raciest of biographies appearing in the student yearbook for 1927 was the following:

> Englishman, but speaks French like a native. University career colored by high marks and a tennis championship. A librarian of much fame. In some ways Guy finds time to indulge in sports of all sorts. Ambition--to see the world.

The author of this casserolette got one thing straight, at least: at this point my ambition was to seek freedom to find answers of my own.

When the opportunity came to accompany a stock freighter across Canada, with the possibility that there might also be a passageway to London, I jumped at the chance. As it turned out later the train was a regular freighter with only two cars of cattle attached. My job was to see the cattle safely from the stockyards in Edmonton to Montreal via the Canadian National Railway.

Roughing it three-quarters of the way across Canada left you with three possible choices: (1) riding the tops of freight cars (which meant that you might have to pay tribute to the brakeman who frequently patrolled the deck); (2) riding the rods underneath each car by lying on your stomach, eyes screwed tight with fear; and (3) hopping a freight in the hope of finding an open boxcar. If you were lucky enough to travel as a watchman with cattle, you took whatever accommodations you could find and hoped that eventually you would be able to find a place in the caboose. But no matter how you rode, it was a grimy, exhausting business.

Just as fatiguing was the length of time it took to make the crossing; in those days it was often as long as a month. Moreover, traveling at this time of the year usually meant company. In the fall there were always a great many migrants moving east across Canada headed for the southern part of the United States in order to escape the harsh Canadian prairie winters. The folk stories about these people were not pleasant. Almost without exception every migrant was considered a witless, worthless, drunken fellow, much given to violence. I was never touched by any of them, but, by God, the thought that they might toss me off the train terrified me.

My family and friends tried to persuade me to abandon the whole idea, pointing out that I was committing myself to something practically unknown and that I would be terribly lonely without my friends and home surroundings. They painted a glowing picture of opportunities in Canada. Where else, they reiterated, would I find a better mix of Old World and modern city life or a land to support everything from grape culture to wheat growing? What country had such immense parks offering grand jobs for outdoor men and women and hunting and sports the like of which brought thousands of tourists fleeing the Volstead Act? They quoted my favorite humorist, Stephen Leacock, as saying, "Beyond it [Canada] till we reach another world, is nothing." I had always had a yen to travel, and the more they talked the more I knew I must cast off the comforting warmth of family and friends to stand squarely on my own. Deep down at rock bottom I wanted to make a bid for complete freedom. I assured my mother that if I needed help abroad, I would not hesitate to call on our friends and relatives in London and Paris.

In a long life I have discovered that experiences that are of a painful nature soon fade from the memory. Consequently I have forgotten much of my adventure in crossing Canada, but a few dominating impressions remain: my first night catching the freight train, the vast emptiness of the country through which we were passing, and my first and only ride in a caboose.

66

Early in September came a hot day and a very cool night when I found myself crouching beside the railroad tracks just a mile north of the stockyards. I waited about an hour beyond the time the train was supposed to be coming, but there was no sign of a headlight as I scanned the tracks, anxiously awaiting its arrival. I had been told that there was a bare possibility of a coach being attached; if so, it would be just ahead of the caboose at the end of the train. When at long last the rails began to hum, I hoisted my knapsack of food and clothing ready to make a run and jump. Finally the huge bulk of the engine loomed into view, a lantern waved, and the train slowly began to pick up speed. Car after car rolled by--C.N., Grand Trunk Pacific, Norfolk and Western, Long Lake Railway Co., and other minor twigs of the Canadian National. There seemed no end to them, but at last the cattle cars and, mirabile dictu, the coach, came into view. I dived into a cloud of steam, ran alongside the train (which was now gathering speed), jumped, made a wild clutch for the handrail, and was aboard. And so were a dozen or more other bodies who came out of the shadows at the very last minute. Finding no open boxcars, they swung aboard the coach with the ease and skill that comes from long experience riding the rods.

In less time than it takes to say Jack Robinson about half the car was filled with men of all ages from forty to seventy, mostly unkempt, with nary a student rider among them. Some were pretty mean-looking characters--what in my ignorance I assumed to be the down-and-outs who float on the outer fringes of society. I tightened my grip on my knapsack and felt in my side pocket to make sure that my summer savings of fifty dollars were still intact. One two-coated fellow sitting down beside me unnerved me considerably. He wore a heavy beard, chewed an old cigar, and looked me over rather wolfishly.

"Where you going?" he asked.

"All the way to Montreal," I replied, surprised that he should ask.

We rode on, neither of us saying anything for quite some time, and then he picked up the conversation from where we left off.

"Tain't all that far," he said, and then added with a grizzled grin, "if you make it."

"Well, " I said, surprised again, "What do you mean, if I make it?"

"Well, " he replied, "I thought you were heading for a funeral when I saw you jump in the coach." And then he added, "You've got to know what you're doing, " and he proceeded then and there to give me a lesson on how to jump a moving train. From then on I changed my ideas about the migrants. Some were bums, some did outrageous things, but by and large, they were a friendly bunch, and they told stories and swore the likes of which I had never encountered before.

Day after day we passed through the Alberta and Saskatchewan countryside, the scenery reflecting what has been most widely trumpeted about the prairie provinces--miles and miles of wheat, oats, and barley ripening in the late summer sun and stretching to the horizon. The scrub grass and flowers that covered the land when my parents made the trek with Barr to the promised land were largely gone. No doubt these boundless fields of grain that replaced the natural flora had helped to clear the debts of many of those same British immigrants. Thus did men and women strike the balance between nature and the need for survival. The view was not entirely a golden monotony of crops. Maple saplings and green willow marked the course of shallow creeks where many a hedge was loaded with clusters of ripe purple saskatoon berries and cranberries. White poplar sheltered the scattered farm buildings and the grazing stock. There were already signs of the migration season on the way--mallards and geese were settling in on the lakes and wheatfields on their way south.

One of the most exciting things I sighted was a prairie wolf, or what I thought was one at least, a shaggy animal much larger than a coyote, which I guess might have weighed fifty to eighty pounds. He was sneaking along the shoreline of a creek where deer were accustomed to make their way, though whether some straggler from an earlier herd passing that way was his quarry I had no way of knowing. Actually I had never seen a prairie wolf before, but I had heard plenty of stories from early settlers about their ravages among the stock.

Close to Saskatoon we entered a large wooded area and shortly afterward crossed the southern fork of the Saskatchewan River. Here we had a short layover, which gave me

time to look around a bit and to find a place where I could
eat without attracting the attention of my hungry fellow trav-
elers in the coach.   The sandwiches were all gone by this
time, but I still had some cheese, sardines, canned salmon,
potted meat, and Swiss milk chocolate left in my knapsack.
Everything was so expensive at the station stops that I was
thankful I had followed my mother's advice and carried a full
load of food.   I found a place down near the river where I
ran into an old-timer who, when he decided that I was not
just another one of "those bums roddin' it," became quite
friendly and told me a lot about how the town was born and
how a large band of crazy English immigrants had had a lot
to do with its commercial success.

One story he told me about the place in its early days
had to do with a fire in the main street at a time when there
was no firefighting apparatus.   In order to save the town a
few quick-witted men upended shacks on either side of the
burning building and moved them into the street.   This they
repeated several times until the fire was isolated and the town
saved.   I took this to be one of those colorful stories that
become part of the legend of every small western town until
some fifty years later, when I happened to read a small book
by a historian in which he gave an account of this very same
fire.

The train left Saskatoon toward evening.   Before climbing on board I took one last look at the sun beginning its
downward path toward the western horizon.   It was a spectacle of incomparable beauty, which I cannot begin to describe
but which is peculiar to this region.   It reminded me of the
colors of the sunset that I used to see as a boy when returning in the evening from a nearby farm where I would often
walk in order to get a warm, rich drink while the cows were
being milked.   It seemed to me then, as now, that the colors
of the sunset in all their diversity were shimmering off the
surface of a great lake.   As far as the eye could see it dwelt
only upon what was truly magnificent.

An hour or two after we left Saskatoon shadows crossed
the moving land to add their beauty to the countryside--a hill,
a bluff, and a smattering of lakes.   In the growing gloom tiny
dots of light from isolated farmers' homes pierced the darkness, while in the sky above plumes of smoke belched forth
like a fiery furnace from the straining engine.   We made frequent stops for what must have been a round-the-world tour

of water tanks or a shunting back and forth on double tracks
to let some fast-flying passenger train go through.   Even
though we were standing still, the coach swayed back and
forth as the express train hurtled by us.   Sometimes in starting up again we seemed to have great difficulty in making an
incline, but on the downslope we shot ahead with amazing
speed.   All night long there was a continuous clanking and
clattering of car rods and connectors, which did nothing to
rest my tired muscles or encourage sleep.   This went on for
two or three days until we reached Winnipeg, then one of the
country's principal cities and sometimes referred to as the
Chicago of Canada.

The name Winnipeg suggests a more modest stature.
It is derived from the Indian word "Ouinipigon," which means
"muddy water."   From its reputation in the West I took it to
be chiefly noted for a very cold climate (the natives insist
that the cold is "dry," by which they mean that you do not
feel it), a worldwide outlook, and the royal ballet.   On arrival I discovered that there would be a layover for two days,
and the thought of spending all that time in solitary so thoroughly depressed me that I called up a friend of the family
who had moved there some years earlier to ask if I might
rest up at his home.

When the Rev. Canon Christopher Carruthers came to
pick me up, I must have elicited the same kind of admiration
that a streaker would at a church supper.   Without a change
of clothing and with very little washing, I had been traveling
for several weeks in a coach through which sand, soot, cin-
ders, and smoke blew continuously.   I was dirty, unkempt,
and greasy.   But the Reverend was gracious and understanding.   When we got back to his home, I had a wonderful shower, clean clothes, and a hearty lunch.   Almost immediately
I fell asleep on the sofa and did not wake up for the next
twenty-four hours.   As a matter of fact, when I finally awoke,
there was just time for another meal and then I was on my
way.   While I was asleep, the Carruthers family had washed
my old clothes and restocked the food compartment of my
knapsack.   I was most grateful.   For an hour or so afterward I had a dull twinge of homesickness, but the rumble of
the train and the scenery spinning by soon made me aware of
the reality of things and quickened my sense of the adventure
ahead.

When we entered Ontario, a short distance from Winni-

peg, the farmlands and wheatfields soon ran out and were replaced by what can only be described as primeval wilderness.
From dawn to dusk the freight pushed its way through vast
unpopulated stretches of subarctic rock sprinkled with thousands of lakes.   It was during this stretch that I had the good
fortune to be invited by the conductor to spend some time in
the caboose and to view the countryside from the vantage of
the cupola or small projection quarters above the front of the
cab.   I sat there for several hours and found my spirits considerably lifted.   Whether it is the prairie provinces with
their vast wheatfields that catch the eye or the unbroken Ontario wilderness of rock and water, there is always magic
from the cupola view.

     The legend is that the word caboose first appeared as
"cambose" or "camboose" in the records of the French navy
in the middle of the eighteenth century.   Its earliest appearance in print appears to be in 1769, according to the "Shorter
Oxford," which also quotes U.S. usage, 1881, as meaning "a
van or car on a freight train used by workmen or the men in
charge."   It is by no mere accident that the word has been
associated with the sea.   Bergen and Cornelia Evans point out
that a caboose in England means a galley, a kitchen on the
deck of a ship.   Most of us, I believe, think of the caboose
as the last car on a freight train--the one you wait for im-
patiently in order to make the grade crossing.

     From a more practical point of view, as I discovered
in talking with the conductor, the caboose is a kind of a second home for the chief crew members.   It provided sleeping
quarters, a place for meals (it was equipped with a coal
stove, from which arose a delightful aroma of coffee brew-
ing), an office and work area for transacting freight business,
and a place to store all tools needed in the operation of the
train: signal fuses, train lanterns, wrecking tools, and the
like.

     The cupola where I spent most of my time in this ca-
boose had its function, too.   It was intended to give the crew
members an overview of the entire length of the train, a vantage point from which they could spot any irregularities in the
operation of the cars.   I also spent some time on the main
floor of the caboose and observed that in addition to the coal
stove there were long, narrow benches on either side.   Several crew members came in while I was there and spent the
time talking, smoking, chewing tobacco, and telling stories.

I had the strange feeling that I was once again in the basement lounge of the Strathcona library branch attending an all-male meeting.

At Sudbury the line divided, one branch going to Toronto and on to the States and the other continuing by way of Ottawa to my destination at Montreal. There were feeding and watering pens at Sudbury, and the cattle cars were detached in order to take care of the animals, who by this time were as weary of travel as I was. Unknown dispatchers, narcissists to a man, rattled out orders over a megaphone, shuffling us to and fro until I felt sure we would never be able to resume our journey intact. But cars were finally marshaled for their destination, the cattle cars were hooked up, and we were on our way to Ottawa.

The seat of the Dominion government was only a stone's throw from Quebec, but still it was in Ontario. As we passed through, I was struck by the similarity of the picturesque setting of the parliament buildings overlooking the Ottawa River to the Alberta parliament buildings overlooking the Saskatchewan. Soon afterward the vast emptiness of Canada began to end. A few houses, then whole villages and railway tracks came racing out of nowhere to converge and slide effortlessly alongside our slowly moving train. Some three days later we arrived at Montreal, where I was informed that my job was completed. Nothing was said about passageway to London. I had only fifty dollars in my pocket, and I was grimy and weary to death of travel. I had not had a decent wash-up since leaving Winnipeg, my clothes were filthy, and I wasn't sure that any hotel would admit me even if I decided to use some of my capital. Finally, after several times being ignored when I stopped someone to ask for directions, I was on my way to the YMCA, where I secured a room for one dollar, showered, and slept once again round the clock.

72

10: THE NEW YORK CONNECTION

Halfway between Winnipeg and the schizophrenic railway center at Sudbury the conductor came up to the cupola of the caboose, where I was enjoying my first comfortable ride since I left home. We were approaching the end of the journey across Canada, and I was beginning to worry a great deal about my future after we reached Montreal. Would I find the passage-paying work I had been led to believe would be available when we got there in order to continue my travels on to London? I asked the conductor's opinion. He seemed to be a brotherly, experienced type of Canadian. He did not answer immediately, but when he did he surprised me by replying with a question of his own.

"Why do you want to go abroad?" he asked.

After weeks of roughing it on a freight my bid for independence and freedom was no longer quite so bold; instead I explained that I wanted to knock about the geography of the earth a bit, to meet people in different countries, and to learn some of those things one did not meet up with in college. Again there was a long pause, and then he informed me that I was not the first college student working his way across Canada who was credulous enough to believe that there would be work aboard ship to pay his ocean fare.

"I've seen a number of them," he said, "and from what I hear tell I would not count too much on your finding work for your passage."

"Well," I replied defensively--I go on the defensive whenever I feel let down--"what would you do in my place?"

73

He thought for a moment before replying. "In the light of what you have told me," he said, "I am wondering whether you might not be wise to postpone your European exploration until you have gained some travel experience in--let us say--New York City."

When pressed for further information, he explained that at one time he had lived some six months in New York City and had found it an amazing place, exotic enough to satisfy the most adventurous.

"New York," he said, "is a nation in itself, a nation of immigrants from all over the world. You can be one of them. You will find Germans in the restaurant business, Irish on the police force, Chinese cooking opium in Chinatown, Greeks operating the fruit stands, Polish girls waiting on tables at Childs, Negroes dancing in Harlem, Jews working in the garment industry, and Central Europeans enjoying the night life after a hard day's work."

He paused for a moment and then concluded, "New York is where I would go. But you must, of course, do what you yourself want to do."

When I woke up after my first night at the Montreal YMCA, my bones ached from the punishment they had taken during the past few weeks. But happily the deep depression that had followed on the news that there would be no job to pay my passageway across the ocean had largely faded. I had no idea what I was going to do, and there were moments on that cool autumn morning when I thought seriously of taking what money I had left and buying a ticket for home. Perhaps it was the sharp sting in the air that reminded me of the harsh winter ahead out West that held me back, but whatever it was I knew at heart that there was no turning back. There seemed to be only one thing to do, and that was to follow the advice of my friend, the conductor. New York might possibly afford an opportunity for work and most certainly would give me a wide variety of experience. Before leaving Montreal I spent a couple of days there and found it a delightful mix of France and Edinburgh. It gave me a chance to try out my French in the coffee shops, although I soon discovered that behind that charming Gallic smile lay a shrewd tradesman's skill in separating me from my money. When I left, my savings had dwindled to about twenty-five dollars.

I bought a ticket and took a window seat on the train

to New York. I hoped that the passing scene would take the
load off my mind. When your mind and your muscles relax,
the view from the train is a pleasant haven of greenery. And
it was a splendid day for viewing. The train rushed through
the wooded country, lakes lying bright in the autumn sun, with
innumerable farms and small towns, and all carefully grassed
and flowered. Compared with the vast emptiness of Canada,
I thought, this land must be very easy and well filled.

When we pulled into Grand Central Station in the late
afternoon, I hesitated to climb to the street level because of
a childish fear that skyscrapers cut off light and air in the
street. Actually my impression of New York was formed
from my boyhood reading of Horatio Alger. I remembered
that the city gave hard-working youths and wayfarers the
quickest chance to better themselves but also that their success was often less dependent on their virtue and industry
than upon luck or some incredible turn of events that brought
them to the attention of a rich man and patron. Also, New
York à la Alger seemed to be full of drab skyscrapers,
thieves, and con men who would stop at nothing to make a
buck. I was taking no chances on luck or misadventure. All
I hoped for was to make my introduction to the city as pleasant as possible, to be able to breathe easily, and to escape
the melee of the multitudes. When the passengers got off the
train at Grand Central, I followed the crowd until I spied a
guard. I explained to him that I dreaded crowds and tall
buildings.

"Can you tell me," I asked, "where I can climb to the
street level and shake off the horror of skyscrapers and
swindlers?"

He batted his eyebrows a couple of times in disbelief
and then pointed to the uptown platform of the nearest Inter-
borough Rapid Transit (IRT) and told me to get change at the
booth in order to pass through the turnstiles. What he failed
to mention was that the nerve center of the IRT divided halfway uptown, one branch of the line going to the West and the
other to the East Side. This oversight cost me four winter
months of the most miserable living conditions I experienced
during my whole stay in New York.

The uptown subway was jammed with passengers. I
stood and kept my elbows as close to my sides as possible.
At 96th Street the people piled out, and instead of getting off

75

and switching to the West line I took advantage of the split-second interval before others piled in to grab a seat. Some four or five stations later I began to feel dizzy from the putrid air and worried that I might be getting too far out of the city. At the next stop I stepped off and followed a young woman up the stairway to the street level. When she paused at the top of the stairs to adjust the heel of her shoe, I took the opportunity to ask where we were and if there was a YMCA nearby.

She replied tersely, "Fifth Avenue and 125th Street. See the street sign up there? The place you are looking for is down 125th, less than half a block."

Without waiting for my thanks she slung her jacket over her shoulder, skipped across the street, and disappeared into an office building.

I found the "Y" and was assigned to a room on the third floor. It was a dingy-looking place with faded yellow wallpaper and a view overlooking an airshaft. For one accustomed to a focused view of white clouds against a sheer blue sky this was bad enough, but instead of waking up to the song of birds I heard nothing but the roar of traffic. The first night I was awakened by bedbugs sucking the life out of me. I was horrified and disgusted. I dressed hurriedly and wandered out into the semidarkness just preceding dawn. It was chilly, and there was hardly anyone around. The shrill horn of a taxi echoed off buildings whose outlines I could barely make out. The sun hadn't come up yet, but as the light grew stronger I felt comforted by seeing the faint grey shapes of apartments and fire escapes and small flights of birds heading to or from some wooded park. After a while I grew tired and hungry and returned to the "Y," where I found my room had already been disinfected and the mattress replaced.

A much more pleasant recollection came later when on my way to Columbia University, I would walk down 125th Street in the early mornings of that lovely autumn to cut across traffic to get to Morningside Heights. Christopher Morley called such days "pluperfect days"; the air was cool from the off-Hudson breeze, and I felt a sense of relief and escape. After the stagnancy and loneliness of my room, where I boarded for several months before moving to the Columbia campus, even the people in the street seemed to be my friends. There's a line in Malcolm Muggeridge's memoirs that confirms this anomaly: "For comfort I turned as usual to the streets, where the endless stream of anonymous people were somehow companionable. " I was glad of the Greek fruit stand I passed, glad of the jolly kids on their way to school, glad of the occasional friendly smile of people I passed on the street. Dodging in and out of the fast-moving crowd, I became accustomed to seeing many of the same faces, with whom I would exchange a cheery good morning. In a kind of impersonal way they became my friends.

In the late twenties 125th Street was a key crosstown traffic artery with buses, trollies, taxis, trucks, and even horses surging back and forth at almost any hour of the day. On my way to Columbia I passed the Apollo Theatre, known as Harlem's "opera, " but from what I saw it appeared to be largely vaudeville. Restaurants, butcher shops, real estate offices, moviehouses, dancehalls, bakeries, fruit stands, and many other small businesses abounded. The eating places got most of my attention. At the time I was living on a very tight budget--one dollar was the limit for the day--and at times I was desperately hungry. One eating place I passed regularly had a huge display window in which an attractive young woman tossed buttercakes on a griddle. This always proved a great temptation, but usually the knowledge of my dwindling savings kept me in line. In this torturing process I frequently ended up buying a large ten-cent box of raisins from a Greek fruit stand or, for a change, a small plastic cylinder of imported figs. I have a bad habit of eating in a hurry, one that I have never been able to overcome, and by the time I bucked the traffic crossing over to Morningside Park I had nothing left for the birds or squirrels.

At this time of the year Morningside Park was a favorite with young mothers and nannies sunning their charges in carriages and strollers. The parks and streets were safe, and sometimes mothers became so engrossed in an exchange of gossip that one of the infants would climb halfway over the gunwale before they came rushing to the rescue. Slightly older youngsters with legs too short or too long were banging their tricycles into one another, causing many a spill and loud yammering for mother. At approximately the center of the park stone steps zig-zagged their way up the rocky cliff to Morningside Heights and 116th Street, leading to Columbia University. After I reached the top and looked downward the people below looked quite remote, as though I had climbed a mountain. The colors and figures--the pinks and blues of the children's wraps, the green and yellow of leaves, and the silvery metalliclike projections of rocks--were very much like the scenes depicted in a Grandma Moses watercolor.

After finding a place to live my first concern was to secure employment. I came into the United States on a permanent visa, available at the time but with certain working restrictions. Although I knew no one in the city, I carried with me a letter from Mr. E. L. Hill, Librarian of the Edmonton Public Library, which I hoped might be of some help in securing advice from friendly librarians about job openings in the city. I was desperately in need of funds and was ready to accept anything that paid room and board. Fortunately my room was very cheap, seventy-five cents a night, as I remember it, and food was good and inexpensive. I soon discovered that one of the wonderful things about New York was the range of its accommodation, which made it financially possible for you to live high or low without sacrificing your quality of life. You could ride almost anywhere on the subway or elevated for a nickel. You could jazz your stomach with Nedick's orange juice and a frankfurter for a dime. A balanced meal of vegetables, meat, and a bun could be obtained behind the glass doors of the Horn & Hardart automat for twenty-five cents. And then, of course, there were the museums, libraries, art galleries, the outdoor music concerts, and the zoo, where you could go for instruction and entertainment without charge. If you loved the outdoors, as I did, there was Central Park and hikes up the New Jersey side of the Hudson River, where you could enjoy the crisp, cool air, the lakes, the crags, and the birds--all in perfect safety.

11: THE NEW YORK PUBLIC LIBRARY

One fine morning I walked all the way down Fifth Avenue, past "millionaires' row, " the Metropolitan Museum, Central Park, the great luxury stores below 50th Street, and found myself facing the façade of a classic, white marble structure extending some two blocks along the avenue, a bit tarnished by the weathering of time.   It was the New York Public Library.   It was not simply the massiveness of the building that caught my attention, however, but rather the scene that confronted the passerby on the forecourt of the Library.   Here were people sitting on the granite steps flanked by two sculptured lions or strolling across the terraced space leading to the main entrance, some as if they had met by appointment ("I'll see you under the lions"), others gathered in small knots discussing the larger life, and still others comprising a goodly sprinkling of drifters such as I had known on my journey across Canada.   I felt right at home.   There was a kind of severe urban coldness about the marble building, more so as one entered it, but the sitters and strollers on the forecourt were very human, and they gave a certain picturesqueness to the scene.   Their leisurely inactivity contrasted nicely with the everlasting flow of traffic on the avenue.   I was glad to rest my feet after a long walk.

The Library was a remnant of the neoclassic style made popular by the Columbia Exposition of 1893.   All around were skyscrapers with soaring spires in the contemporary mode.   When I screwed up enough courage to rise from the steps to enter the building, the uniformed door guard, the immensity of the entrance hall, and the cold austerity of the marble stairways leading to the floor above, so intimidated

me that I wavered and almost left. Then in a fatuous moment I climbed the stairs and found a young woman in one of
the offices, head bent over a typewriter and banging away
fiercely. When she did not look up, I interrupted her with
an exaggerated cough.

"May I speak to the librarian?" I asked.

Still without raising her head she said, "You have an
appointment?"

I thought I was done for and would soon find myself
out in the street again looking for work. I was afraid to say
anything so I just stood there. When she finally looked up,
I could tell by the severity of her expression that she was
waiting for my reply and that it had better be pronto, or
else. . . .

"I need a job and I thought one of the librarians might
be able to advise me," I stammered, at the same time placing
Mr. Hill's letter of reference on her desk.

She glanced at it and told me to take a seat. She then
made several calls, and a few minutes later I found myself
in the office of a rotund, friendly-looking gentleman, telling
him all about myself in response to his amicable questioning.
Out of the Canadian northwest, college, roughing it across
Canada, the whole caboodle. . . . After reading Mr. Hill's letter he nodded appreciatively.

"We have some part-time jobs in the stacks, and we
could use a person like yourself if you don't mind starting at
the bottom," he said. He then went on to say that there were
already thirteen of my native countrymen on the staff and that
they liked Canadians very much.

I can only describe my response as ecstatic. I didn't
even ask about salary. But it was at this very moment that
I remembered the restriction in my visa about not being permitted to work in a job supported by public funds. For a
minute I was torn between a desire to say nothing about the
restriction and fear that later discovery would result in de-
portation. I decided to play it safe. As it turned out I had
nothing to worry about, but I was thankful that I mentioned it.
Charles Shaw, the urbane and friendly gentleman who interviewed me, explained that the New York Public Library was
really made up of two separate types of libraries.

"The New York Public Library in its present form," he explained, "is a consolidation of two famous private libraries and a foundation established to support science and popular education. The Astor Library and the Lenox Library merged with the Tilden Trust to form the Reference Department of the New York Public Library. It is maintained by private endowment and is housed in this building. This is where you would be working. The confusion arises because the New York Public Library also consists of a series of branch libraries supported by public funds. If you enter this building from the 42nd Street entrance, you will find one of the smaller branches just inside."

I was not sure that I fully understood, but I could breathe again. I thanked him profusely, skipped down the marble stairway, found my way to Grand Central, and sent a telegram to my mother giving her the good news.

I began work in the stacks a week later. There were seven decks or floors in the stacks that extended and supported a two-block-long reading room above. With the exception of the two lower decks, which were not in use for book storage during my term, the stacks were lined with steel shelving--fifty-five miles of it--broken by gangways and having aisles two to three feet wide. Four electrically driven book lifts of more than normal size, narrow stairways, and a pneumatic tube system for conveying readers' book needs to the stacks, provided communication with the principal service points of the Library. The stacks were entirely closed to the public. Readers wanting books filled out "call slips" after consulting a card catalog of more than ten million cards in a room just outside the Main Reading Room. At the center of this room was the Information Desk, where a small staff answered a diversity of questions in addition to sending the readers' call slips, by means of a pneumatic tube system, to the stacks. These assistants must have had Indian blood in their veins. They were experts in tracking down answers to difficult questions. One unusual inquiry I remember hearing about ran like this: "Please give the name of a bandit driven out of Mexico or Spain some time ago--fifty to a hundred years." Cross-examination finally revealed sufficient clues to determine that the name wanted was Don Quixote.

Robert W. Henderson was in charge of the book stacks. I do not know how many persons have succeeded him in this position since his retirement, but as long as the present building lasts the stack operation and management will be in-

81

separably connected with this man, who came to the job from South Shields, England, in 1910. He worked in several positions in the Library before being made Chief of the Stack Division in 1919. Robert was a rather slender man with an expressive face and heavy eyebrows that always seemed half-raised in a questioning mood. His hair was black with considerable gray in it, brushed straight back. He wore tight-fitting suits and almost invariably a bow tie, which I thought at first marked him as a New Yorker. Although slight and of medium height, there was about him a quality of distinction that derived from his natural energy and efficiency. As an administrator he was exacting but benignly so; he had a way of combining authority with sympathy and understanding for those who worked under him. At least I was always conscious of his personal care and concern for staff members. Long after I left the Library I received a letter from his attractive wife in which she mentioned how proud he was to read of any little success of his former "stack boys." Some did quite well. I read recently in "The New Yorker" where fourteen future college presidents were among the boys who worked their way through college in the stacks of the New York Public Library. I also owe a great deal to him for guiding me into the library profession and making it possible for me, as night supervisor of the stacks, to attend classes at Columbia's School of Library Service.

Knowing of my love of sun and greenery, of which I saw very little in the city, he would frequently invite me on weekends to his home in White Plains, where we would play deck tennis and occasionally swim at nearby Rye Beach. Thus I came to have an exceptionally vivid sense of this wiry Englishman, who seemed to have done a bit of everything in his busy life: administered two major departments of the New York Public Library, served as Librarian of the prestigious Racquet and Tennis Club of New York, formulated a standard of book-space measurement in stack shelving, earned a high place in the hall of fame for his book and journal writings on the history of sports, and probably had many other achievements that he was too modest to talk about. His early upbringing had indelibly stamped a Scottish Calvinism imprint upon him that left him outraged by much of the superficiality, vulgarity, and immorality of the modern age. This did not embitter his personality in any way, however; he was far too witty and fine a man to indulge in misanthropy, but he had a very deep faith.

My work at the New York Public Library as an ad-

ministrative cub entailed sending to the Main Reading Room
hundreds of volumes that readers requested during the evening
hours, sorting and shelving returned volumes as quickly as
possible so that readers next day or next hour might get what
they wanted, maintaining the seven-to-eight minute average
for the delivery of books to the readers, and accounting for
books called for but not delivered. My actual supervisory
duties were minimal because on the whole the stack boys con-
ducted themselves well and worked hard. New stack boys
were sometimes the object of harmless pranks, but I remember one incident that might have resulted in tragedy and that
caused me to lose my temper completely. It occurred when
a small chap, during his first evening on the job, was
squeezed by the older fellows on a lower book level into one
of the book lifts and shot upstairs to the Main Reading Room.
I can imagine the surprise and amusement of the readers
when this poor youngster fell out of the lift as the door was
raised, but the Supervisor of the Main Reading Room was
anything but happy, and he took his wrath out on me--rightly
so. Another incident occurred of quite a different nature, for
which I secretly thought an apology was due us. The only
source of ventilation in the low ceiling stacks was the windows overlooking Bryant Park. On warm summer evenings
we kept them open. On this occasion a sudden rain squall
lasting only a short time blew water into a dozen or more of
the open windows on each floor. I rushed to close the windows on stack six myself and yelled over the balcony to the
stack chiefs above and below to close their's. It was impossible to close all the windows without some rain blowing
in and wetting the marble floors nearest the windows. It
could have been a major calamity, but as it turned out it
wasn't. Fortunately no books were damaged, and the boys
quickly mopped the floors when time could be spared from
"running slips." Moreover, at my insistence, they exercised much greater care than the janitors, who regularly
splashed their soapy mops against the bottom shelf heedless
of the damage to the spines of the books. Our debacle, however, was reported by some busybody to one of the top administrators in the Library, whose gauleiter scolding was so
gratuitous that it rubbed and rankled me for years afterward.

On long summer evenings when the work was not too
heavy, I would take a break by leaning out of a stack window
for a breath of fresh air and a view of William Cullen Bryant's park from the sixth floor. If it was not exactly mountain air, it was better than the suffocating stagnancy of the
stacks. As I watched the park benchers below, drifters,

dropouts, winos, and other kinds of broken down and lonely people--some obviously in pretty bad shape--I thought of the poet's advice to those of us who are about to depart this earth:

> "...approach thy grave,
> Like one who wraps the drapery of his couch
> About him, and lies down to pleasant dreams."

At least I hoped their dreams were pleasant. There were so many of them--in so small a space yet without disorder. The only noise was the crackling of newspapers, which they spread out to lie on, or, if the evening were cool, to use as a cover. I'd gotten to know such folk in my journey across Canada, which made me feel more sympathetic perhaps than most people. There, I fancied, but for the grace of God I might be lying myself. "If you have no anguish of your own," wrote Christopher Morley, "hurry to find one."

Toward the end of my employment I was transferred to the Main Reading Room, where my work at the delivery windows was even more mechanical in nature than the job in the stacks--but it had one great advantage. For here, at last, I came into direct contact with the readers, and it gave me an opportunity to observe the multiplicity and variety of books and subjects in which they were interested. The head of the Main Reading Room made a study of a single hour's use about the time I was there; in his report he said that he considered the study fairly typical of a winter afternoon's demands. A total of 498 volumes were issued to readers at the delivery windows, and these, it should be borne in mind, represented only books consulted in the reading room during a single hour out of the thirteen hours the Library was open and not the use recorded in other reading rooms in the Library, such as Economics and Science. Edward Bellamy's "Equality," Kropotkin's "Mutual Aid," and Robinson's "Mind in the Making" were among titles called for in the social sciences. Works on marriage and divorce laws were so popular that it was found necessary to keep handbooks and digests covering the subject at the delivery desk. Poetry was represented by Arthur Chapman, John Masefield, and Robert Service; novels, by Willa Cather, Upton Sinclair, and Arnold Bennett; and essays, by Havelock Ellis and Don Marquis. One reader asked for and got eight books on memory. Biography was perennially popular; in this study Dreiser's "About Myself," Emma Goldman's "Living My Life," and Visconti's "Memoirs of

Youth" were fairly typical of the requests. An interest in
certain aspects of crime was responsible for a friend of mine
being asked for a book on how to poison someone without
leaving a trace. She took it in stride. A librarian is committed to equal time for all parties.

Charles Flowers McCombs, the headmaster with the
slight body, large head, and eyes that, in Emily Dickinson's
fine phrase, "hurried all abroad," was the chief of the Main
Reading Room. He was considered an outstanding scholar and
a good, practical administrator by his colleagues. As evidence of the former he served for many years as visiting
professor at the Columbia University School of Library Service, where he taught a course in bibliography. I am sure
he was considered an ornament to the profession, but at that
time in my life I found it a little difficult to see why. I
think it is fair to say that the working atmosphere at the Main
Reading Room staff area was impersonal and sophisticated,
but even sophistication needs a little warmth. It was not
there. In the bibliographical course at Columbia I was impressed by his knowledge of foreign languages and the ab-
struseness of his reference-question assignments, but the
course did nothing to stimulate my interest in bibliography or
to develop my bibliographical sense. On the other hand I
was probably one of the most fervid admirers of the major
exhibitions of the Library, for which he was largely responsible and which drew the eyes of New Yorkers if not the entire
country to the wealth of material possessed by the New York
Public Library. I remember especially an exhibit that marked
the three hundredth anniversary of John Bunyan's birth, in which
one could view the original editions of "Pilgrim's Progress,"
first editions of Bunyan's literary contemporaries (notably
Milton), portraits, relics, books owned by Bunyan with his
autograph, and even the original warrant for his arrest. One
reason for remembering this exhibit was the vivid way in
which it portrayed the background of seventeenth-century life.
It brought home to me that well-planned and arranged exhibitions in a library could contribute in an exciting and popular
way to the average person's understanding of history.

There were several seminal and lasting gains from my
association with the New York Public Library. Among these
were what to do with books you don't know what to do with,
recognition of the fact that libraries have to learn to live with
the frustrations of ever-increasing space limitations, some
understanding of the principles of good organization, and an

85

appreciation of the amazing variety of materials that make up the book world. These perhaps deserve a further word of explanation.

About the first. On stack six were a number of sections of shelving fenced off and referred to as "the cage," although I thought of it as "the pantry" because it held so many goodies. As night stack supervisor I had a key to the cage and was responsible for getting books housed there and called for by readers. I soon discovered that the majority of these books were not in the approved taste of Anthony Comstock and the U.S. Customs. Should you want to know the erotic fancies of women or how to castrate bulls, or study the sexual positions portrayed in some photographs of the Pompeian frescoes, this was the place to go. I spent a lot of time there and concluded that if I never read anything else I would still gain a large education.

The New York Public Library was in its sixteenth year in the Central Building when I began work there. Six years earlier the Director of the Library was already calling attention to the serious problem of overcrowding. After spending hundreds of hours in the stacks shifting books to make room enough to squeeze in "just a few more" I was impressed by the fact that there is no way to prevent reaching the saturation point of existing space in a library long before the planners and architects anticipated. Librarians who get this principle firmly in mind will save themselves a lot of psychological problems.

A third element in my learning process was the growing realization that, much as I sought personal freedom and independence, it took organization and teamwork to get the job done. Obviously no one could be familiar with every phase of the work of a large research library like the New York Public Library. The pattern of service in the Library included such broad areas as general services (Main Reading Room, Information Desk, Stacks), subject divisions (Economics, Science and Technology, American History), ethnical collections (Jewish, Slavonic, Orientalia), and special collections of types of material (Rare Books, Manuscripts, Prints), to mention some of the larger categories. The director and his administrative staff had to have help, and this meant organization. A workable division of labor with appropriate procedures in the stacks under a head who coordinated and delegated duties seemed to work well; a more diffuse organization pattern in the Main Reading Room, perhaps better suited to the type of work there and the personality of the head, seemed to me to be less satisfactory. In any event, when I left the Library in 1929, I had gained some conception of the importance of organization, and I was beginning to suspect that practical wisdom and moral integrity were more important in successful administration than the mechanics of organization.

When I think of the New York Public Library today, as I often do, I think also of New York itself. In the late twenties it was a wonderful show. Unfortunately I sampled very little of it, even though I lived there for two years during my first stay. There never seemed much time left for exploring the city after classes and thirty-five hours a week working at the Library. However, in going to and from work--116th Street to 42nd--I thoroughly scrutinized everything to be seen by the varied routes of bus, trolley car, elevated, and subway. If I had plenty of time, I frequently rode a trolley all the way down Broadway, combining viewing with study and enjoying the fresh air blowing in through open windows. More often I chased home up Broadway on foot after the Library closed at ten o'clock. To fortify myself for the long trek I would stop at a small health bar on Amsterdam Avenue for a bowl of graham crackers with half and half and perhaps a wholewheat honey bun.

I do remember one rather exciting incident that took place after I had finished my evening stint in the Library. It was election night, and the candidates were Al Smith and Herbert Hoover. The crush around Times Square near midnight was so thick you would think you were in the midst of the subway rush hour. The Governor was the favorite, of course, Manhattan versus Main Street. He had the vigor and personality to win, but he lost. I couldn't believe the returns as they showed up on the Times news belt. In college I had studied James Bryce's "The American Commonwealth," the authoritative work on U.S. politics. "The ordinary American voter does not object to mediocrity," wrote Bryce, "he likes his candidate to be sensible, vigorous, and above all, what he calls 'magnetic.'" Now if there was a man who was sensible, vigorous, and magnetic, it was Governor Al Smith. He had both the personality and frankness to win. His defeat was explained on the grounds of religion, Smith a Catholic and Hoover a Protestant. Even if this made no sense, it had the ring of truth for me, who knew something about religious big-

otry from my experience at home. On the whole it was a
very happy evening for me. I became crowd happy. I guess
I may have had a couple of cheap gin drinks from a local
speakeasy, but I found it exciting to join the flowing mass of
orderly people. It was my first campaign experience in the
United States. I think it was probably the first time I really
felt what democracy was all about. Everyone was there--
from street cleaner to college president. All life pressed
around one. Who could be at odds with life, who could be
without hope in such a pageant of democracy?

I chose cool, clear nights for walking home after work,
and I always chose Broadway. What a sight that great street
presented against the background of night with its belt of electric bulbs girding the Times Building and spelling out the
latest news; its pageantry of running-fire advertising--beer,
Coca Cola, the most beautiful girls in the world; its thea-
ters--Loew's State, the Palace, the Strand, the Rialto, and
the Continental; its automobile row, where one could view
the kingdom of Cadillac, Packard, and Franklin; and further
north, at 59th, Columbus on his granite monument presiding
over "Hyde Park" orators declaiming on everything from the
Greenland ice cap to the latest in vegetable diet.

Continuing beyond Columbus Circle, I passed several
dancing academies, which made me think of Sullivan's in Edmonton, and I wondered if the folks here could do "the right
and left turn in the Two Step," which I never mastered at
home. I noticed that the girls entering the Broadway dancing
academies had less on than the girls at Sullivan's and that
they were quite young--no doubt a reflection of my Canadian
four-ply morality. If I needed a short break from walking,
there was always a Liggett's drugstore where I could browse
among the thermos bottles for some of that manly outdoor
stuff by Zane Grey, James Oliver Curwood, and the like. By
way of contrast there was a Childs restaurant that I passed
further uptown whose interior seemed to me to be as surgi-
cally antiseptic as a hospital. It had something to do with
the white walls and white porcelain tabletops. Anyway I always stopped long enough for a view of the pancake exhibition
and then hurried on. If I tired of walking or window viewing,
I would descend to the stale depths of the nearest subway station and take a Broadway local to 116th. It was often so hot
down there that I had to anchor myself long enough to reach
my destination. When the blue and white colors of Columbia
showed up on the station wall, I staggered out and labored up

the long stairway.   The old man who sold horse chestnuts at
the entrance was usually the only person about.   We exchanged a few words, and then I made for my room in Furnald, completely pooped.   I had studying to do, but when I
glanced at my wristwatch, I saw that it was already well past
midnight.   So I gave up all pretense of study, lay down in
oafish slumber, and didn't think of anything.

12: BACK IN THE CLASSROOM: COLUMBIA UNIVERSITY

When in 1883 Melvil Dewey, Librarian of Columbia College (renamed Columbia University in 1896) made proposals for establishing a School of Library Economy as an academic department, librarians for the most part were learning their craft as apprentices in academic and municipal libraries or in training classes associated with a few of the larger libraries. Little by little this occupation took on more of the trappings of a profession, or so it was claimed, which demanded of its practitioners some special knowledge and a strong liberal arts background. Dewey presented his case for a School as an academic department at a propitious time, and such was the plausibility of his argument that President Barnard and the Trustees of Columbia College agreed that the School should, both in fabric and fact, be an organic part of the whole institution. When it opened some four years later, Dewey served as its Director, but shortly thereafter he accepted the post of Director of the State Library of New York and took the Library School to Albany with him. Talented, persuasive, and a master of the expedient, he soon built up the New York State Library School into a position of leadership in library training throughout the United States.

In the early years librarianship moved about as slowly as a glacier. It was not until some forty years after Dewey had established his Albany School that the American Library Association proposed that all library schools with graduate programs be associated with an approved degree-conferring institution, and as a result the New York State Library School came back again to Columbia University. About the same time an important library training school associated with the

New York Public Library arranged to move its program to Columbia, and the two recent transfers were then merged to form the School of Library Service at Columbia University. The School was officially opened at formal exercises in 1926. President Nicholas Murray Butler made a felicitous address in which he paid tribute to Dewey as "the originator of the idea and the first formulator of all those instrumentalities ... which together made up a great group of carefully planned and well-thought-out agencies for [the] advancement of adult education in the United States." The School opened in temporary quarters with a registration of approximately a hundred students and a faculty that included E. J. Reece (Library Management), Mary L. Sutliff (Classification), Isabella Rhodes (Cataloging), John S. Cleavinger (Public Libraries), Lucy E. Fay (Bibliography), Margaret S. Williams (Reference), Alice I. Hazeltine (Children's Literature), and the Director, Dr. C. C. Williamson. Other luminaries associated with the permanent teaching staff were the fabulous Isadore G. Mudge, one of two angels in white guarding the entrance to the circular reading room of the Low Memorial Library; Charles Flowers McCombs, Keyes D. Metcalf, and Frank Weitenkampf, all three associated with the New York Public Library; Linda Morley, a widely respected librarian in the special-library field; and Minnie Earl Sears, editor of the Standard Catalog series of the H. W. Wilson Company. The drawing of such outstanding library practitioners to supplement the faculty did much to increase both the power and prestige of the School.

I registered in the newly reorganized School of Library Service in September 1927, the second year in its morning of new life. The first year had not passed without some grumbling from within and without, but on the whole it appeared to have been exceptionally successful. There were a few who shook their heads over the alleged neglect of "practical work" and others who questioned awarding a Bachelor of Science degree after only one year of graduate library study, but this was largely nit-picking in view of the high quality of graduates entering the first year and the practical fact that all the graduates readily found jobs. The most obvious sign of progress was in brick and stone. The School had acquired East Hall, completely redecorated, although it was still necessary to schedule lecture rooms in other buildings. In addition the full program of courses leading to the degree of Master of Science was offered for the first time.

During my first semester in the School my education

in library science, at best, but limped along. One reason
was that I was constantly on the run from my room on 125th
Street to classes, from Columbia to downtown, and from the
New York Public Library back to my room. This left no
time for anything but classes, no counseling or personal talks
with instructors and no extracurricular or social life with my
fellow students. I felt like an outsider and more isolated with
each month that passed. More importantly, perhaps, I found
the courses in library school so different from what I anticipated in a graduate program, so far removed from the knowledge of books and the living contents of libraries as I knew
them, that I developed a bad case of Winter Chill. I became
increasingly lax about attending class at a time when tardiness
and attendance seemed to be one of the chief preoccupations
of the staff. Our newly decorated quarters in East Hall, I
was told, had served at one time as an asylum, and I felt the
ghosts of former occupants erupting every time I entered the
place. I did very little work, and my grades were barely
good enough to get a pass.

Suddenly all this changed. I got a lucky break. I received word that a room had become vacant on the top floor
of Furnald Hall, where graduate and professional students
were housed, and that I might move in immediately. I rushed
to claim it as if just released from the Gulag. I wish I could
describe how I felt about my new home. But I cannot. I
lived there for almost two years and chased its personality
all around Amsterdam and Broadway from 116th to 114th
Street. All my simple needs were met by small but genial
shops on Amsterdam--stationery, laundry, shoe repair, drugs,
and a small delicatessen that sold the best cheesecake in town.
My room on the seventh floor was small, about ten by fifteen,
but it had hot and cold running water and there were showers
on the same floor. The east view from the window overlooked South Field--tennis courts, wide swathes of surrounding
green grass, walks crisscrossing the campus between classrooms and residences, trees set beautifully against a background of burned brick and limestone in the residence halls,
tall John Jay just completed and standing out like a skyscrap-
er on the southeast corner of Amsterdam and 114th Street,
and the inviting archway just outside Furnald leading to the
Bookstore and University Press. Entering Furnald one was
greeted by a large foyer and a fireplace. Often when I returned home from work late at night there was someone playing the piano, and sometimes a saxophone provided accompaniment. I loved the place.

92

My change of residence marked a turning point in my attitude toward library school instruction. What I regarded merely as technical, trivial, and obvious--what might largely be left to the common sense of any intelligent person--now took on greater importance. I realized for the first time that it was not just skills, technique, and "know-how" that my instructors were trying to instill but, more importantly, a sense of the whole system of ideas, values, and judgments that constituted librarianship. It may not have been apparent at the time how well attuned the introductory courses were to this objective, but if to any degree I attained a sense of the basic principles and aspirations of librarianship, I owe it to the careful tuition of Reece, Rhodes, Williams, and Fay, who gave personal guidance during the first two years of my studies. What they had to offer was what I needed to knock out my pretentious superficiality. The acquisition of these and others of the best teachers from the two library training schools that had merged to form the new Columbia School did much to raise the status and quality of its faculty. But Dr. C. C. Williamson, the Director, was also in search of immediate reinforcements from distinguished practitioners, and the accession on a part-time basis of such notables as Weitenkampf in the book arts, Melcher in publishing and bookselling, and Oswald in printing, greatly enhanced the reputation of the School. My regret is that the Director did not insist that the students should take courses in printing and the book arts, if not in the first professional degree offered by the School (B.S.), then at least in the master's program.

Among the part-time luminaries brought in for a summer teaching course was Dr. Harry M. Lydenberg, Director of the New York Public Library, with whom I was fortunate enough to take an advanced course in the history of books and libraries. Dr. Lydenberg was then approaching the height of his powers and was in full career as a leader in the library world. He had served as president of the American Library Association and was active in a number of prestigious bibliographical and learned societies. Five universities conferred honorary degrees upon him in the thirties and forties. I was a bit overwhelmed by his reputation when I first entered the class, but not for long. He was never the formal teacher, always the friendly adviser, the energizer, and the listener. He taught his students to go adventuring among subjects of their own choice but insisted on the use of original sources without language limitations. I chose to investigate George III as a book collector because from my college reading I

93

remembered that Dr. Johnson considered the King's Library more interesting and valuable than the limited stock in the British Museum. Dr. Lydenberg accepted my selection and then in the very same conference, to my utter astonishment, directed my attention to the principal English and French government and learned-society publications that I would probably do well to consult. Friendly and modest, in spite of his rather stern appearance, he staggered me by the range and grasp of his varied and glowing mind. He was not only a remarkable teacher but, as Frederick Keppel pointed out in a volume of essays compiled in his honor, he was one with whom you could discuss your problems, your hopes, and your dreams. I can attest to the fact that he renewed in me a youthful desire to write, to create something worthwhile. If I have contributed anything to professional literature, I owe it to his inspiration.

Living so contentedly in Furnald Hall did not mean that I had more time to make friends with my fellow class members. I knew few of them well, partly because I did not try hard enough (British reserve, perhaps) and partly because professional school students always seemed poised for flight. This was particularly true in East Hall because our class lectures were given in different buildings due to a shortage of space in the home port. Even at mealtimes, when you might expect to make friends, an air of exclusiveness was evident. In any case I took most of my meals downtown at the automat on the way to work. Among my classmates was Charles (Chuck) Mohrhardt, who was a general favorite with everyone. He was a short man with a quick but uninhibited sense of humor, which was emphasized by cocking his head to one side, looking at you with a kind of cherubic innocence, while reciting the limerick about the young lady from Exeter. His inseparable companion was Ralph Ulveling, tall, good-looking, square-shouldered, bespectacled, and dressed at all times as though he belonged at a convention of bankers rather than in the company of librarians pledged to disorient society through the reading of books. The faculty all agreed that Ralph was the man to watch.

When I first met Ralph Shaw during my second year in the School of Library Service, he struck me as being energetic, opinionated, and possessed of sufficient arrogance to compensate for the peasant qualities in most of us. His character was further particularized some fifteen years later when I came to know him better. His friends spoke of his probing mind and restless energy, but his greatest strength lay in his complete intellectual integrity and his willingness to lay it on the line. He knew right from wrong, the authentic from the counterfeit, and was never afraid to apply his judgment to a specific case. On one occasion I asked him for advice regarding my manuscript of a bibliography of Christopher Morley. I explained that it had been rejected by the Louisiana State University Press on the advice of Columbia's famed Lionel Trilling, on the ground that it would be a disservice to literature to publish a bibliography of Morley. Ralph asked to examine the manuscript and later offered to publish it without even mentioning a word about Trilling's rejection. I often wondered what inward pangs of despair led him to choose the name Scarecrow as a moniker for his press. A friend suggested that he should change it to Eagle Press--"the eagle sees further and it would have patriotic connotations." According to Ralph's own account, Earl Schenk Miers, his friend and an author, perhaps a trifle grimly, suggested the name because "you're talking about a scarecrow; it has no overhead; it pays no rent; it is not responsible for somebody's future clothing or shelter. It's a scarecrow."

Tall, handsome Henry Brimm was a prime favorite with the faculty and students. He had a shy look of spirited gaiety, especially when speaking, and an accent full of Southern lingo that delighted women. I do not remember the specific occasion, but one summer session we must have been roommates in one of the few suites in Furnald Hall. I marveled how Henry managed to keep up with his studies and win such high regard from the faculty. Whenever I returned late at night from work downtown, I seldom if ever found him in his room. Yet the following morning, around ten or eleven, he could always be found lying in his bed, face down and dead asleep. As I mentioned, he had an unusual attraction for women, and on one occasion, because he felt sorry for the old plodder, he arranged a blind date for his roommate. After the theater we rode around Central Park in a taxi or horse cart until the early hours of the morning. All I remember of that evening was that my date's name was Zoe, that she possessed a very special glow, and that she left for Paris the following day. After Henry graduated from the School of Library Service and gained some experience in the library world he went on to carve out for himself a quiet but apparently prosperous little realm as librarian of the Union Theological Seminary in Richmond, Virginia.

13: WITH ARTHUR E. MORGAN AT ANTIOCH

Although I had no particular idea what I should do after graduation from the School of Library Service in the spring of 1929, I now felt that in addition to having a fair grounding in history, literature, and philosophy from my undergraduate studies, I had acquired the vocational know-how for earning a living. Yet there was something more needed. Almost unconsciously I felt that what I still lacked was a knowledge of how to bind all this training together to form some constructive purpose in my life. Once again, as when I first entered college, I had a lucky break when an opportunity arose to join a venturesome educational activity that would in the end bring much happiness and helpful direction to my life.

About a month after graduation I received a call from Columbia informing me that Arthur E. Morgan, President of Antioch College, was interviewing candidates for a library position, and if interested I should see him that afternoon at the Waldorf. Since I was most anxious to leave the city for the sights and sounds of the countryside, and, I hoped, work that would bring me into more intimate contact with readers than my job in the New York Public Library, it seemed only prudent to follow up this lead and to learn as much as possible about Mr. Morgan and his College before the interview. What I already knew was mostly ancient history. In preparing a paper for one of my courses I remembered reading about Horace Mann, an educator of worldwide reputation in the last century, who left his native Massachusetts to establish a college named Antioch somewhere in the Midwest. Famous, fearless, and full of progressive ideas for a coeducational, nonsectarian college, he gave up assured success for the unknown only to be smothered under board domination and, as one writer put it, to be "worried into his grave by an imperial college janitor."

I did my homework as thoroughly as possible in the time available before the interview. It appeared from what I read that Antioch College continued to survive for a number of years on Horace Mann's reputation, but by the second decade of the twentieth century it was about to close its doors and call it quits. Then something of a miracle happened. A new board of trustees engaged Arthur E. Morgan as President in 1921. He was the Chief Engineer of the Miami (Ohio) Conservancy District and had made an outstanding reputation for his work in drainage and flood control. In fact a few years earlier he had saved Dayton from a devastating flood. In the course of his work he had had an opportunity to observe hundreds of young college-trained men, whom he supervised in the construction of levees, sluices, spillways, and bridges, and found them, mostly graduates from engineering schools, rather narrowly trained in technical efficiency but lacking in breadth of knowledge and the adventurous qualities that he regarded as necessary in his profession. He found that those who had graduated from a liberal arts institution fared better, but even they had acquired a background based on a more or less accidental accumulation of courses without broad, direct contact with affairs. Perhaps the most extraordinary thing about Morgan, however, was why he ever chose to become a college president. He had less than a year of college education, still less in teaching. But he had what one experienced educator regarded as the most important qualification a president could bring to the job, and that is a philosophy of education. The central tenet of Morgan's educational philosophy followed Horace Mann's creed--that a college education should properly concern the whole individual and not the mind alone. In Morgan's view this could be accomplished in two ways: first, there had to be a strong liberal arts program that required all students to take courses in the major fields of knowledge, and second, all students should be given experience in jobs of their choice during the college career. The dovetailing of theory and experience, known as the Antioch cooperative plan, was first conceived by Dean Herman Schneider of the University of Cincinnati, who applied it to engineering students only. His purpose was to give them practical experience in engineering. At Antioch the scope of the plan was enlarged to include all students above freshman rank, and the emphasis was changed. Morgan saw in the cooperative

97

plan a means to develop maturity of judgment and personality as well as the habit of thinking in terms of reality.

Punctually at five o'clock I presented myself at the door of Morgan's room at the Waldorf and was greeted by a tall, stooped, and rather burly man who looked to me more like an English countryman than an American college president. He had large ears and a prominent nose and he looked straight at you from behind steel-frame glasses, a certain hardness and reserve in his features. He wore tweeds, which I thought a bit informal for the haut monde of the Waldorf. He smiled disarmingly by way of greeting, but his first questions were rather upsetting to one who hoped to make a good impression by his knowledge of Antioch's history.

"Do you smoke?" he asked.

I confessed that I smoked a pipe.

"You should leave tobacco alone," he warned. "Our studies show that it greatly lowers the chance of success."

His next question confirmed that conviviality was not his long suit.

"Do you drink?" he asked.

And from the emphasis he placed on pronouncing "drink," you might have thought I was running a distillery in the basement of Furnald Hall.

"Drink!" I exclaimed. "No, I don't drink," I replied. It was obviously difficult for him to conceal his contempt for frivolity. Even the rough life of an engineer had not eroded his inveterate puritanism.

After we talked for half an hour or so, during which time he divulged that he was seeking a head librarian for the College, I asked about the two things that concerned me most, the salary and life at Antioch. My query produced the fact that the salary was two thousand dollars and the College was located at Yellow Springs, Ohio, a small village near Xenia and Springfield. Both could be reached by the interurban electric. If one had an automobile, there was a shortcut to Dayton, but the road was unpaved. He also informed me that the village was named for an iron spring located in a beauti-

ful thousand-acre glen. From the way he spoke about the
glen I knew that he loved natural beauty, and this had a greater appeal for me than the salary.

When I asked about the Library, Morgan mentioned
that it was built on the foundation of Horace Mann's house and
that it contained a large reading room that was unusually attractive, with a fireplace and free access to all books. I was
working weekends at the Racquet and Tennis Club in New
York, and the idea of open shelves and comfortable reading
surroundings sold me on the job. When I asked about the
book collection, Morgan's knowledge of what the Library had
seemed to me to be about as slender as that of most college
presidents, but his acquaintance with the classics, such as
Thoreau and Huxley, was evident in his speech. It was encouraging to learn that there was very little dead wood in the
collection. There was mention of portions of the old library,
including unopened gifts, stored in the towers of the main
building.

About the time I was beginning to wonder whether
Morgan knew I was still in the room--he had a disconcerting
habit of making notes during the conference--he rose from
his chair, checked his watch, and said: "Do you know a good
place to eat dinner?" On my limited budget I was certainly
not the best person to ask, but I took the plunge and replied,
"If you do not mind a short walk, there is a good French
restaurant near Vanderbilt and 42nd." Not wanting him to
think that I indulged in high life, I hastened to add, "I recently enjoyed the hospitality of my Uncle August and Aunt
Isa [Poirier] from Paris for a couple of days. They chose
this restaurant near where I work and thought it quite satisfactory."

Morgan seemed satisfied, and we left promptly for
what I anticipated would be the first good meal since my relatives left New York. I kept wondering when he might approach the question of a job offer, but as yet, not a word.
In fact Morgan seemed wholly absorbed in his own thoughts
and had very little to say as we walked along. I noticed that
he looked around several times, almost as if seeking a land-
mark to determine where we were, and then suddenly, within
a short distance of our destination, he stopped short.

"I have been here before," he exclaimed. "I recognize
where we are. Would you mind if we had dinner at a place
I know just around the corner from here?"

"Of course not," I told him. I could not very well do anything else, but my instinct told me that I had just said goodbye to a good meal. When we rounded the block, Morgan came to a full stop in front of a Horn and Hardart automat. My heart sank. "No, oh no! It can't be," I said to myself. But unfortunately it was, and here is my Olympian host explaining just how an automat works.

"You get change when you enter, at the cashier's desk," he explained, "and then you proceed to the little glass doors all around the room where the food is on display. You make your selection, drop your coin in the machine slot, and carry your tray to one of the stand-up tables." With great formal courtesy, he offered to get the change.

After we ate what Morgan termed a "good and nourishing" meal we returned to the hotel, where to my great surprise he asked if I would be interested in coming to Antioch. He prefaced this offer with the observation that my record at Columbia was by no means the best among the applicants who had been recommended to him. I accepted and thanked him, and he said he would send me confirmation of an appointment, along with literature about the College, when he returned to Yellow Springs. I could only guess why he had selected me above others with better records. The value of experience in the New York Public Library may well have appealed to him. Aside from the fact that the "work-study" idea fitted into his theory of educating the whole person, I think it is probably true that experience in the New York Public Library was more widely recognized as an asset in placement than at any time since.

In the early summer of 1929 I left New York to come to work at Antioch College. I was twenty-two years old, with a lot of ambition but only a vague notion about the nature of the work I was about to undertake. I was excited but apprehensive about having the responsibility to administer a college library. I was also a bit self-conscious about becoming a head librarian. After all, in the New York Public Library I was about as far down on the totem pole as one could get.

My first consideration was to find a place to live. I was fortunate enough to be assigned a room in what was known as the Mills House, with the understanding that I would serve as a kind of monitor to the Antioch students who lived there. After

100

reading the bulletins that had been forwarded to me it was exciting to have a glimpse of the place where I was to work for the next six years. The village truly had a quiet New England air, which the College catalog suggested "was first imparted by families that came from the East while Horace Mann was president of the college." The four or five students living in the Mills House were upperclass members and therefore participated in the cooperative or "work-study" program. Under this plan two students held a single cooperative job. One student studied on the campus while his or her "coop" worked on a job either on or off the campus. At the end of five or ten weeks, depending on the distance of the job from the College, they reversed their roles. All the time I stayed at Mills House I never quite became accustomed to waking up in the morning and finding new faces sleeping in the beds occupied by their coops the day before. What was perhaps even more surprising was the fact that their program of study and recreation appeared to proceed normally in spite of the five-week change.

Built in 1842 by Judge William Mills, the man most influential in securing Horace Mann to be the College's first President, Mills House was in its time the showplace of Yellow Springs. Located on a fifteen-acre tract in the heart of the village, it had a natural setting of great beauty, a gravel road sweeping in a wide curve to the front door, many fine old oaks gracefully proportioned, and a large expanse of lawn bordering all sides of the House. Rooms on the first floor were assigned to the Antioch School, where primary and elementary grade work was being done. The Antioch students in residence there occupied the upper floors. My bedroom was small and somewhat bare, but I was fortunate, with the coop changes taking place every five weeks, to have a room of my own. Nearly half the space was taken up with a bed and study table, a desk chair and an easy chair, and a low bookcase extending half the length of one wall. The view from the single window in the room overlooked the lawn at the front of the house. There was no closet, but someone had erected a rod across one corner from which dangled half a dozen empty hangers. Directly across from my room was the bathroom shared by all occupants, and from its window, which extended almost to the floor, one could climb out to a kind of catwalk running the full length of the roof. On hot summer evenings we would drag our mattresses out onto the roof and sleep there all night. I remember four of the students very well, although I cannot remember their names:

one was a red-headed, lanky engineering student; another a chemist--dour but brilliant; a third majored in business but held views that seemed to me to be more attuned to Karl Marx than Adam Smith; and the fourth, a bearded chap from California, studied oysters under Professor Federighi and claimed that their reproductive organs were in their feet.

My next concern was to get started in my work, and to this end I paid a call upon President Morgan to let him know that I was settled in and ready to go to work. Unfortunately, as it turned out, Morgan was not in Yellow Springs and was not expected back for a week or so. His secretary assured me that he was expecting me and would see me as soon as he returned. She arranged for a student to show me about the campus and to take me to the Library. My first encounter with the Library stands out in great distinctness. The brick building had dignity and simplicity, its numerous windows shaded by fine old oaks and elms and foreside set off by a small, second-level balustraded balcony, which I believe was intended more for ornament and viewing than for any practical purpose. The entrance door, badly in need of paint, opened onto a rather shabby hall with a metal staircase leading up to the second floor. On the left wall inside the front door hung a handsome portrait of Horace Mann that my guide said had been there for many years, yet she had no idea who it was. Inside the inner door on the first floor was a large reading room with a fireplace at the far end, a davenport and easy chairs arranged in front of it, and the librarian's desk and a checkout table to the left. Around the room were double-faced bookcases, crowded with books, projecting from the walls to form small reading alcoves. It was all quite as attractive as Morgan had pictured it in our first interview. At this point a rather stern, middle-aged lady approached and introduced herself. I knew from her look and tone of voice that this was not going to be a howdy-do meeting. My student guide took this opportunity to excuse herself and departed. Without any of the usual amenities my new acquaintance, full of attack, informed me that she was THE Acting Librarian and that the Librarian, a Miss Emily Turner, was ill and in the hospital. A kind of hunch or instinct warned me that this was not the time to reveal why I was on the campus, but a few minutes later she asked me what I was doing at Antioch and I felt that I had to inform her that I came as the new Librarian. I noticed that the normal half-meek look in her eye now took on an icy and challenging gaze. I've forgotten what the rest of our conversation was about, but I'm sure it included an invitation to make myself scarce.

I returned to the President's office, feeling as though a meteor had hit me in the head, and asked for an explanation. I was told that everything would be straightened out when Mr. Morgan returned. Meanwhile, would I care to look over the books and journals stored in the twin towers of the main building, Antioch Hall? Morgan was anxious to have this material looked over by someone who could judge what would be needed by the Library and what could be disposed of for money to supplement the present book budget. This seemed to me to be the only thing I could do, and I expressed my gratitude to the President's secretary. I was not only glad to have something useful to occupy my time but I foresaw in this task an opportunity to get acquainted with some of the faculty whom I would have to consult before disposing of specialized material in their fields.

One afternoon when visiting the Library to check dealers' catalogs for prices of back files of journals, I once again ran into the Acting Librarian. She was tiptoeing up the stairway and asked me to stop by her desk a minute. Her office turned out to be a reading table on the second floor where she had spread out a dozen or so order cards, business records, and other paraphernalia associated with the acquisition process. She then plunged into a prolonged discussion of the steps that she considered essential in ordering books, checking invoices, and so forth, ending with this question:

"Are you familiar with these procedures in a college library?"

"Not those," I responded shortly.

"It is as I thought," she exclaimed triumphantly. She then proceeded to undo me with her final coup de grace:

"Look here, my friend," she said. "You seem to be a nice young man, but obviously you know nothing about the procedures in a college library. I know that you are accustomed to working in a specialized department in a large library. That is quite different from a college library. You're not ready for this job, and besides you would not like the salary. I'm thinking of your future and I strongly advise you to return immediately to your job in the New York Public Library."

I was a bit shaken at first by the directness and unexpectedness of her attack. She had not seemed to me to be
a vindictive person, and perhaps there was some truth in
what she was saying. Maybe I wasn't "ready for the job. "
This much I will concede. But as mature as she was she
ought to have known better than to expect that I would retreat.
There must have been something resilient or devil-may-care
in me that saved me from becoming resentful and making a
fool of myself. I merely thanked her for her advice, and our
paths never crossed again.

When Morgan returned to the campus, the problem of
who's who in the Library was quickly settled. As it turned
out, Emily Turner, the Librarian who was ill in the hospital,
had no intention of returning to work because of failing health,
and the Acting Librarian, whom no one seemed to know much
about, departed unceremoniously. I who had been busy as a
bee in a clover patch among the nineteenth-century journal
files in the twin towers was now obliged to step down to the
level of administrative work, hiring and training student coop
assistants, rearranging spaces in the Library to make better
use of the second floor, finding a place for the staff to work
without interfering with readers, and participating in meetings
and student counseling. For a time I felt like the man who
got himself a hearing aid, only to find that he could now hear
much more than he wanted to.

The obvious physical changes were not difficult, and I
was fortunate to have the cooperation of several faculty members in bringing them about. Dr. William M. Leiserson,
professor of economics and a nationally known figure in labor-
arbitration cases, occupied a small office on the second floor
of the Library, which he voluntarily surrendered to me. He
had been allowed the special privilege of smoking in his office provided he keep the door leading to an external fire escape slightly ajar. He was generous enough to hand this office on to me with all the rights and privileges pertaining
thereunto, including smoking and utilizing the fire escape to
avoid unwelcome visitors. Dr. Leiserson was the head of a
large and talented family. When the great Depression caught
up with Antioch, married faculty members had their salary
cut to nineteen hundred dollars, with an allowance of three
hundred dollars for each child, and single persons at thirteen
hundred. Under this regulation Professor Leiserson received
the largest salary on the campus, but no one begrudged him
this bonus for a very good reason. Antioch College had a

regulation at this time that required a faculty member to share outside income, no matter what the source, with indigent colleagues. From his earnings in arbitrating labor cases Professor Leiserson brought in more money to the College coffers than he was paid in salary.

It was largely because of this share-the-wealth requirement that my friend Tom Cox Lloyd, an electrical engineer, gave up his teaching position at Antioch for a deep-carpeted office in Springfield in the firm of Robbins and Myers. When I first met Tom, he was an instructor at Ohio State University who commuted twice a week to Antioch to offer an evening course. He maintained a room in the village on these nights, returning to Ohio State and his home the following morning. Almost invariably, it seemed to me, he would pop into the Library just about closing time to get something good to read before going to bed. After he had selected what he wanted--usually in history, biography, or the personal essay--we would close up the Library and sit around and talk in front of the fireplace. He always had fascinating bits of useful knowledge to talk about from his reading. I remember once his telling me about a mathematician named Robert Record (circa 1660), who wrote a book on algebra and was the man who first used the sign (=), adopting it, he said, because "noe two thynges" could be more equal than two parallel straight lines. Tom said he would write an article about it someday, and he did, many years later, entitled "Whetstones of Witte." He was a wide-awake figure, entertaining, witty, and well liked by everyone, especially women. His wife, Martha, whom I got to know very well when Tom decided to cast his lot with Antioch and move to Yellow Springs, was sociable, generous to a fault, and a trifle snobbish. She enjoyed a ceremonious display. Once when she went to England, she created quite a court for herself, where her cooking and entertaining among the local gentry caused more of a stir than the divorcee from Baltimore. Her two young sons, Tommie and Davy, returned home from their short overseas visit as little Englishmen.

The faculty at Antioch at this period formed a powerful nucleus to support Morgan's innovative ideas in higher education. There were men like Lincoln R. Gibbs in English, whom a colleague described as "so fine and complete a human being that he brought us a realization of how life and literature intertwined"; William M. Leiserson, who built up a widespread reputation in his field and later became the first

105

chairman of the National Labor Relations Board under Roosevelt; Algo D. Henderson in Business Administration, who succeeded Morgan as President of Antioch after the latter became Chairman of the Tennessee Valley Authority; Austin McDowell Patterson, an inspiring professor who brought a broader concept to the teaching of chemistry and wrote the seminal book on "The Literature of Chemistry"; Ondess Inman, who headed research on photosynthesis; Clarence Leuba in psychology; J. D. Kingsley in government; and Herman Schnurer in romance languages. The Chairman of the Library Committee during my period at Antioch was Dr. Albert W. Liddle, an English professor richly endowed with humor and one who liked his comfort. Underclass members rated him rather poorly as a teacher ("like sophomores who nodded in your classes, unequal to the challenges you posed"), but a few with Milton or Chaucer in their blood assured him that "your life was music in the dark." His talk among friends, somewhat waggish, and his letters, always fascinating, make one wish that he had bestirred himself to write for publication. Often the letters describe some phase of his travels, and, as in the following excerpt, are revealing of his wit, sensitivity, and gifts as a letter writer.

Dover Beach
12 July 1937

Dear Guy and Margaret:

  I cannot leave England without sending you a stamp for your collection and some documentary proof that we have travelled under the flag you have renounced.

  For five weeks we have gone up and down the roads of this country until, after 2,500 miles of it, I am a perfect left hand driver. We have virtually drawn a spider's web over it from the tip of Cornwall to the Scotch highlands, dipping into North Wales as far as Caernarvon to see the place that gave the world Billy Owen, and into the Burns country, leaping over Hadrian's wall both ways, and so down through Cambridge and London to this place, where we sit gazing over the channel ready to cross to Belgium tomorrow. We have seen every cathedral and castle and birthplace of importance in England. I have been photographed where all the great have trod for 13 centuries. I now look at nothing which hasn't an authentic history of at least 700 years. I have haunted the paths of Dr. Johnson in

Fleet Street, following him to his very garret in
Gouph Square where he labored at the "Dictionary";
I have clambered up the stairs in All Hallows'
Church up which Pepys ran to view the London fire,
and down again "as fast as ever he could"; I have
seen the place in the Tower where Walter Raleigh
whiled away his last four hours, and the spot where
Anne Boleyn, Lady Jane Grey, and others lost their
heads; I have gazed on the tombs of everybody of
importance in British history; the chairs in which
Milton, Burns, Shakespeare, the Archbishop of
Canterbury, or any other celebrity ever sat have
also felt my weight; I have seen enough stained
glass windows to surround the whole state of North
Carolina, and enough statuary, monuments, paintings, and first editions to fill it; I have seen enough
hedges, gardens, thatched stone cottages, and historic streams and bridges to do an ordinary person
the rest of his life; and we have laid eyes on royal-
ty on at least three distinct occasions. In fact, we
have seen more of England than the average Englishman knows there is. We have heard the King's
English spoken in I know not how many ways. And
we have drunk tea till our insides are rusty with it.
I cannot begin to tell you all we have done; but if
you ever come our way I shall be able to give you
a detailed account, for every night records the do-
ings of the day. We have been well; and motoring
is the grandest way imaginable to see a country
such as this....

Yrs as ever
AWL

One of the most interesting and unusual of the younger
members of the faculty was Walter Kahoe. A man of infinite
intellectual resources and tireless energy, he began publishing
fine books when a student at Antioch; secured an A. M. (Harvard) and Ph. D. (University of Pennsylvania); taught philosophy at his alma mater; carried on experiments in cross-
breeding flowers, birds, and animals that often struck me as
slightly macabre; published each year a finely printed book as
a Christmas gift for his friends; wrote and published a biography of Arthur E. Morgan and his writings; was undoubtedly
Morgan's closest friend and confidant; established a private
press in Moylan, Pennsylvania; and ended his career in busi-

ness and education as director of medical publications for the J. B. Lippincott Company. I think it is fair to say that not everyone thought as highly of Walter as I did. I remember thinking about inviting him to speak to the young women of a college with which I was later associated and wrote to a friend at Antioch to ask his opinion. With wry humor he replied, "Imagine Kahoe at a tea for women. Better make sure he shaves and gets the hot potato out of his mouth. He'll pontificate like nobody's business."

At the end of my first year at Antioch I left Mills House to join a group of faculty bachelors at the home of a former postmaster of Yellow Springs. Here I learnt something about the feelings, characteristics, and eccentricities of young faculty members. Most were men of undisputed ability and most were critical of administration whether in government, business, or education. A few were arrogant, an occupational hazard of the teaching profession; others showed the strain of being driven by their feelings of inadequacy. For the most part they were men of imagination and originality, and all were good company. Among them was one very special Irishman named Kevin Guinagh. He was brought to Antioch by Morgan to tutor his youngest son, who was having some difficulty with courses in mathematics and English. Kevin was a classical scholar and was completing the writing of his dissertation at this time. Although not the most practical person in the world, he was a general favorite in the postmaster's household, where his gift of Irish blandishment and wit contributed much to the pleasure and harmony of its occupants. We became close friends. What made him particularly delightful as a companion were his manifold gifts--his knowledge of many languages, his easy flow of conversation, sparkling wit, and lively letter writing. Colleagues of his have spoken handsomely of his "urbane humor and charm"; a monograph on the history of Eastern Illinois University, where he taught after leaving Antioch, speaks of him as "educator, scholar, wit, and author." In all their comments, however, friends have been a little puzzled as to how to describe him and have usually fallen back on some witty quotation from his conversation or books. There is, for example, the occasion when someone asked Kevin how many Latin majors he had at Eastern. He replied sadly, "Once I had two. Now I have one, and you, being a philosopher, will know that the difference between one and zero is infinitely small."

Antioch's concern for the individual student projected

itself in various ways in the Library and more or less determined my thinking about the purpose and administration of
college libraries throughout the rest of my professional career. A major feature of the Antioch course program in the
late twenties was self-directed study. Under this plan the
courses provided for not more than one weekly lecture, and
students were not even required to attend. Instead they
worked independently from a syllabus prepared by the instructor for the entire semester. Of course they were expected
to confer as often as needed with their instructor, and, at
the end of the semester there were rigorous examinations.
The effect of this program on the Library was to make it a
kind of laboratory or workshop for practically all courses,
which in turn meant that we had to develop a strong reference
collection, a wide range of nontechnical books, and a generous
selection of journals to enable students to investigate, cur-
rently and retrospectively, any topic pertaining to their courses. This impact on the use of the Library was not limited
to the nonscientific courses. For example, the collection in
mathematics had to be enlarged to include general reading
covering the development of mathematics in relation to such
other fields as music, architecture, and biology. Students
were asked to write in each course at least two papers that
required a reasonable measure of thoroughness and depth in
their research. This offered a challenge to the staff to ac-
quaint the students with the indexes to recorded knowledge
and to help them in evaluating the relative importance of the
materials for their purpose. This responsibility fell largely
on me, and it gave me both confidence and a sense of ac-
complishment.

In the administration of the Library I discovered how
helpful faculty members, alumni, and even the students themselves could be in developing and broadening the resources
of a small college library. It was through Walter Kahoe's
knowledge of the making of fine books that the Library was
able to enlist his sponsorship of a collection of finely printed
books that would give interested students some firsthand
knowledge of the graphic arts. Robert L. Straker, an alum-
nus, combined efforts with Bessie Totten, Associate Librarian, to build the foundation of a special collection that with
later additions has come to represent an important research
collection of historical materials dealing with Horace Mann
and the early history of the College. Robert cast a wide net,
as evidenced from a letter he wrote July 7, 1938, while serving as textbook representative with the firm of Longmans,
Green & Sons:

This summer I am laboring away at gathering still more Mann and Peabody material. At the moment I am wading through about a hundred closely written letters that passed between Mary (later Mrs. Mann) and Elizabeth Peabody, while Mary and Sophia (later Mrs. Hawthorne) were in Cuba in 1833-35. Elizabeth tells in minutest detail almost everything that went on in Boston, a great deal about Brother Mann and Waldo Emerson and Dr. Channing and other worthies of the period. I find it most interesting but damned hard on the eyes.

Then, there was the interest of a student in music who persuaded the Class of 1928 to make a contribution for music appreciation. In 1929 this amounted to a fairly sizable sum, enough in fact to buy a phonograph and albums for the Library. The following year the Student Government continued the support of the collection, and it was decided to circulate albums in the same way the Library circulated books. Phonograph collections existed at other colleges, but so far as we were able to determine, these collections were restricted to use by music appreciation students.

No doubt the most significant improvement in the library service during my period at Antioch was the elimination of six small departmental collections in different classrooms, offices, and buildings into one consolidated science library in the new science building. At first, of course, there was the usual round of uninformed criticism about giving up the departmental collections, but once the science library was firmly established and a reference librarian employed with proper scientific background, the stimulus to faculty and students was justification enough.

Antioch seemed to me to have admirable ideas about athletics and religion. If the College ever had intercollegiate contests and "varsity teams," it had abandoned them. Intramural sports, participated in by faculty and students, constituted the athletic activities. I encountered handball there for the first time in my life and continued to play it four or five times a week for the next twenty years. After that my fingers began to play out and I gave it up for squash.

The essence of Antioch's attitude toward religion was, as stated in one of its admirable bulletins, contained in the

110

following biblical quotations: "Prove all things; hold fast that which is good." and "I am come that they might have life, and that they might have it more abundantly."

Arthur E. Morgan was a deep man with a very deep faith in hard work and discipline. He did not mind using the word "drudgery," which most educators would shun. This did not mean that the seriousness of purpose so admirably expressed in his leadership, writings, and way of life subtracted from the high spirits of the faculty and student body. I am reminded of the epigram of a bearded chaplain of Lambeth Palace, who on meeting a reporter come to interview the Archbishop of Canterbury greeted him with the observation that "to inhabit a museum does not necessarily oblige one to turn into an exhibit."

The Glen was a lovely and secluded spot for walking, picnicking, swimming, studying nature, skating, or just sitting on a log smoking and enjoying the wild roses beside the still waters. It consisted of a tract of forested hills and streams, and it extended over a length of three miles. Occasionally we took a dip in a deep pool beneath the springs for which the village was named. The water was icy and one dive was enough, but when we came out we felt refreshed and ready for the arena. Connected with the Glen was the Clifton Gorge, perhaps the wildest and most rugged rock formation in Ohio. A few of the more hardy souls would hike over the rocks and rivulets until they reached the main stream of the Gorge, which must have been thirty or forty feet deep with rock side walls extending a hundred feet or more from the surface of the water to the top. A good swimmer would swim up against the current for several hundred yards, then turn and scud back with the force of a big dam broke loose from everywhere at once.

On campus there were the usual attractions of college life, theater and opera rehearsals, bridge, house parties, dances, the Town and Gown club presided over spaciously by Lincoln R. Gibbs, sports of all kinds, political meetings to fume against injustices in the village and nearby towns, poetry readings, radio listening, record playing, and just plain amiable loafing on campus, during walks, or in the Tea Room presided over by Rod O'Connor. On special occasions there was "high tea" with Nurse Bingle. As an ice breaker for new faculty and foreign students, Nurse Bingle's "high teas" had no equal.

14: MARRIAGE AND OTHER PLEASURES

With my work beginning to shake down into a less dramatic
fashion by the summer of 1929, my life entered upon a new
emotional center. It all began with attendance at my first
American Library Association meeting, in Washington, D.C.,
where twenty-five hundred librarians poured into the city by
automobile, train, and bus for the week's debacle. I had
been encouraged to attend the meeting by my friend and neigh-
bor Paul North Rice, Librarian of the Dayton Public Library
and formerly a department head in the New York Public Library. A chubby man with a network of wrinkles at the cor-
ners of his bright eyes, he had a way of holding his head
when looking and speaking to you as if to say, "You agree,
don't you?" He had a genius for friendship, perhaps because
he was so generous with his time and money. When I asked
about the annual conference, he assured me that it was important in my work not only to have close academic relationships on campus but to seek the company of my fellow practitioners, and not only those in my special field.

Since Linda Eastman of the Cleveland Public Library
was the President of the Association at this time, page 1 of
the "Conference Chronicle" carried her picture--under the un-
imaginative title "Miss Eastman says 'Good Morning.'" She
is shown flanked by two local lady librarians and one lissome
lass from Honolulu holding a tennis racquet. I do not weep
for male librarians, but the editor of the "Chronicle" evidently thought it desirable to balance "numero uno" with a photograph of eight male librarians on the back page. These were
no lackluster fellows. Only Andrew Keogh of Yale unfurled
a slightly quizzical smile; the others showed a network of de-

112

termined heads, with tightly wrapped mouths. As I now look over the names in the photograph--Joseph Wheeler, Theodore Koch, Andrew Keogh, Charles Rush, and the others--I genuinely feel the loss among the great personalities who used to dominate the library scene.

Somehow--I forget the precise circumstances--I met a fellow librarian, Harold Brigham of the Nashville Public Library. Perhaps it was Louis Shores who introduced us, because as librarian of Fisk University in the same city he was undoubtedly well acquainted with his public library colleague. I knew Louis from Columbia library school days, and I heard some fine things about him since then from my friend Professor Leiserson of Antioch. As a result of this meeting I was invited by Mr. Brigham to join a party for a dance that climaxed the social events of the week. He had brought his secretary and children's librarian to the meeting and asked me to make up a foursome for the dance. At the last moment, following a long grueling business meeting, I discovered to my dismay that I hadn't time to return to my hotel to change and spruce up. But here once again my friend Louis came to the rescue and produced the proper apparel. Mr. Brigham and I met the girls at their hotel shortly after nine o'clock, and I was surprised and delighted to find my date for the evening a very beautiful young woman, about my height, with fine features and dark brown wavy hair. Her long eyelashes hung over brown eyes, and she wore her hair in a way that was half girlish, half womanish. I do not recall too much about the evening, but I remember her soft southern accent when she greeted me and my own self-conscious feeling of inadequacy for the occasion. I suspected that she might also feel a little self-conscious on a blind date, but apparently she did not. She was quite relaxed and showed a surprising self-command in her kind welcome. The events of the evening may have escaped my memory, but I do remember that we had a wonderful time together, and, since it turned out to be the most important event in my life, I quote--at the risk of appearing vulgar and indelicate--from her own diary account of the happenings:

> Mr. B. brought a young librarian from Antioch College, Ohio, to take Susie and me to the dance.... He was a nice blond about my height. After we danced for several hours, he asked me if I would like to see some more of Washington at night. I was charmed, so we got in his Ford and rode

around for several hours. We got started about 1
a. m. ... Such a wonderful climax to the trip. He
was the sweetest person on earth--just enough not
too much. And he was very much the gentleman--
never pressing himself. He said he would write.
I hope he will. I got to bed about 4 o'clock. When
I got to my hotel, Susanna was waiting for me. She
was worried to death and had even called Mr. B's
hotel to ask him what to do. He reassured her
that it was all o. k.

I should add that neither of us thought of the event as anything
other than a grand evening--as Margaret put it, "a wonderful
climax" to the conference--but the stars in their courses that
night were conspiring.

It was something of a relief when the College year
ended and I was able to give full attention to things that ur-
gently needed to be done but could not be undertaken until
classes were over. We made changes and renovated the entire second floor, which had only been partially available to
the Library before. Staff working space, a room for the Antiochiana, a desk, and reserve-reading requirements were
provided here. A reference collection, occupying an entire
alcove on the first floor, was established. Finally, but perhaps most difficult of all because of the cost, we arranged
for special cataloging help to incorporate the materials that
I had selected and brought over from the twin towers in Antioch Hall. On impulse, halfway through the summer, I decided to motor to Nashville to see Margaret, who wrote that
she would be happy to have me come. I took a student along
for company and to help with the driving. We drove in the
cool of the night for comfort, covered miles and miles of
curved and crooked roads, some of them unpaved, and finally
reached Nashville fourteen hours later. No matter what route
I took on future occasions, I could never beat that time.

I met and had dinner with her parents and learned
quite a lot from seeing them as a family. Margaret had a
talent for drawing and showed me a sketch of her home, a
lovely Queen Anne-type of residence with multiple gables and
a balustraded veranda curving around two sides. I suspected
the neighborhood to have been fashionable at one time but now
undergoing the inevitable changes that come with a rapidly
growing city. Her father, John W. White, an employee of the
Veterans' Administration, was tall and handsome like his

beautiful daughter, but in character quite different. He was more the extrovert although I'm sure a solid citizen underneath a jocular exterior; she was more like her mother though not nearly so reserved. Margaret showed me a picture of her mother, who was strikingly beautiful as a young woman. I suspected her early married life must have been a bit of a struggle financially, and it showed. Some of the love of life and joy of her youth seemed to have drained from her in later years, and she was not easy to draw into conversation. Both were very kind to me and made me feel at home, although it was quite obvious they were not thinking of me as a match for their beloved daughter. Neither was Margaret entertaining any such thoughts. She apparently had a number of suitors and many girl friends to keep her occupied socially, and she was having a good time. Had she given me evidence of encouragement I am sure I would have responded. For one thing, judging from the questions asked, she probably felt that she did not know enough about me. I sensed this and wrote her later telling something of my family background, my intention to become an American citizen, and my hopes for the future. In her replies there was both advance and retreat.

Life is a curious succession of contradictions. Here I was strenuously courting Margaret by letter while at the same time becoming more and more fascinated by a young woman who had recently come to Antioch as secretary to the President. Her name was Deryl Clark, and she was also a Southerner, from Blythe, Georgia. Deryl was attractive but not beautiful. Her genius was her wit and sophistication. She had a social gift to a remarkable degree, which may have been one reason Mr. Morgan hired her. He was incapable of small talk. I believe that what I liked most about her was her relaxed, almost languorous manner, yet she had great ability and commanded respect. She was also a cool one. On one occasion, when she was returning from her home to Antioch by way of Nashville, I gave her a lift after visiting Margaret. It was another all-night ride, and half way home the car lights burnt out. I spent the rest of the night until dawn chasing the taillights of trucks. It was nerve racking and dangerous. Deryl's only comment when we reached home was, "It's a pity we weren't arrested in Bowling Green so we could at least have got a chance to go to sleep in jail." We spent a good bit of time at the home of our friends Martha and Tom Lloyd and could often be found there, having dropped in for an hour or so after work. Sometimes we stayed for supper or perhaps all of us would go out for dinner if there

were a sitter available to take care of the children. The
longer I got to know Deryl, the more inaccessible she seemed
to me. I don't remember her going with a lot of other men.
She was not capricious, but if she was in love with anyone,
it was Tom Lloyd. They were two of a kind, two of the
most delightful people I have ever known.

After several more visits to Margaret's home, including one in which we spent a week together with her friends
at a camp on the Cumberland River, we became engaged and
were married November 27, 1930. The ceremony was performed in the Woodland Street Presbyterian Church before an
an assemblage that included all of Margaret's friends
and relatives and her parents' friends. William Haury, Margaret's musical instructor, arranged the music, and her
friend Charlotte Caldwell was the vocalist. Mr. White gave
his daughter away; Kevin Guinagh served as best man. His
surname seemed to be the only wrinkle in what otherwise
turned out to be a very smooth affair. Some of the guests
addressed him as Dr. Ginar, others as Dr. Ginagle, and
still others as Dr. Goonaw. A reporter for the local newspaper referred to him as Dr. Gurnaugh, but Margaret's parents wisely stuck to the "best man," whom they regarded as
"a most agreeable gentleman" and one whom they "thoroughly
enjoyed." A number of Margaret's friends wrote later to say
how beautiful she looked at the wedding, which to me was
rather like saying it was sunny in Sarasota. Only her dog,
Cop, appeared to take a dim view of the proceedings. When
she did not return home, he looked around for her in and
outside the house, repeated this several times, and then lay
down in front of the fireplace with a mournful howl.

Following the ceremony we drove to Louisville, Ken-
tucky, for three days and nights. I am sure we saw all the
major tourist points of interest (Churchill Downs of Derby
fame, the library and museum of the famous Filson Club,
homes and tombs of famous pioneers, and so forth), but the
thing I remember most pleasantly was eating, sleeping, and
the continuation of creativity. Kevin came to Louisville by
train several days later bringing a bottle of champagne, and
we all drove merrily back to Yellow Springs in our well-worn
Ford. On our return we took up residence in an apartment
owned by a friend who was spending the year in the East,
opened the boxes of wedding gifts forwarded by Margaret's
parents, went shopping for the essentials we lacked, and set
up house. About this same time Kevin married Marie, an

116

old friend of Pittsburgh days, and brought her back to help fill our lives with happiness and peace.

Antioch was an energizing place to work, the faculty lively, productive, and devoted to their students. In such an atmosphere it is not surprising that several months prior to my marriage I had already given thought to returning to Columbia University for a summer session. I was driven partly by the feeling that I was inadequately prepared for academic library work; partly by the need for a broader acquaintance with the leadership in the field and courses in American literature that would fill a gap in my undergraduate studies. I felt particularly the need for a greater familiarity with the writers in American history and literature of the past two decades, which would help me to sharpen my critical judgment in book selection. When I learnt that Charles B. Shaw, librarian of Swarthmore College and well known in the world of letters, was to be at Columbia for the summer session, I signed up immediately. I ended by enrolling in the master's program because of the leeway provided by the School of Library Service in allowing students to elect a reasonable number of courses outside the professional field. I was fortunate in getting a room once again in Furnald Hall and my old job back in the New York Public Library. After our marriage, with Margaret's encouragement, I continued my studies in the summer of 1931 and again in the spring semester of 1932, on which occasion she joined me in New York, rendered valuable assistance in preparing my thesis, and helped to make living there fun.

In the fall of 1933 our first child was born. We named him John Donald, after a young political scientist friend at Antioch whose career, we felt, was indubitably marked for a brilliant future. My first reaction was one of parental pride. Margaret had done all the hard work, of course, but I took pride in helping to contribute to the stream of life. I rushed out to announce to the world: "It happened." But then the phone calls started coming in, and I was completely mortified. Phone calls on such occasions consist of three questions: sex, weight, and how's the mother getting along. Well, authorities do not like husbands--one is not even allowed to hold one's own kid--so I hadn't a definitive answer to either the first two questions, and, as to the third, I wasn't allowed to see my wife after the delivery. And here were all her friends, burning with curiosity and getting no answers, immediately calling one another to say, "You know the dumbest

117

thing in the world is not a chicken or a horse; it's men."
So I hurried back to the hospital for a second look, and this
time my reaction was what a marvelous creation a newborn
baby is. I was prepared that ours might be a bit ugly because forceps had been used and his lips, at birth, were
slightly puffy. Either my sense of beauty was distorted by
having a child of my own or else he now seemed beautiful.
Whom did he favor? A slightly sinister nurse suggested me--
at eighty. But in my eyes he was fine and healthy and his
skin fairly glowed. What seemed truly amazing was the miracle of his perfect formation--tiny ears and fingers, how he
was equipped with the instinct to use his mouth for food, and
so forth. It had a kind of humbling effect to think one had a
part in such a wonderful creation. And as to the questions
of her friends who had been deriding me earlier, the baby
was a "he" weighing nine pounds, and his mother was doing
nicely. As a matter of fact when I last saw her she was
lying with hands folded on a flat stomach, luxuriating over
being once again in normal shape.

After having succeeded in becoming a parent, I found
that the desire to write, which had been inspired by Dr. Lydenberg's class, might be useful in my career as a librarian.
During the academic year 1931-32 I had contributed articles
to the "Wilson Bulletin" on the selection of journals for the
college library, and these were published, with substantial
revision, by the F. W. Faxon Company in book form in 1934
under the title "Classified List of Periodicals for the College
Library." Later revisions of this book, in collaboration with
Virginia M. Trumper, were published in 1938 and 1948. The
"cacoethes scribendi" was still with me in 1934 when I con-
tracted for a book with the Faxon Company that was published
in 1935 under the title "College Library Publicity." The distinguishing feature of this book was the illustrations by my
wife.

15: INTERLUDE: UNIVERSITY OF ILLINOIS

It took the Midwest, even at its most eastern fringe, some time to realize that the collapse of the '29 bull market was more than a temporary decline. When the shock waves finally reached Yellow Springs, with a consequent reduction in my salary to twenty-two hundred dollars, part of which was paid in script, we could no longer afford to eat and pay the rent. The mood at Antioch since Morgan left to become head of the newly created Tennessee Valley Authority is better expressed in a letter from my friend Albert Liddle than I can do by anything written now:

> Yellow Springs
> March 29, 1936

Dear Guy:

> ... What a moving time this spring is! Every other person one meets here is suspect. When Algo recently made it known that the only way to balance the budget was to make a drastic reduction in what he rather impersonally called "salary items," one tends to look at all one's best friends as people must have done during the great Plague, not knowing which one may be seeing for the last time! Some, like T.C.L., with good press agents, have given advance notice of their taking off; but the majority remain mysteriously silent, as if in good time we shall know. Your countryman, ----, was being prepared for the skids, but I am told he is thumbing his nose at them by leaving immediately for a job in Washington that pays twice what he is getting here. Perry Mason is voluntarily seeking

119

a year off to go to some new school of Commerce connected with the University of California.... An open season on deans caused a little stir, but most of them are merely going to work teaching. Walter is going to Harvard (Mildred should go somewhere, for she doesn't look like an office girl anymore!). Miss Marine is leaving.... The new head of that department, I am told, is Alexander. Clarence is angling for something at Columbia, I believe, and Kingsley has accepted the Fellowship for a year's study in England. So you see, the old place won't be quite the same.

Kevin had long since departed for Eastern Illinois State Teachers College (now Eastern Illinois University).

A young son meant new responsibilities. One does not analyze too carefully what one is best fitted to do under such circumstances. When the opportunity to become an Associate in Library Economy at the University of Illinois presented itself, I grasped it. I had no teaching experience and no idea whether or not I would like it. What appealed to me was the salary. Being interviewed and accepted was only a beginning. After a month or so of experience in the classroom I knew that teaching was not my cup of tea. I lacked the essential mark of a good teacher--a philosophical turn of mind. If I couldn't be a Harry M. Lydenberg, a William H. Alexander, or a Kevin Guinagh, I didn't want any part of it--on a permanent basis. I sweated over my lectures, often wrote them out at full length and memorized them, and tried for a style that would appeal to the students, all the time building up guilty feelings of ideas inadequately formulated and things undone. Actually I had had enough experience of a practical nature and enough enthusiasm for my profession to hold the students' attention at one meeting, but I was constantly apprehensive that I might flop at the next. There was no self-satisfaction in this. Moreover, I felt that when it came to an analysis that would evoke new insights and perspectives into the topic under discussion, I fell short.

The man who provided me with the Associate position was Phineas Lawrence Windsor, Ph.B., Professor of Library Science, Director of the Library, and Director of the Library School. Either he offered me the job because I had employed his daughter two or three years earlier as Science Librarian at Antioch or else he figured I was on my way to the Librarianship of Congress--I suspect the former. In any event from

the very first time I met him I liked him immensely. In
spite of the fact that he was the head of a great institution
I felt completely at ease in his presence. He was perfectly
natural, first and last himself, modest, quiet, judicial,
Phineas Windsor. With a brilliant staff both in the Library
and in the Library School, and the hearty support of his administration, he made the University of Illinois Library one
of the great research libraries in the country, ranking with
Michigan, Chicago, Columbia, and Pennsylvania. You might
say that in his quiet and modest way he had a flair for ad-
ministration--the wise executive who makes a careful distribution of any work that could possibly turn up to well-chosen
subordinates. In appearance and manner--tall, with a Vandyke beard, friendly eyes behind steel-rimmed glasses,
and tactful, he was well equipped by nature to work his spell
on the great variety of people who make up the librarian's
world. I have heard it said that when he went to the Faculty
Club for his favorite luncheon and bridge with senior administrators and faculty--sometimes an alumnus--he frequently
returned with the promise of new riches for the Library's
budget or shelves. Formal academic honors came late, but
in 1939 Columbia University offered him "summos honores"
as Doctor of Literature.

The actual operation of the Library School was left in
the capable hands of Amelia Krieg, Assistant Professor and
Assistant Director of the Library School. I was especially
grateful to her for her patience and assistance in helping me
to get started in my new work. The School's program and
requirements were similar to Columbia's, a bachelor degree
for admission, professional training leading to a bachelor and
master's degree in library science, but differing from Columbia in not providing for studies leading to a Ph.D. in librarianship. The Library School staff also assumed responsibility for a course for freshmen and sophomores in the use
of the Library, a responsibility generally undertaken by the
Library staff in most colleges and universities. My teaching
assignment was twofold, library administration (a general
course) and college and university libraries. In the summer
of 1936 I gave the course in library architecture and buildings. The faculty of the School, though small in number in
relation to the student enrollment, was assisted by several
members of the Library staff in special areas.

On the whole my first year and a summer session of
teaching was not notable in any way, but it was instructive.

It widened my acquaintance with the entire family of librarianship. It knocked out the mistaken notion that professors only believed they were working terribly hard when no one else could see that they were doing anything. And it may have led to an invitation from the poet Stanley Kunitz, in his new editorial job with the H. W. Wilson Company in the mid-thirties, to contribute a column to the "Wilson Bulletin" on the efforts and experiments of librarians in popularizing library services. I hope my bimonthly eructations left a favorable impression, although it was as obvious to me then as it is now that no amount of public relations palaver could take the place of the quality of the staff. In the seven years I continued the column before running out of gas I never had the good fortune to meet Kunitz except through his published poetry and biographical works. One reason perhaps was the unusual terms of his editorship, which he reveals in a short autobiographical sketch for "World Tomorrow":

> With the first money I saved from my editorial job with the H. W. Wilson Company I departed for Europe, fully expecting to be fired; but Mr. Wilson surprised himself by giving me permission to edit the "Wilson Library Bulletin" (then the "Wilson Bulletin") from abroad. When I returned a year later, I moved to a one-hundred acre farm in Connecticut ... and continued to perform my editorial duties in absentia.

1. The S.S. "Lake Manitoba," which brought the Barr Colonists, March 31, 1903, from Liverpool to the Port of St. John, New Brunswick

2. Barr Colonists waving from the Canadian Pacific Railway "colonial car" that brought them from St. John to the village of Saskatoon

3. Barr Colony Camp at Saskatoon, April 1903

4. Those Englishmen! Even on the prairie they felt obliged to shave

5.   "Soddies" and tents were the first homes of the Barr Colonists when they reached the colony site.

6.   Log cabins, chinked with mud, replaced the soddies and tents of the colonists.

7. Lloydminster, 1905: Broadway Avenue

8. Devonshire House _circa_ 1907

9. Father, World War I

10. Mother

Clockwise from above left:

11. My brother, Ken, and I

12. My step-brother, Pat

13. My sister, Molly

14. Tennis Club, 1925-6, University of Alberta

15.   Margaret, November 1930

16. Arthur E. Morgan, President of Antioch College (1920-1936), a man of magnificent character who believed in the purposefulness of the universe, freedom to doubt, and the sacred responsibility of each of us to make one's life count in the struggle for human advance

17. Horace Mann Library, built 1924 on the site of former Presidents' house, burned January 1924

18 and 19.   Margaret and I at Antioch College (1933)

20.   Friend and mentor, R. W. Henderson, New York Public Library

21.   My friend Kevin Guinagh (Antioch)

22. 1946 (LSU): Margaret, Don, Christopher (with football), Jennifer, and I at home, Baton Rouge

23. Emory's beautiful ten-story Woodruff Library ranks as one of the great libraries of the South.

Sons and daughters

Clockwise from above:

24. Don
25. Jennifer
26. Christopher
27. Ellen

28.   At retirement (1972)

29.   Writing and Teaching
(Office of Mitchell Reames, Director, Francis Marion College Library, Florence, S.C.)

30. Squash (with partner Ralph Davis)

31. Riding

Awards

32. (Above) LL. D. University of Alberta, 1964

33. Joseph W. Lippincott Award (American Library Association), 1972

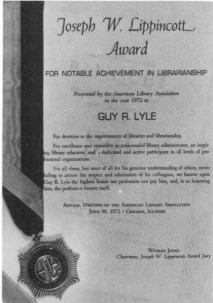

Joseph W. Lippincott Award

FOR NOTABLE ACHIEVEMENT IN LIBRARIANSHIP

Presented by the American Library Association in the year 1972 to

GUY R. LYLE

For devotion to the improvement of libraries and librarianship.

For excellence and versatility as a successful library administrator, an inspiring library educator, and a dedicated and active participant in all levels of professional organizations.

For all these, but most of all for his genuine understanding of others, never failing to arouse the respect and admiration of his colleagues, we bestow upon Guy R. Lyle the highest honor our profession can pay him, and, in so honoring him, the profession honors itself.

ANNUAL MEETING OF THE AMERICAN LIBRARY ASSOCIATION
JUNE 30, 1972 · CHICAGO, ILLINOIS

WYMAN JONES
Chairman, Joseph W. Lippincott Award Jury

16: THE WOMAN'S COLLEGE OF THE UNIVERSITY OF
NORTH CAROLINA AND OTHER MATTERS

In the early spring of 1936 I received a letter from the Woman's College of the University of North Carolina asking if I would be interested in the position of librarian of the College, and what did I know about the South? The day the letter came was windy, cold, and overcast--a day when with Robert Frost "you're two months back in the middle of March"--and so for my wife's sake if for no other I replied "yes" to the first question. But as to the second, I felt obliged to reply that I knew "practically nothing, " except, of course, that I had married a Southerner from Tennessee. I went on to explain that while I didn't expect this marital alliance to change the alchemy of my British blood, I had sworn to uphold the United States Constitution, and I understood this act of fealty applied to all states and not just to the "Nawth. " And then I promptly forgot all about the matter because I was engaged at the moment in two time-consuming projects in the Administration class.

In the thirties there were many innovations to help make the academic library and general cultural reading more attractive to students--exhibits, dormitory libraries, browsing rooms, and the like--but in all of these little attention had been given to the students' first introduction to the library. Most students in the Administration class felt that when they were freshmen their trek through the library during orientation week had left them with the impression that the library was a rather dull and dispiriting place. Some of the students felt also that there was too much emphasis in college on what G. K. Chesterton described as "bad good books"--those that

123

are studied rather than read--and not enough on "good bad books" --those that are not necessarily highly regarded from an intellectual and literary point of view but that are extremely readable and long remembered. These seemed to us to be lacunae in the educational process that the librarian might be able to do something about. The Administration class recognized that there was no one solution to the problem, but they felt keenly that freshman students needed a more informal and friendly approach to the library than they were getting. So the class went to work and produced an attractive, pleasantly informal leaflet that they entitled "Greetings to Freshmen!" and that was written from the point of view of a senior student addressing his freshman brother and sister. The leaflet was illustrated with five original drawings by Margaret Lyle, James Baker, and Jean Wilder. The American Library Association thought enough of the flyer to publish it.

The second project, a more ambitious undertaking, had as its purpose helping students use the library more effectively and efficiently in connection with their regular course work. So far as I could determine this had never before been done using a movie as the medium. In the Administration class there was a bright young man, Ralph Esterquest, who possessed plenty of self-confidence and genuine, innate sangfroid, and who, I believe, had had some previous experience in public relations. His dapper appearance, bow tie and all, was as conspicuous as his wide-open smile, although I could never be sure whether he was smiling with me or at me. In any event I saw great things ahead for this young man, and I invited him and five other students in the class, Lewis Bright, Olga Schevchik, Bernard Foy, Mildred Easton, and Martha Sanford, to produce a movie presenting the highlights of an intelligent technique for using the library in the preparation of college themes and other types of class work. My hope was that in addition to giving college students specific information in library research technique, the movie would afford a general overview of what a library was really all about and accustom the students to thinking of the library and its use as an integral part of their education. The chosen five under Ralph Esterquest's direction wrote the script, students in the dramatic school of the University took the leading parts, the University photographer shot the film, and Mr. Windsor provided the financial support. The scenes were photographed on successive Sunday mornings when the Library was closed.

"Found in a Book," the title given to the film, had no startling climax, but it had a certain measure of dramatic sequence. Tested out by a critical audience of University undergraduates, it was awarded a "B+" grade. In the words of one observant student, it gave "a definite sense of the concreteness of library tools and their use, something which no amount of verbal classroom instruction" could give him.

The "Christian Science Monitor" for October 13, 1936, gave it a lengthy spread under the title "Hollywood Comes to the Library." The film was taken over by the American Library Association and made available to libraries on a rental basis. Later on Bell and Howell took over the distribution of the film.

Late March or early in April I received a letter from my friend Professor Liddle of Antioch College that reminded me that I had heard nothing from the Woman's College since the initial inquiry some months before. Albert wrote:

> A couple of days ago I had an inquiry out of the South from a Miss Cornelia Strong, who appears to have a more active function than the chairman of the Library Committee at Antioch College, asking many personal questions about you as if she feared that the young "woman" of the "Woman's College" in N. C. might be in some danger of getting for the custodian of books there a lacklustre, effeminate fellow with long hair and a Windsor tie who should be "indiscrete" (sic) and humorless into the bargain! She particularly wanted to know if you had dignity, tact, and were masculine. Masculine, quotha! and discreet!!

Shortly after Albert's recommendation to Miss Strong, I received an invitation to join the Faculty of the Woman's College as Librarian and Professor of Library Science. I accepted, Margaret got started on plans to ship the washing machine, and this left only the difficult task of informing Mr. Windsor that I was leaving after only one year of teaching. I am sure he was not thrilled about this, but he understood my reasons and was kind enough to say that he thought my classes had been unusually successful. Since I felt terribly uncertain about my success or failure in the classroom, this word from Mr. Windsor was as good as Jove's nod. No wonder he was so widely admired and beloved by his staff.

The final summer session (1936) in Urbana was a hot

125

one.   We moved to the basement of our two-story rented
home to escape the heat; air conditioning in residences was
unheard of at this time.   However, we did not mind the bodi-
ly discomfort too much because we had already in our con-
sciousness moved into another, and more preferable, condition of life.   We had pinned on the wall of the basement a
huge map of North Carolina, which showed there was not one
but three North Carolinas, a mountain region, the piedmont
region, and the coastal plains.   Greensboro appeared to be
pretty much in the center of the state, in the piedmont region, about equidistant from the Blue Ridge and Smoky mountains and the historic coastal towns on the Atlantic where settlement in this part of the country first began.   From further
study of the map and the help of a guidebook we discovered
that we were about to enter a very serious-minded portion of
the state, with Quakers a few miles away at Guilford College,
Moravians to the east at Salem, Methodists from within at
Greensboro College and still more emerging from J. B.
Duke's palace in Durham, and the ubiquitous Calvinists and
Baptists all around.   Were we headed for the Sahara of the
Bozart?   We certainly hoped not, and our fears proved
groundless.   Less than a year after we moved to Greensboro,
if someone had asked what we thought was the chief charac-
teristic of the people there, the answer would have been con-
geniality.

Our first contribution to Greensboro was our second
child, Jennifer Anne, born November 10, 1936.   I was too
busy with the new job to make a proper record of the event,
but fortunately there were others, sufficiently knightly, to take
up pen and send us a word of congratulation.   From these I
share one from Kevin:

7th day before the Kalends of Dec.

Dear Guy, Marge, & Donald:
      Well, we want to congratulate you all.   It's
pretty nice to see your roots deepening in the soil.
You people must have a feeling that you belong to
this world.   We felt of course that everything would
be successful.   You have managed, too, to take
care of the proper distribution of the sexes.   This
is especially gratifying to you, I imagine.   About
spelling the young daughter's name with two n's, I
understand that this is very Cornish.   With your
British background you will naturally approve of this
spelling.

I am interested to see that you have become folksy with Chris Morley. Cultivate this contact, my friend, water it with the dew of remembrance, hoe it with comment on what he writes, manure it with the sweetness of a little flattery and betimes you will find your column in the "Wilson Bulletin" will find a place in the "Sat. Review of Literature." Don't forget your old friends is the moral principle that you should apply here.

Best
Kevin

Kevin's good-humored raillery regarding Christopher Morley and my connection with his visit to the Woman's College campus was inspired by these events. A reprint of Morley's most popular early novel, "Parnassus on Wheels," a story about a vagabond bookseller that has perennial appeal, appeared in a dollar series shortly before he was scheduled to deliver a lecture at the College. I wired to ask if he would autograph copies of his novel before the lecture, in the late afternoon at the Library, explaining that I was trying to raise money for the annual student prize award that we sponsored for the best collection of books formed by a student during her term at the College. He promptly wired back, "Of course, be glad to help!" Several hundred copies of "Parnassus" were sold at the autographing party, and the difference between what I paid for the books with discount and the list price provided sufficient money for both a first and second prize that year. Following the lecture there was a reception, and after that a select few met at one of the faculty homes, where Morley persuaded the group to take part in impromptu Elizabethan charades. Some of these struck me as a little rich for some of the virginal minds present, but everyone had a good time and enjoyed the evening immensely.

Morley was a great fan of O. Henry, so naturally he stayed at the O. Henry Hotel and remained over the following day for as long as his schedule would permit to see something of O. Henry's town. One of the first places he visited was the drugstore where O. Henry worked at one time, and here he found "O. Henry's own favorite" book behind the hot water bottles. It was Webster's dictionary that he presented to the Quill Club at the College. Before leaving he was kind enough to autograph one of his most recent books, "Ex Libris

Carissimis," the Rosenbach lectures delivered at the University of Pennsylvania. His inscription reads:

For Jennifer Anne Lyle
(who is today Four Days Old)
this signed with love from her father's friend

Christopher Morley

(who wonders if this little book will still prove
readable when she is old enough to read it!)

Greensboro, N.C.
November 13, 1936

Well, I am getting ahead of my story. Back to the Woman's College and Greensboro. The College itself is located on a hundred-acre, beautifully wooded campus. We were fortunate enough to find a house for rent within walking distance--303 Woodbine Court ("where the woodbine twineth") in a relatively new subdivision, Sunset Hills. On my way to the College I cut across a couple of streets, followed about a quarter of a mile up Market Street, and then took the lovely shade of a winding, wooded, uphill path leading to the dormitories and the Library.

Although part of the school system of the state with the responsibility to provide instruction for those training to be schoolteachers, the Woman's College had developed a liberal arts program comparable to the best of other fine women's colleges throughout the country. The faculty were certainly not intellectual giants, but they included some distinguished teachers and researchers--Benjamin Kendrick and Alex Arnett in History (joint authors of "The South Looks at Its Past"); Calvin Warfield, John Tiederman, Lawrence Ritchie, and Helen Barton in Science and Mathematics; Allen Tate, Caroline Gordon, Marc Friedlaender, and George P. Wilson in English; Albert Keister in Economics; Mereb Mossman in Sociology; Charlton Jernigan in Classics (later President of Queens College, North Carolina); Meta Miller and Malcolm Hooke in Romance Languages; and Gregory Ivy in Art. There were many others, of course, more than half women, and most of them brought recognition to themselves and credit to the College for the quality of their teaching. The student body numbered a little more than two thousand and, I imagine, came largely from the South.

One of the good things I discovered about the College was its spirit of tolerance. The quest for reputation and power that plagues the faculties of larger universities did not exist, or if it did, I was unaware of it. To be sure we all wanted more and better things for our respective departments, but as Harold Stoke of Queens College, New York City, succinctly put it, "Every college and university is always short of money." I did not observe the intense interdepartmental rivalry for money and status that I have in some other institutions. There was no pressure on the faculty to do research; good teaching rather than publication was the goal sought by the Administration. Nor was there any compulsion to engage in outside activities, professional, civic, or religious. So far as I was able to determine there was no serious cleavage between faculty and administration, although some members of the faculty felt that the Dean of Women, a politically powerful woman of undisputed ability, exercised more power in College policy and administration than was desirable. One reason for campus harmony, I believe, was Dean W. C. Jackson's extremely tolerant and sympathetic attitude in dealing with problems of the faculty and staff. In all my conferences with him regarding the Library and my own professional activities I found him easy to talk to, reasonable, and more than willing to help move my recommendations ahead.

If I were to pick out one person who seemed to be representative of the spirit and character of the faculty during my time at the College, I would select George P. Wilson, professor of English. He was a charming, witty, energetic man, ever thoughtful of his teaching colleagues and the Library staff, who managed without strain to accomplish a good deal of research and writing along with his teaching duties. And he was a very successful teacher. His favorite specialties were folklore, southern pronounciation, and the English language. His son records that his teaching was not restricted to the classroom:

> ... he taught at the dinner table, regaling his family and friends with selected tid-bits on the English language, folklore, and the uniqueness of Southern speech patterns and pronounciation. And these "informal students"--family, friends, and casual acquaintances--admired and loved him for his erudition, his never-ending stream of quotations, stories, literary allusions, and pedagogical points.

G. P., as I used to call him, may have been a little more industrious than some of his other colleagues--he had no relaxing vices other than fishing and hunting--but I think that he shared with them a love of teaching, an ability to communicate their ideas, and a generous tolerance of human frailty in colleague and student.

The Library when I arrived was far from adequate. A devastating fire in 1932 had resulted in serious book losses. The Depression years had brought about a reduction in book funds, curtailed services, and low staff morale. Some faculty members had lost interest in recommending books for purchase in their fields because they said the Library had no money to buy them. In two years we were able to turn this poor condition around. In my second annual report I was able to report that a substantial increase in the overall Library budget had stimulated faculty interest in book recommendations, led to an improvement in current book and periodical acquisitions, provided some increase in staff salaries, and strengthened the service of the Library in direct assistance to students and faculty. Help arrived unexpectedly the following year when the Library was selected as one of ten state institutional libraries in the country to receive the maximum grant from the Carnegie Corporation for a three-year period.

With the restoration of book funds the first practical problem to be resolved was shelving for more books. Space was at a premium, but there was room above the three existing stack levels to add a fourth, and within the third year we were able to install steel shelving for another twenty thousand volumes. When these shelves became full, we informed the administration, the Library would need a new building.

No library service is better than the quality of its staff. The nucleus around which we endeavored to build and strengthen the staff were the five department heads inherited from my predecessor. They were Elizabeth Sampson, head cataloger, meticulous and demanding of her staff but quite attractive in a quiet way; Virginia Trumper, in charge of periodicals, a formidable but exceedingly competent woman in her field of work; Sue Vernon Williams, reference librarian, loyal, unassuming, shy to the point of self-torture, technically skilled, but not well suited to head a reference department; Marjorie Hood, head of circulation, amazingly industrious, a good organizer and teacher, and quite obviously capable of making anyone like her; Minnie Hussey, reader's

130

adviser, a southern lady with a sparkle and a broad and deep knowledge of contemporary belles-lettres. There were others, such as Treva Wilkerson, circulation assistant, known for her diligence and beauty, who contributed their full share to providing good library service. In future years we were able to add new staff members who brought experience and ideas from different schools and backgrounds, which helped to offset the tendency of earlier years toward inbreeding. Among these were Roseanne Hudson from Illinois, Ruth Worley from North Carolina, Sarah Bowling, and Margaret Moser.

The "Crow's Nest" column, which appeared in the "Wilson Library Bulletin" without interruption from 1935 to 1942, projected me into a number of professional activities outside my job that were exciting and maturing but consumed a great deal of time I might better have used in private study and reading. I served as Chairman of the College Library Advisory Board, a predecessor of the Association of College and Research Libraries (ACRL), from 1938 to 1940, and as a member of the Council of the American Library Association during this same period. In 1941-42 I served as President of the North Carolina Library Association, and as Chairman of the ACRL Publications Committee from 1941 to 1943. In the summer of 1937 I taught at the Library School of Louisiana State University, where most of the faculty thought well of Huey P. Long, and about which I shall have something to say later. In the following summer I taught in the School of Library Science at the University of North Carolina, Chapel Hill. During this same period I was reviewing books for the National Parent-Teacher magazine and started work on a book, "The Administration of the College Library," commissioned by the H. W. Wilson Company.

In the fall of 1938 I accepted an invitation from Dr. Louis R. Wilson, Dean of the Graduate Library School of the University of Chicago, to participate in a survey of the University of Georgia Libraries along with Dr. Harvie Branscomb, then lingering between divinity and presidential duties as Librarian of Duke University, and Ralph Dunbar, Chief of the Library Division of the U.S. Office of Education. My responsibility was to spend a week ahead of the first meeting of the surveyors to collect information needed for making recommendations and to prepare the final draft. A survey of the University of Florida Libraries followed in 1940 with Dr. Wilson, Dr. A. F. Kuhlman (the distinguished Librarian of the Joint University Libraries, Vanderbilt University), and myself, with responsibilities comparable to those assigned in the previous survey. Dr. Wilson served as chairman of both surveys. I am quite sure that thesis after thesis has been made of the technique of university library survey-making so I shall not comment on the subject here. These two surveys, though expensive and the process somewhat clumsy and sluggish, were pioneer works and were said by kindly reviewers to "set the pattern in this important trend in university library administration." More important was Dr. Wilson's general approach to the survey. I had never met the gentleman before, although I was well aware of his reputation as the "Dean of American Libraries" and his great successes in Chicago and North Carolina before and after. I observed him closely and learned something that was valuable to me in my work afterward. His approach was to delay involvement in the actual library situation until he had fully assessed the forces within and without the university that might have a bearing on the success of the library. He made this assessment as warily as a hound dog circling a porcupine--a trial run here and a trial run there--but before he was through he knew precisely where the authority and the influence and the power lay within the institution and what the library might reasonably be expected to accomplish in the local situation. When his mind began to work in this way, when his engagement with a particular problem was strong and spontaneous, there occurred to those who worked with him, and to the officials and faculty he came into contact with at the university being served, an experience that I can only describe as one of opening and enlargement.

By 1942 we were at war with Japan and the other Axis powers. Up until this time England had pretty much fought the war alone after France and Russia were largely overrun. For one who had close connections with England and particularly with the Canadians who were already in combat overseas, it was an uneasy time--being concerned over whether England would be invaded, hearing rumors about heavy casualties, not knowing what to believe about conflicting reports from the war zone, and feeling a sense of guilt and inadequacy for not being more actively engaged in the war effort. For a few short months my stint as state director of the Victory Book Campaign to collect books for the troops here and abroad helped to make the passing time more endurable. When this work was finished, I made strenuous efforts, supported by recommendations from Frank Porter Graham (President of the University of North Carolina), Dean Jackson, and friends elsewhere, to secure a commission in either the Army or the Navy, but this failed--in the case of the Navy the stumbling block was my refusal to have a prior operation for a hydrocele. Then quite unexpectedly I was offered an Assistant Professorship in the Library School at the University of Illinois, which I accepted for 1942-43 after talking it over with Dean Jackson and securing a leave of absence from the Woman's College for the year. I was most grateful to Dr. Jackson for his understanding and approval. I felt certain that the sense of being inadequately prepared each day I faced the class--a feeling I was never able to shed during my entire teaching experience--would be more than enough to drive every other kind of worry out of my mind. The year at Illinois was also an opportunity to continue my studies in the field of American literature, begun at Columbia University. My family went with me, of course, and we were fortunate in securing a very comfortable home to rent for the year. The man who served as Deputy Director of the Library School under Dr. Carl White, successor to Phineas Windsor after his retirement, was E. W. McDiarmid. He and his wife helped to make our stay a very happy one. He was a good-looking man, above average in physical vigor--to judge from his performance on the tennis court and on long treks with Professor William A. Oldfather's weekend safaris into the wilderness surrounding Urbana--and unusually patient and optimistic in his relation to students and the faculty. His leadership had much to do with the cordial relationship that existed between the faculty and students and the staff of the University Library. No doubt the fact that both the School and the University Library were under the direction of Carl White had also something to do with closing the gap that frequently exists on university campuses.

In the year and a half following our return to the Woman's College we moved from Woodbine Court to our own home located still nearer the campus. I turned down the position of University Librarian at the University of Georgia and offers to be considered for a similar position by the presidents of Colgate and the University of Nebraska because, for the time, at least, this seemed to be our permanent home. I should admit, of course, that both the new house and our Ford were jointly owned by the finance folk. We lived modestly but with plenty of enjoyment. There were dances, formal and informal, which the younger members of the faculty were often invited to chaperone. The boys from Chapel Hill came up on

133

weekends, and these were festive occasions for the girls.
There were plays, noted speakers, and musical programs
sponsored by the College--no preaching or revivals. The
College owned a cottage in the country, with a small spring-
fed lake, where we spent many a weekend in an endless round
of swimming, eating, reading, talking, playing canasta, and
sleeping on porches that extended around two sides of the cottage. We had a faithful maid, devoted to the children and a
wonderful cook, but an absolute tyrant when it came to de-
ciding when and what we should eat. Either you accepted
Rena on her terms or you did without her. If I was not
teaching during the summer vacation, we often spent two or
three weeks with our friends the Warfields and the Tiedermans
at Cedar Beach, the former's summer home, a few miles
south of Tappahannock on the Rappahannock River. We have
never forgotten those vacation weeks or cease to marvel how
the children and everyone got along so beautifully; how we
bought fresh vegetables from the gardens of neighboring farmers; how we swam and fished and built castles with the children on the sandy beach; and how after a marvelous evening
meal we all gathered on the screened-in porch, sheltered by
friendly cedar, oak, and gum trees, and rocked and watched
the Rappahannock flowing southeast to Chesapeake Bay. Talk
of a fine vacation! There may be things better than a sprawling cottage with a screened-in porch overlooking a beautiful
river, watching the buoyant flight of gulls and the steady upward push of a returning fishing boat, and meals of pork roast
with sweet potatoes, blackberry pie, and homemade bread--
but I have not experienced them.

17: THE "LONG" ARM OF THE LAW

Maybe this is scarcely worth mentioning. It had nothing to do with books, libraries, or teaching. But whenever anyone mentions Louisiana to me, and especially when the weather is blisteringly hot, as it is this day in Atlanta and has been for the last ten days, I think back to the summer of 1937, when I accepted an invitation from James A. McMillen, Director of Libraries and Director of the Library School of Louisiana State University, to teach during the summer session. I had no noble motive in accepting the offer, simply that I wanted to feed our two fast-growing children, to buy Margaret an oriental rug she had set her heart on having some day, to pay the final installments on the car, and to learn something about the customs and folkways of the irreverent infidels who lived in the Pelican State. In my mind's fancy it was exotic, shadowy, and somewhat violent. Although Huey P. Long had been assassinated two long years earlier, Baton Rouge, the home of Louisiana State University, was still very much in the news. The capital city took its name from the Indian word "Istrouma" meaning "Red Stick," later translated into the French.

Louisiana State University and the University of Chicago have two things in common--they were both built with Standard Oil money: philanthropy in the case of the latter, extortion in the former. I was not long on the campus before I discovered that the ghost of Huey P. Long still hovered over the "Ole War Skule," whose first President was the same fiery general, William Tecumseh Sherman, who burned Atlanta and devastated Georgia from Atlanta to the coast during the Civil War. Politics still honeycombed the campus. Rumor had it

135

that there were certain political comers among the student
body; it was wise to clap those boys on their broad backs.
To be sure the Kingfish was buried under several tons of concrete, but I noticed that some faculty members still glanced
over their shoulders when asked about the assassination or
some of the peculiarities of campus folkways.

One day I was getting ready to leave the campus for
my apartment in downtown Baton Rouge when I spotted a motorcycle cop at an intersection.   I made the required stop at
the corner, put out my hand to signal a left turn, and released the clutch.   Immediately the cop pulled alongside of
my car and then swung in front to cut off my advance.   He
climbed off his machine, deliberately, came over to my car,
and without any form of greeting, snapped:

"Your name?"

I gave it.

"Address?"

"410 St. Hippolyte Street."

He then demanded my driver's license and I showed it
to him.   I was a bit staggered by the precipitateness of it
all, but when I found my voice, I asked what the charge was.
There was no response, only a curt, "Be down at the courthouse tomorrow morning at 10:30."

With this display of boorishness, he thrust the ticket
in my hand, climbed onto his motorcycle, gunned the motor,
and disappeared at the turn of the University gate.

I drove back to my apartment, past the gates, down
the old blacktop Highland Road, which led to Baton Rouge,
some two miles or so distant from the campus.   There was
a market in progress, and I had some difficulty in avoiding
the carts and goods or the dark-skinned youngsters and their
barking dogs as they scooted back and forth across the road
between the booths anchored on each shoulder.   When I arrived home on St. Hippolyte Street, I climbed the iron stairway to my second-floor, tin-roofed apartment, opened the
door, tossed my briefcase on a chair, and lay down on the
couch.   It was terribly hot; once again the temperature had
climbed to a hundred or more, and, of course, there was no

air conditioning. I was so dog tired I slept for an hour or so. When I awoke, I splashed water on my face and called the Director of Libraries on the phone to ask his advice about the traffic ticket. I had a class at the hour I was supposed to report at the courthouse; of even greater concern to me was the blistering heat. I wanted to avoid any unnecessary trips if possible.

Subsequent events may be briefly summarized. The Director said he would check into the matter and call me back. When he did, about an hour later, he said he was sorry, but he had been advised by the University authorities that it would be best for me to respond to the summons and be at the courthouse in the morning. He said if I missed a class to let the Library Office know in advance so a proper notice could be posted. I hung up wondering why in God's name I had ever come to LSU when at this very moment, frying in hundred-degree heat, I might be cooling my heels in a mountain stream in North Carolina.

It was still early next morning when the milk round brought me to the surface. The heat was already oppressive, even on the screened porch. After breakfast I felt better and was determined that nothing, at least, should interfere with my first class of the day. But in spite of good resolutions my performance was below par. I didn't even make the customary effort to pronounce some of their unfamiliar and exotic names, and the students' ill-concealed snickering did nothing to improve my disposition. I was about to leave the room at the end of the class hour, and was getting out the traffic summons to check once again the exact time I was supposed to be at the courthouse, when my eye caught Jim Thorn approaching from the rear of the classroom.

I was never quite sure what Jim was doing in the class, anyway. He was older than I, much older than the other students in the class, a shy, heavy-set man with broad shoulders huddled in a way to suggest he was carrying part of the world's burdens on his back. His face seemed rather raw and scarred, and on one cheek he had a nasty scar. Perhaps he was a veteran of World War I or had been in an accident, I thought. In dress, he was careless to the point of slovenliness. Judging from his seersucker suit, he had little use for cleaning and pressing. But then again who could wear a suit in such weather and have it look like anything after half a day's wear? Jim sat alone at the back of the

137

classroom, took no part in the discussion, and appeared to have developed a protective lacquer of silence. But here he was now, practically blocking my exit, and seemingly getting ready to say something to me. Finally he spoke, and his voice had a curious rasp.

"Professor," he said, "I hear you ran into some trouble with the state police yesterday. Is that the summons you have in your hand? It looks familiar. May I see it a minute please?" Before I could respond he took the ticket from my hand, paused a moment to read its message, and then said:

"Ah, yes! Just as I thought. Ridiculous, of course. Don't you bother about this. I'll take care of it. I know you are anxious not to miss your next class."

It all happened so suddenly that before I had a chance to remonstrate with him, which I probably wouldn't have done anyway, we were caught up in the conflux of changing classes. He waved the ticket in his hand, smiled ingratiatingly, and disappeared in the crowd.

I felt a little humiliated. I pretend no particular solidarity with high principle but felt a little guilty. After all the University authorities advised that I appear in court and here was a student in my class, with whom I hadn't exchanged more than a dozen words the whole time I had been there, telling me to forget all about the traffic ticket, saying he would take care of it as casually as one might light up a cigarette. Slightly oppressed by my thoughts, I wandered out on the campus and sought the shade and obscurity of a small group of live oaks. I settled down against one of the tree trunks. Above me low-hanging moss clung to dead branches, giving the tree an almost sinister look. I felt a bit spooky myself. How had Jim learned about the summons? And why was he putting himself to all this trouble on my account? I managed to upset myself.

The following day I stunned the students by dismissing the class five minutes early, and I fixed Jim Thorn with a look that clearly meant that I wanted to speak with him. As usual, he brought up the rear. I wasted no time.

"I want to thank you, Jim, for taking care of my problem with the police. I am most grateful. I was able to meet my class and you probably saved me from heat prostration.

138

But I wonder, would you mind telling me what this ticket business was all about?"

"Oh that," he said, "It was nothing at all! No trouble at all. You were simply ticketed for a half-year's license fee for driving with an out-of-state license. I spoke by phone to a friend of mine and that's all there was to it."

He snapped his fingers as though the law was only a pet irritation--to be pushed aside if it got in one's way. I wanted to ask him what he would have done if the summons had been for a serious offense, such as leaving the scene of an accident, but of course I did not pump him. I think I already knew the answer. I thanked him once more, he smiled graciously and shook hands, and then departed.

A couple of days later the State Highway Board sent out a report to the University that the Attorney General was reconsidering an interpretation of the law with respect to licensing vehicles that would exclude visiting summer-school instructors from out of state.

Jim's connection went right to the top.

Christopher arrived December 1, 1943, without taking much
toll of his mother's energy or strength even though he weighed
in at nine pounds ten ounces--one ounce less than his brother.
A little late for tax exemption in 1943, but welcome just the
same.   As Kevin pointed out in his congratulatory note, he
earned us honorable mention:

> ... In effete Rome, a man might be given the "jus
> trium liberorum" as a kind of political favor even
> if he didn't have three children.   But you earn the
> rights of three children legitimately, whatever those
> rights might be.   From your population altitude you
> must look down upon a one child sterility and ask
> what people are doing to fulfill the biblical injunc-
> tion to "increase and multiply and fill the earth."

Whether or not Christopher entitled us to the "jus
trium liberorum," his entry into the family circle marked,
as did his brother and sister, the end of one period and place
in our lives and the beginning of another.   When Don was
born, we left Antioch for Illinois; when Jennifer came along,
we departed Illinois for the Woman's College; and now with
Christopher's entry we were considering a move to leave
Greensboro for Baton Rouge.

In 1943 James McMillen of Louisiana State University,
becoming more conscious of the strains of his office on his
failing health, decided to resign his position as Director of
Libraries to continue as Bibliographer without administrative
duties.   This left open the librarianship of one of the largest

universities in the South, one of the few state institutions that combined both the land-grant college and the state university. It also had well-advertised imperfections. Typical was a "Time" magazine report (November 12, 1945):

> Huey never went to college, but he knew what he wanted. With the help of his hand-picked president ... he spent $13,500,000 on a building plan, blew another $3.5 million a year for such furnishings as professors, a football team, a country club for students, a high-brow quarterly, and a university mascot--a Bengal tiger in a $12,000 cage.

In 1941, when the position of Director of Libraries became vacant, the University was beginning to make a comeback, but it still had a country-club-image hangover. It was considered an upstart by certain state universities that had their mushroom growth several decades earlier, and it was still subject to public and political pressures. All this did not prevent Louisiana State University from being a pleasant place to attend college, to teach, or to do research. For one thing it was fortunate in its setting. It lay well outside the city of Baton Rouge, with a two-mile frontage on the Mississippi River. The buildings, erected on a plateau some distance back from the river, were attractive, with red tile roofs and connecting archways in the domestic style of northern Italy. Dominating the campus, a hundred-and-seventy-five-foot War Memorial Tower afforded a good view of the surrounding country, chiefly oaks, elms, and magnolias. All this plus the genuine distinction of many of its professors, the excellent reputation of its University Press, and the University's effort to carve out a significant role in international relations, particularly with reference to Central and Latin America, helped to make up for the deficiencies it inherited.

Out of a clear sky I received an invitation to come down to Baton Rouge to talk with the officials regarding the vacancy caused by McMillen's decision to relinquish his administrative duties. Before leaving I checked the statistics on the library situation and discovered that while it was a modest seventh among southern university libraries in number of volumes, it was significantly higher in current expenditure for books and journals. Only Texas and Duke were higher. I discovered later that this favorable ranking was largely due to a special supplementary grant. After giving the matter a lot of thought, and in spite of my recollection of the sizzling heat in Baton Rouge in the summer of 1937, I decided to go down and find out more about the job and living conditions. I was met by Dr. Richard Joel Russell, Professor of Geography and Chairman of the University Committee on Libraries, who arranged for me to stay at the Faculty Club, which had comfortable accommodations for guests of the University. Dr. Russell seemed to be very well informed about library matters and genuinely concerned about increasing library resources not alone in geography and geology but other fields as well. It was his perspicacity and persuasiveness that had secured the supplementary grant for library resources that had inflated the statistics of expenditures and given Louisiana State such a high ranking. In fact his familiarity with the funding and operations of the Library made me wonder if he would be willing to relinquish the administrative responsibilities he had assumed since McMillen's retirement. Fortunately his administrative grasp and tireless energy were soon absorbed in the dual capacity of Dean of the Graduate School and his regular teaching, but he continued to remain an indefatigable and helpful Chairman of the University Committee on Libraries.

At lunch I met with members of the Library Committee, enjoyed the company of a lively group of scholars, talked about library matters in the Southeast, was informed and tried to be informative in about an hour's time before most of the committee members had to leave. It would have pleased me to go on all afternoon, but the depressing demands of interviewing required that I keep moving. And so on to the Library, where I met a few members of the staff, renewed acquaintance with faculty members in the Library School, and met the Director of the School, Florrinell Morton, who had not been present in the summer of 1937. She was most gracious in her welcome. I had no time, of course, to get a coherent picture of the Library building and its operations, but then nothing about an overcrowded library in an old building is coherent. The essence of librarianship under these conditions is to do the best one can with makeshift arrangements, and a somewhat war-depleted staff was certainly doing its best in the Hill Memorial Library. Space had run out, staff working quarters were crowded or completely lacking, and the books in the stacks had already been shifted several times to make room for new titles. No provision, apparently, had been made for shelving the thousands of volumes that might be anticipated from the special grant, which I had now learned was in the amount of a hundred and twenty thousand dollars.

The following day I visited several of the branch libraries scattered in buildings throughout the campus and then attended a luncheon with deans and directors. There were so many of them that I felt like Daniel being thrown to the lions. Generally speaking deans and directors in a university have no experience and little knowledge of the problems of administering a university library. Their rule of conduct is to hang on to what promotes their private interests. The deans and directors of Louisiana State University, with two or three notable exceptions, followed this same pattern. The majority were individualistic to a degree that would have aroused the admiration of the Talmadges of Georgia. Socially, their hospitality was refreshing and genuine. During the luncheon they made me feel right at home, but afterward, when they got to talking about "their" libraries, they made it quite clear that they favored separate branch libraries under their control to a centrally administered library system. I minded my own business. I knew perfectly well that in any discussion of the administration of branch libraries the librarian could at best pull off a Pyrrhic victory. With some show of good manners, however, I managed to switch the talk to the state of the collections and their adequacy for teaching and research in their respective fields. This was an area in which they had only vague, general opinions but one in which I felt thoroughly at home from my experience in surveying other university libraries. I felt that I had a pretty good idea where most of the major deficiencies would occur, and so, with the poet Leonard Bacon, "I rode triumphantly into the tourney, not only visibly a master in my own field but with one foot in theirs." Shortly thereafter the deans and directors left for their respective satellites.

For my final interview I was taken to the President's office. Meeting university presidents is not my forte. I fear the office. I think they will be bored talking to me and that I shall find myself rather awkwardly trying to keep up appearances. I looked up President Hatcher in the catalog before going to his office, discovered that he had received three degrees from Louisiana State University, that his field was history, and that he had only just been made President in July. This gave me no clue to his thinking about libraries, but generally historians were on the right side. When he rose to greet me, I was struck by his height and build--visibly the kind the crowd at the stadium might be expected to admire. His greeting was warm and friendly. After we had talked for a few minutes he asked me how I liked teaching. Evidently

143

someone had tipped him off that I had spent a summer on the campus. "Oh, I am not exactly a teacher," I told him, "I've taught a few times in summer session and found it a bit like mountain climbing. When you get to the top, it's fine, but it's a struggle getting there." I was about to ask him why he singled me out as a teacher when he gave the answer in his next question.

"Do you think teaching interferes with the library job?"

It was a good question and a practical one, which I had already faced in my work.

"Yes, I think it does if one attempts both at the same time. My feeling is that unless one is a dedicated teacher, loves his work, and gives his all to it, he probably doesn't deserve a place on a college faculty. If such a person has a library job also, the latter will suffer."

He next asked me if I had had an opportunity to look about the campus and see the branch libraries. I told him I had and that I found the library system more complex and more widely dispersed than I had supposed. I had met up with the same problems on a much smaller scale at the Woman's College and libraries I had visited as a surveyor. Quite frequently I found that the problem of decentralization resulted from an overcrowded building, a weak library administration, or poor support from the university administration. I told him as much.

Dr. Hatcher then brought up the matter of the special book grant, and we talked about it and related problems until his secretary interrupted to remind him of his next appointment. Before leaving I managed to convey the message that a large supplementary book grant had concurrent obligations for staffing and shelving. I told him quite frankly that it was my offhand opinion that this need had not been taken into account in the present instance.

Two or three weeks after my return to Greensboro I received an offer from the President inviting me to become Director of Libraries effective October 1, 1944. At the same time I received a personal note from Dr. Russell assuring me that if I accepted, the University Committee on Libraries would fully support the Director in building one of the major research collections in the South. With the reluctant approval

144

of my family, who had found great joy in living in Greensboro, I wired my acceptance. From what I sensed in talking with members of the faculty, President Hatcher, and particularly with Dr. Russell, I saw a challenging opportunity to build a great library.

It was not easy to take leave of the Woman's College. My friends wanted to know, Why? When the Library was running smoothly, when the administration had demonstrated its readiness to support good library service, when the staff was excellent and loyal, and when I had two books in preparation, why would I abandon a promising career in North Carolina? I could not tell them that I felt I was falling into too easy an acceptance of the good life in a woman's college, that I felt the need to switch to something tougher and more challenging. Elinor Wylie may have said it all in her poem about the peach country:

"... we'll swim in milk and honey till we drown."

Yet sensing the impermanence of too much of a good thing, she adds:

"Down to the Puritan marrow of my bones
There's something in this richness that I hate."

Well I certainly did not hate my work, and it did not seem routinelike, perhaps because I had not been there long enough. The faculty were all so friendly and sociable. We enjoyed great times together. But my work perhaps was a little too easy. I felt that the opportunity to tackle a university job in which I had to deal with the problems of graduate students and research workers would afford the kind of challenge I needed at this point in my life. Also, to be quite honest, I was not all that sure that a woman's college was "a good place to go from."

Leaving the family in Greensboro, I drove to Baton Rouge in late September to look for a house. I was driving a car without a spare, with as many ration cards as I could extract from friends, and with one smooth tire. An incident is perhaps worth recording. I was approaching Athens, Georgia, when the smooth tire blew out. Fortunately I knew that Wayne Yenawine was Acting Librarian at the University of Georgia. I called him, and he hurried to the rescue. We went from one store to another and finally located a tire at a filling station. Our next hurdle was to get the operator to fill out a form for the Ration Board stating that I was in dire need of the tire. We then proceeded to the Board's office, where after prolonged discussion we finally got the clerk to schedule a meeting with the Board that afternoon at 3 p.m. It was then 10 a.m., getting hotter by the minute. I was desperately anxious to be on my way, so Wayne, who appeared to know everyone in town, volunteered to talk with a member of the Board before the afternoon meeting, hoping to strengthen my case before the full Board. The upshot of his visit was that he persuaded the Board member to approve the request on the spot. We returned to the filling station, purchased the tire for seventeen dollars and fifty cents--an enormous sum in those times--and replaced the blow-out on the rear. The tire was much bigger than the other three, but I was lucky to find a friend and a tire and to be on my way shortly after noon.

After being driven from pillar to post by real estate agents in Baton Rouge wanting to sell me a house at inflated prices, which had doubled in the past year, I found that I was looking at rental property in the University Hills subdivision. The house was quite large, perched near the front of what appeared to be about an acre of land. There were swings and slides and a trailer in the backyard, which I knew would make a dream-playground for the children. Water oaks, magnolias, and fruit trees roughly marked the property line on two sides. The backdrop was the only thing that bothered me. It was a bit eerie, similar to what Harnett Kane portrayed incisively in describing a bayou as "a place that seems often unable to make up its mind whether it will be earth or water." By day, from the picture window of the kitchen overlooking the backyard, one could see the edge of a cypress swamp; white egrets picking their way with high strides through a lacework of grass, sedge, purple hyacinth, and moss; large black buzzards holding conference in the dead branches of oaks; and towering above all, on the rim of the swamp, an open-burning oil well. By nightfall the flames shooting up from the top of this structure lit up a stage for a thousand bellowing bullfrogs. I wasn't sure how Margaret and the children would take to this combustible display, but the agent said I had better take the house while I still had a chance. I was the first of twenty-five parties applying to be shown the house in the first hour it was announced for rent. The terms of renting allowed us only forty-five days to evacuate when the owner returned from military service.

The scene of my action in the Hill Memorial Library was a suite of offices on the north mezzanine, balanced by the Library School quarters on the south mezzanine. I think the faculty of the German Department had previously occupied this suite because I was informed that they would be moved to quarters outside the Library before I began my work there. Another professor, Walter Prichard of the History Department, occupied a large room on the first floor of the Library. He weighed in at about three hundred pounds and was harder to dislodge.

My first concern was to provide space in the Hill Memorial Library for books and staff working space. Something had to be done, but ever present in my mind as I conferred with Dr. Russell, numerous faculty groups, and administrative officers, was one thought--whatever was done to relieve the current situation must in no way interfere with or postpone the construction of a new library building, which I anticipated might be needed within five years. The consensus was that the full stack space in the Hill Memorial Library should be utilized; that additional reading space could be secured by remodeling and rearrangement; and that rebuilding a war-depleted staff should not be blocked by lack of working space and equipment. Secondarily, it was felt that any reorganization of space should serve as a countermove to existing and continuing pressure for further decentralization of the Library's book collection.

A major and unexpected obstacle was the fact that the stack companies had yet to begin reconverting their plants from wartime to peacetime production. We were fortunate. The officials of Library Bureau of Remington Rand saw in our major stack project an undertaking of mutual benefit to both parties, enabling them to begin reconverting immediately to stack manufacturing. We, on the other hand, got a very attractive financial offer, which within a month of the completion of the plan was approved and funded by the President and Board of Supervisors. A factor leading to general support for the plan was the abandonment of the multitier type of stack construction and the use of new stacks and equipment of a type that could be readily converted for use in a new building.

When the work was completed in the summer of 1945, the capacity of the stack was increased by a hundred thousand volumes, a specialized area was provided for rare books scattered throughout the collection, processes relating to the acquisition of library materials were consolidated in one area, and movable study carrels were made available in the stacks

147

for those students and faculty requiring constant use of library materials. It was only a beginning, of course, not comparable to the facilities of some of the major universities in the South and East, but it made possible a considerable improvement over conditions as they existed in the fall of 1944. It would serve for a while.

In the reallocation of reading space the Louisiana Room was moved to larger and newly decorated quarters. The Latin American Room, which under an overly ambitious custodianship had begun to look like the Hill Memorial Library all over again, was restricted to Romance languages and literature and renamed the Romance Language Room. It was in this field, particularly in linguistics, that the Library possessed one of the major collections in the country.

A step in the direction of coordinating library materials was made when the "monumenta" of bibliographical works, many of them acquired in the thirties by my predecessor, James A. McMillen, were assembled from scattered locations and placed in a Bibliographical Alcove, convenient to readers and to the staff who made continuous use of them. Here, as in other specialized areas of library development, we relied on consultants to advise, strengthen, and sometimes to confirm our own opinion as to what was needed. Among the luminaries who shed light on our darkness were Charles B. Shaw, Librarian of Swarthmore College (to advise on policies for the development of the bibliographical collection); Herman H. Fussler of the University of Chicago and Ralph Carruthers of the New York Public Library (to review plans for a microphotographic laboratory); Charles H. Brown, Librarian Emeritus of Iowa State College (to survey the science collections and draw up priority lists of scientific journals for purchase); Dr. Louis R. Wilson and Dr. C. C. Crittenden, head of the State Historical Archives of North Carolina (to establish policies governing the scope and administration of archives and manuscripts); Robert B. Downs, Director of Libraries of the University of Illinois (to survey the need for a new library building); and several others. Recognizing the need for such help at the very beginning, I was fortunate in securing a grant from the General Education Board. I am sure that the Board was pleased to be able to shed light on my own ignorance and that of others.

At the same time as the reorganization and enlargement plans were being carried on the University was able to recruit for its Library staff a rare and fine company of young men and women. The first to arrive was Robert Maxwell Trent, one of the most attractive men I have known in the profession. He came from the City College of New York Library after graduating with a B.S. and M.S. degree from Columbia, with varied experience earlier in a bookstore and newspaper library. His main contribution to the Library's development was his reorganization and streamlining of all procedures relating to acquisitions and overseeing the establishment of a new microphotographic laboratory. An excerpt from his published account of the laboratory speaks of its launching:

> ... Armed with proof of need and practicability, the Library was able to convince the University Administration of the merits of the plan and funds were made available in the Spring of 1947. Not quite a year later, in February 1948, the first roll of film was photographed and processed. Appropriately enough this was a film of one of the most important source materials for students of the South, a record which had left the region years before, the 1850 population census of Louisiana now in possession of the Duke Library.

Max was popular on the campus. Staff members spoke with emotion of his thoughtfulness and encouragement; members of the faculty voted him Vice-President of the Faculty Club. In 1949 he became Director of Libraries of Southern Methodist University. We certainly missed him.

Wholly different but equally indispensable to the Library during this period was Andrew J. Eaton. Quiet, judicial, and obviously unprejudiced, he could be counted upon to weigh all the facts carefully before reaching a decision. He came to Louisiana State University with degrees from Wooster College and the University of Michigan Library School and with a doctorate from the Graduate Library School of the University of Chicago. In addition to serving as administrator of eleven branch libraries and assisting in the formulation of policy governing the acquisition of research materials in all their varied formats, he edited several important finding lists of newspaper and serial holdings of the Library. He also directed the program of filming Louisiana newspapers, which he described in the article "Toward a State-Wide Newspaper Microfilming Program" ("College and Research Libraries,"

January 1953), and served during his last year at the University as Chairman of the University Press Committee. In May of 1953 after seven years as Associate Director of Libraries at the University, he resigned to accept the position of Director of Libraries of Washington University, St. Louis. I cannot be but eternally grateful to him for the support he gave through his thoroughness, leadership, and good humor.

As important an influence as any in this period of the Library's development was a young woman from Texas who came to Louisiana State University to take charge of the circulation services of the Library during the absence of T. N. McMullan, who was away on military leave. It is perhaps worth noting that Ruth Walling held three degrees, the last from the Graduate Library School of the University of Chicago. More important than the technical and administrative skills that her library school training provided were her intellectual and moral qualities. She had a wide and varied reading background, the patience and capacity to understand the needs of another person, and the ability and passionate desire to respond to those needs. Her positive empathy with young people made her the confidant of staff and students alike. It was these qualities that shaped her career later as one of the great reference librarians of the country and the winner of the Isadore Mudge Award of the American Library Association in 1964 for outstanding work in the reference field. The following year she received the Savannah (Georgia) State College Library award with the following citation:

> for: "the quiet, steadfast, and overwhelmingly effective role she played, both locally and nationally, in the successful drive toward the racial integration of the American Library Association and its affiliated chapters."

When McMullan returned from military service, Ruth Walling transferred to the position of Chief Reference Librarian, where she won for herself a reputation as "primum inter pares." This is attested to by the enthusiastic testimonials of the faculty and library staff of the University.

There were others, of course, who contributed to this fine company of librarians. Besides the personable Elliott Hardaway, who succeeded Andrew Eaton as Associate Director and later migrated to the University of South Florida as Director of Libraries, it comprised Lucy Foote, Head Cataloger, who trained some of the best catalogers in the profession and also edited the basic bibliographies in Louisiana State documents; Richard Klenk, who presided over the sprawling Acquisition Department and its many divisions and who proved himself a scholar-bibliographer in the humanities; Roseanne Harrington and Helen Malone, who successively handled personnel matters and edited the Library bulletin besides adding a good deal of excitement and joy to an office that badly needed it; and Helen Forsberg, Gertrude Minsk, Louise Ward, Marguerite Hanchey, and many others who made their mark in the branch library field.

In the spring of 1947 President Hatcher, who had been failing in health, resigned and was succeeded by Dr. Harold Stoke, who was chosen in an executive session of the Board of Supervisors, James M. McLemore, Chairman, from a large number of candidates screened by a faculty committee. It was not long before the new President gave the University a tone no earlier administration provided. He wanted Louisianans to think of their university as a serious place of education and not as a playground or as an object of political interference. He wanted scholarship substituted for "candy and cake." Among other things he sought the best instructors regardless of where they came from, he revived faculty meetings, and he enlisted the help of faculty committees in running the University. During his short term of office he brought about a period of intense educational activity, stirring incidents, and almost continuous intellectual excitement. He was a brilliant speaker, independent thinker, and a liberal, though not in any radical sense. On the contrary he was a hardheaded realist who dealt with serious matters with humor and sound, practical sense. His wit was always at instant command. One incident, admittedly trifling, may illustrate this trait. We were playing a foursome in handball. Dr. Stoke and I were partners, and after an exhausting first game we managed to edge out our opponents 21 to 19. My friend Jim Coltharp immediately prepared to serve in the second game, ready for revenge, when Dr. Stoke leaned heavily against the sidewall, raised one hand, and exclaimed with a roguish smile, "Jim, leave me enjoy this moment."

In this period when Dr. Stoke, with enthusiastic support from the faculty, was trying to remold the character of the University, the Library was bound to make progress. As Helen Malone once wrote, "The quality of a university and the quality of the library go hand in hand. A good university

151

will create a good library, and if a good library cannot create a good university, at least a good university cannot be created without one." The President secured a grant of $75,000 from the General Education Board, matched by an equal sum from the University, to carry out the recommendations of the Brown survey in filling in important scientific research journals. The American Association of University Professors, the University Committee on Libraries, and the Faculty Council each sent resolutions to the President and Board of Supervisors requesting top priority for a new library building in the University's building program. However, in debate by the Board regarding priorities for spending construction funds to be derived from a multimillion-dollar bond issue, the Library lost out to the pigskin, with emphasis on the pig, even though, at the Committee hearing in the House, the Chairman of the Appropriations Committee was openly critical of the fact that the University had postponed the building of an adequate Library in favor of other projects.

Later the Board debated whether funds left over from the two designated purposes (Medical School and stadium) should be used for a library or an auditorium. President Stoke made a good case for a new library building, and the Board resolved in favor of the library, even going so far as to authorize the appointment of a committee to begin making plans. Dr. Stoke appointed a nine-member committee with Dean Russell as Chairman. Unfortunately, before the Library Building Committee's report was submitted, the President resigned because of "a fundamental incompatibility" between the views of "a substantial number" of Board members and himself on policies and procedures. Transmitted by Dr. Stoke's successor, Lt. General Troy Middleton, the Committee's report received a negative response. The Board resolved that "the proposal for a new library building is considered premature."

The note struck in the Middleton administration was one of harmony, cooperation, and Louisiana for the Louisianans. When it finally became apparent that the University had reached a point where unless further provision was made for library growth the University would find itself seriously handicapped in even securing the faculty necessary for its operation, the President appointed a Library Building Committee composed of Board members, administrators, members of the faculty, and the Director of Libraries. This was a good idea, which had been advanced more than once by the Stoke-appointed Library Building Committee in order to enlarge the thinking of the members of the University who could be most helpful in funding the building.

It became apparent during the first meeting that if the Board chairman appointed by President Middleton and the Board were not to plan the entire library building, floor by floor, room by room, on free weekends, it would be well to arrange for the Committee to visit some of the newer modern university libraries. I made arrangements with the head librarians at six recently constructed university library buildings to receive as many of the members of the Library Building Committee as could make the visits, pointing out in my letter of May 29, 1953, that "Dr. Russell, Dean of the Graduate School, and I have had the pleasure of visiting your new libraries and we think nothing would be more helpful to the other committee members than to see these same libraries." The itinerary suggested for the visits included Princeton University (William Dix), Harvard's Lamont (Keyes D. Metcalf), MIT (Vernon Tate), University of Georgia (William Porter Kellam), Oklahoma A&M (Edmon Low), and Rice University (Hardin Craig, Jr.). At an all-day meeting in late August of the same year the Committee adopted four important resolutions that were eventually incorporated into the architect's final concept of the building: first, the site of the new library should be in front of the present building so that facilities can be appropriately integrated; two, that branch libraries should be centralized, as far as possible, looking toward a more complete unification of library resources; three, that the building be designed as a modular-type building to secure economy and flexibility; and four, that the building provide for at least one million volumes and accommodate twenty-five hundred readers. It was pointed out that the Committee could not give a reliable estimate of cost without the services of a consultant, and Board member Lewis Gottlieb offered to pay personally the expenses of a consultant so that the Committee could expedite the submission of its report. I recommended either Angus S. MacDonald, architect-stack manufacturer, who first introduced the idea of modular planning for libraries, or Russell Bailey, an experienced Virginia architect. In September of 1953 MacDonald estimated the cost of the building at $3.6 million. In the spring of 1954 the Louisiana State Legislature appropriated the money for a new library building for Louisiana State University.

Before leaving this abbreviated case history of a dec-

ade of effort to strengthen the library resources and to secure
a new building for Louisiana State University, I should like to
pay brief tribute to Richard Joel Russell for his seasoned, indispensable, and continuous support of the Library during my
entire period at the University. Dr. Fred Kniffen, a friend
and colleague of his and the kind of man any good librarian
is always happy to see come into the library, wrote a splendid account of Dr. Russell for the "Annals of the Association
of American Geographers" (June 1973), in which he particularly stressed his scientific achievements. But he also
touched on the man himself, and from my acquaintance with
Dr. Russell I can do no better than to underscore some of the
distinguishing traits that he pointed out: Russell was a man
of acute judgment, a good organizer who put in long hours
but used his time to the best advantage, and a superb teacher; he was articulate, forthright in speech, fond of classical
music, and much interested in the culture of the inhabitants
in the many areas of the world in which he did his research.
These are Dr. Kniffen's observations, which anyone who was
fortunate enough to find an empty chair around the table at
the Faculty Club, where he happened to be eating his lunch,
would endorse. I would like to add that he was always crackling with energy, that he talked a great deal but was never
wearisome, and that he was generous with his time no matter how busy. From the time I arrived at Louisiana State
University in 1944 until I left in the summer of 1954 he gave
me the aid and comfort that I badly needed due to my own
ignorance and that of others.

19:   THREE BOOKS AND PERSONAL SIDELIGHTS

Such time as I could spare from the activities of the Library
I spent with my family at home, where I wrote books and
helped with the chores around the house.   Pipe smoking was
a great help to me in writing.   It relieved the boredom of
repeated typings and enabled me to work late at night without
falling asleep.   Handball two or three times a week, a grueling game giving one plenty of exercise in an hour or less,
and an occasional game of tennis offered a release from the
worries of Library affairs.   It was at Louisiana State, also,
that I was first introduced to squash by a retired University
of Chicago professor, William Fielding Ogburn, who came to
the University to shed light at a time when it needed all the
light it could get.   He was looking around for a squash partner, and Joy Kistler, Head of Physical Education, suggested
that he get in touch with me.   I agreed to a game provided
he would give me some instruction.   Because of the difference
in our ages, it was not long before I thought that I could
probably beat him at his own game, but for months afterward
his winning style had a lowering effect on my morale.   I opted for speed, while he "read" every shot I made and was
always in position to make the return.   And while I slugged,
he positioned himself for corner shots.   Eventually I learned
to calm down, to move to center court without blocking, and
to anticipate Ogburn's moves.   Many years later, when my
fingers became too tender to play handball without pain, I
switched to squash and have played it ever since.   For me,
like handball, it provides the flow of energy and the discipline
of concentration needed in writing.

"The Administration of the College Library," published

155

by the H. W. Wilson Company, was largely written in the spring and summer of 1944, before I arrived at Baton Rouge, but the galley and page proofing were done there. It was a straightforward attempt to give students a simple, logical, self-contained introduction to college library administration. Four chapters were prepared by librarians who were well known for their competency in the areas covered: Paul Bixler, my successor at Antioch College, Marjorie Hood of the Woman's College, and Arnold Trotier of the University of Illinois. The book had some noble reviews in "College and Research Libraries" and "North Carolina Libraries"; the "Library Quarterly" and the "Library Journal" said some nice things about it; but a couple of "furriners" in England and Scotland blasted the hell out of it. In its fourth edition, in 1961, I was not quite so long-winded, but I have never bothered to look up what they said then. Perhaps most important to me was the encouragement I received from friends who took time out to write: Bob Downs, Blanche Prichard McCrum, Charles Rush, Thomas Barcus all the way from Saskatchewan, and many others. One guy wrote a four-page letter asking for a job. He was probably tanked when he wrote.

In the course of collecting the writings of Christopher Morley I managed to gather together a bundle of bibliographical notes about his novels, poems, essays, and ephemeral writings, which eventually led to the compilation of "A Bibliography of Christopher Morley," published by the Scarecrow Press in 1952.

My interest in Christopher Morley was more than a bibliographical whim. I have already said something about his visit to the Woman's College, when he autographed copies of a reprint of one of his early novels to help the Library make enough money to provide a student library prize award. So my personal acquaintance on that particular occasion was followed by meeting the man once again--from the third row of the balcony of the college auditorium. I was listening to a soliloquy at two dollars a minute. It was not I, let me hasten to add, who received the two dollars; and I speak of Morley's discourse as a soliloquy because he seemed more interested in listening to the pleasant sound of his own voice than in reaching any particular destination. He might have been chasing butterflies, for all of that, for whenever he caught sight of an especially bright-winged idea he pursued it with much glee, quite careless of where it might lead him. Exactly what he said on the subject of "Streamlined Writing"

I am unable to recall, but it was most entertaining; and the throng that stormed the hall, packing the doorways and overflowing the well-supported balcony--almost letting themselves down, biblical fashion, through the roof to touch the hem of his garments--was uproarious. He proved himself to be just as charming and brilliant a speaker as he is, in his best moments, a writer. No one on this occasion seemed to care that he had no burning message.

"A Bibliography of Christopher Morley" was compiled with assistance from H. Tatnall Brown, Jr., as a supplement to the Lee bibliography published by Doubleday, Doran & Co. in 1935. The Lee bibliography describes the first printing in the English language of the writings of Christopher Morley down through 1934, books to which Morley made contributions, ephemeral writings, and books by other writers containing comment on Morley's work. "A Bibliography of Christopher Morley" continues the bibliographical record for each of the four sections down through 1951 and lists, in addition, the periodical articles by and about Morley from the beginning in 1908.

Wishing to pay some testimony to this many faceted genius with a gut feeling for literature and a skillful and loving pen for etching the foibles of human beings, I quote here from several of his letters that relate to bibliography, librarians, and the making of my own bibliography. The comment of a writer on the maturation of his own bibliography I found to be helpful, highly amusing, and instructive.

2 December, 1947

Dear Mr. Lyle:
    I wasn't as rude as you may have supposed. I am just back from two months in England. What is so incredibly surprising and thrilling as what grows (in any man's life) while he is briefly off the map.
    And I suppose that the career and curiosity of the Bibliographer is to see that nothing does get off the map?
    I am affectionately embarrassed by yr suggestion, because although nothing has ever been said in a statutory and establishable way, I have a feeling that my old friend, a very handsome and sturdy man, H. Tatnall Brown, of Philadelphia, has had in mind for many years to do something in the realm

157

of bibliography. He is a most humorous and temperamental creature, he rings like a highball glass tickled on the rim with a knife-blade, he has a quite incredible garner of my lesser casuarina, and I have a sort of feeling that if you and he (he and you) were to collaborate something might Come to Town. So capricious is he, he doesn't answer my letters anymore, but I have a notion that if you were to write to him, c/o Haverford College, Haverford, Pa. ... it wd reach him somehow....

E. V. Lucas could have told you about this, but blessed bullheaded Butch Lucas died too, some 10 years ago. I know, because when I was in London lately, Lucas wasn't there. If he didn't die, at least he went elsewhere. He and I had much that was common, in common.

I wonder sometimes about Librarians, and I hope they do too?

And I wonder about myself, more sourly than anyone else is likely to, because I was never properly and completely incarnated as a human being; am still considerably a gnome, shilling off my carcase, the primordial clay; or what our Hebrew classics call a gonoph, a spiritual pickpocket, rifling the pants of the universe, making off with little silver sixpenses it didn't know it had.

I have also just remembered my first bibliographer, Aaron Mendoza, of Mendoza's Bookstore, 15 Ann Street, New York City. He too should be consulted.

Another thought: my only resolution for 1948 is to try to reduce, so far as myself am concerned, the world's overload of Paper Work. I have spent the past two weeks almost entirely in contemplating, with marvel and misery, what has been laid end to end in the local P.O.

... I don't propose to be interrupted again and I ring down.

Good luck to you Where the Bayou Begins.
Merry Xmas,

C. M.

Roslyn Heights, N.Y.
Jan. 24, 1949

Dear Guy:

Your kind letter, which I much appreciate, reached me at a busy time so I will try to be brief-- for your own sake?

... I have made some suggestions on the carbon copy of yr preface. I have tried so hard the past 15 years, to reduce the necessary output of "the Morley writings" (grim phrase indeed!) that even if the volume since 1934 equals all previous (which I doubt?) let's not say so! There is always a danger of annoying the really judicious friends by paying too much heed to run-of-the-mind stuff. That was why I implored no circumstantial analysis of my Evening Ledger--Evening Post--Sat. Rev Lit series. I am not the least ashamed of the stuff; I think it was as well done as powers and circumstances permitted; but it is not important enough for detailed report.

I have a hunch that the new book (which will be pub'd June 13 by Doubleday) will get a fairly sour reception from most reviewers. But (don't quote me!) I myself believe it goes about as far and as fast as I am likely to achieve. You and Tat will quite properly form yr own opinions .... I think whatever its fortune that book should be the climax of your compilation. It nearly killed me to write it, and will probably quite kill me to read the reviews.

... I'll send a copy of this to Tat for his info. In haste, yrs indeed--the only picture, by the way, shd be (if you wish) Joe Hirsch's portrait. Harcourt can send a print.

C. M.

P.S. Photos of Knothole only increase the horror of casual visitors who come and park to see what an author's home looks like. The only answer is a shot-gun.

Green Escape
Roslyn Heights, New York

Dec. 6, '49

Dear Guy:

As I'm sure you know I am greatly touched

(and perhaps a little agitated too) by the huge time and effort you have been spending on the bibliography. Since getting home (after near 3 months absence) last month I've been grievously busy trying to catch up--to do a little more work to give you more pain! But I have been able to talk with Tat Brown, whom I saw in Philadelphia recently, and also consult my friend and assistant Louis Greenfield. I think that both agree with my feeling, which briefly is this: -

A list of contributions to periodicals, particularly in the case of a writer who does much miscellaneous work, can never be complete. I think you have done a marvellous job of compilation. I find myself reminded of things I had quite forgotten--sometimes a twinge--but I am sure that to attempt to include so large a supplement wd make the book practically unpublishable. All mfrg costs are almost prohibitive.

I suggest there is only one practical solution: to make a note in yr preface that you have compiled such a list which can be supplied, if desired by librarians or fellow-bibliographers or hyperthyroid collectors, in mimeographed form for $1 a copy-- or whatever the cost might be. But I do urge you not to include all this subaltern matter in the bibliog itself. It's going to be hard enough to find a publisher anyhow.

... Greenfield hopes in a few days to have first copies of the little privately issued POETRY PKG. by Wm Rose Benet and C. M. I believe he plans to publish on Ja 1st so as to be the first book of 1950!

All kind regards, and please believe that I am trying to simplify your self-imposed task--in every possible way except to quit writing altogether!

C. M.

Green Escape
Roslyn Heights, New York

July 13, 1951
Dear Guy:
My letter last night wasn't nearly as andante

160

affetuoso as I meant it to be. If I had known the
bibliogr was still in consideration I'd have contrived
to send you a copy of A Pride of Sonnets last Xmas,
but I had only a few, and all went off to family &
oldest friends. I sent one to Tat, who cd collate
it for you. It was printed at his own suggn by my
friend Arthur Rushmore, on his private press in the
cellar, Madison, N.J. Immediately thereafter he
had a heart attack, like mine. I shd ask forgive-
ness for seeming rudeness; but with a semi-paralyzed
arm even typing is slow & laborsome. I told hardly
anyone about my disability, because friendly inquir-
ies wd have slaughtered me entirely. But think how
shrewd and keen is Nemesis: what a sonnet she wd
make: you spend 40 yrs in writing too easily or
glibly (the collar of Needs - Must on yr neck) so
by the time you have some things you've learned
how to say, and must say for yr honour & conscience, the overworked nerves of the R. hand
crack wide, & then you are damned for piggish in-
dolence!
        ... Good luck, old boy

                    Chris

                         Roslyn Heights, N.Y.
                         May 18, '53
Dear Guy:
        I'm thoroughly ashamed of my delay. I can
only offer in excuse my humble pleas that since my
serious illness 2 yrs ago I have a semi-paralysis
in R. hand, which makes everything (and most of
all, writing) disastrously slow....
        Yr bibliography is a labor of love if there
ever was one. Of course I haven't vetted it in detail: but I can see with what extraordinary com-
pleteness & conscience you have worked. Not in
any sense as a correction, but just for yr own info., I shd note that the BOM Club connexion began
in 1926, not 1928 (p. ix). I think the Club's first
selection was for April '26.
        ... Who is the Scarecrow Press? How did
you come across him?
        I enclose, to amuse you, a proof of a sonnet
that was in NY Herald-Trib on May 5, 1953--my

                    161

Grand Climacterie--it was the Trib that added the
subscription about the 63rd birthday, wh was not
intended by me. They took advantage of private info., which was corny.

All kindest thoughts, dear fellow, and much
gratefulness for your long and unselfish devotioneer-
ing. It is only my lame hand, and general decline
in physique that have made me so slow.

Afftly indeed,
Chris

The third book to appear during my period at Louisiana State
University was "I Am Happy to Present," a book of introductions, published by the H. W. Wilson Company with Kevin
Guinagh as coauthor. I cannot remember when it was that
Kevin and I first felt within us the stirrings of a conviction
that what the world needed was a good book of introductions.
There was none, so we decided to contribute our mite of experience to the enigma of the introduction to speeches. In the
beginning, at least, we thought of the introduction as a neg-
lected form of literary genre, no less important even though
ephemeral, than other literary genera. No one who has not
tried it, however, can form any conception of the difficulty of
finding introductions worthy of the masters of the art, such
as Samuel Clemens, William Lyon Phelps, Louis Nizer, Sir
Owen Seaman, Walter Prescott Webb, or Will Rogers. After
turning over the pages of a large library we decided to settle
for a handy little book of reference that would help sensible
persons to make an introduction without embarrassment to
themselves or without annihilating the speaker with politeness.
In an introduction to the book Kevin warned that "unless you
are one of those who make their living by talking ... you
may begin to walk the floor, to bite your nails, to wake up
at four in a cold sweat. However, if you go about readying
for the ordeal in a capable way by reading a few simple rules
and studying the models set forth in 'I Am Happy to Present'
... you have nothing to worry about." That sounded reassur-
ing enough for readers and speakers to demand a second edition in 1968.

At all stages in the preparation of books that were published by the H. W. Wilson Company I benefited by the pain-
staking assistance of John Jamieson, Editor of General Publications. He corrected errors, suggested new interpretations,

and helped to unify and condense the style and expression--all
considerable tasks calling for judgment, editorial precision,
and great stamina.   The pleasure of working with him and
his encouragement and untiring assistance will never be forgotten.

If a state university library is to take a commanding place
among educational institutions in the state and region of which
it is a part, the Director of Libraries is expected to make
contributions to the profession by working with organizations.
I served on committees of the Association of Research Libraries, as Chairman of the College and Reference Section of
the Louisiana Library Association (1948-49); Chairman of the
University Libraries Section of the Association of College and
Research Libraries (1949-50); and President of the Association
of College and Research Libraries (1954-55).   One is also expected to hit the speaker's trail and, at moments of high visi-
bility, if you wish to live to be a respected senior member
of the profession, be seen enthusiastically applauding the lead
of the right people.   I did a fair amount of this during my
ten-year stint at Louisiana State University, but only once
did I thoroughly enjoy myself and feel the audience's warm
response.   That was on the occasion of the dedication of a
new library building for Oklahoma A&M College in May of
1953.   I called the address "The Launching" because of the
happy symbolism it suggested of a library carrying a cargo
almost as wide and deep as the ocean itself and one that if
wisely and widely used was life's most serviceable piece of
machinery.   The address was published in the Phi Kappa Phi
"Journal" for October 1953.   Edmon Low, or Mr. Oklahoma
Librarian, as he was known in Oklahoma and by his friends,
demonstrated not only his skill in planning and building but
also his superior ability as host to the large gathering that
came to inspect the new building.   He was a master of the
art of flattery, but he could also administer the rabbit punch
to hypocrites.

While engaged in these extracurricular activities, I was not
completely neglecting the family.   A charming letter from my
seventy-three-year-old mother attests to the fact that Don and
I were building a concrete-block garage on the rear of our
lot, and I am sure I got encouragement from all the children
repairing the screen porch that ran around two sides of the
house and cutting out the cane bordering one side of our lot.

163

But the main event was the arrival of our fourth child, Margaret Ellen, who was born a beautiful, strong, and bright baby on June 1, 1948. Fortunately nobody had snatched up my services that summer. With Margaret in the hospital, university events grew dim for a week or so. Things began to hum around the house, not a dull moment in the day, although by the end of the week I felt that I could use a few. The emphasis was on food for the family, when to get it, how to satisfy the lusty and individual appetites of three children, and how to pay for it. Don was as tall as I was, Jennifer was a bit of a tomboy but awfully good at helping around the house, and Chris knew only enough to eat and occasionally comb his hair. The ordinary events of our day--menus, private quarrels, bathroom priorities, dishwashing--all took on a lost freshness. Drinking, violence, broken homes, arson, police brutality, General Wainwright, Madame Chiang, Harry Truman, road casualities, and the wailing of farmers all receded over the horizon. Hamburgers at McDonald's shed their secondhand quality. But when Margaret finally arrived home with the new baby, we all breathed a sigh of relief. I vowed to disabuse Ellen and Chris of the idea of a Santa Claus and once again settled down to life on the rockpile.

As a family we also made frequent excursions, taking our lunch, along the Old River Road, which wound its way close to the levee south of the University. In season we picked blackberries and dewberries, but just as often we went for a picnic and to enjoy the peaceful view of the river from the top of the levee. One recollection is particularly vivid. We were approaching the levee and had started to climb the bank when we were astonished to look up and see the superstructure of a tramp steamer passing slowly before and above us. For a moment we gazed, hypnotized, at the sight of moving flags and blackened funnel tops and sky and nothing else. Apparently on this occasion the river was high, the waterline just a few feet below the levee top; consequently all we could see were the moving parts of the superstructure moving along quite independently of the ship itself. I had never seen such a sight before, but I witnessed the same scene many times afterward and never ceased to be startled. One of the children said it wasn't an honest ship.

Often we would find cattle grazing on the slopes of the levee, and on a good day we might even see them drifting in single file along the summit. Silhouetted against the sky, they were as dominating as the ship's superstructure. On another

164

occasion, picking blackberries, one of the children stooped to climb under the arch of an overhanging branch covered with ivy only to discover a yellow and black snake peering down on him from above. He let out a yell that scattered every kind of wildlife within a mile, including a deer. In my memory, which is of course fallible, I remember only one other unpleasant incident. We were returning from an afternoon picking berries and found the windshield of our car shattered by a blow from a large stone. The evidence lay on the hood. Someone told us later that the people who lived in the shacks along the River Road were sending us a message to stay out of their berry patch.

An interesting estate we always admired on these trips was somewhat incongruously referred to as the "Cottage." It was a lovely two-story plantation-type home that at the time was occupied by a well-known novelist, Frances Parkinson Keyes. The Cottage was said to be haunted, but there is nothing that I can say about it that has not been said much better by Mrs. Keyes herself:

> Like every other well-equipped Southern house, the Cottage had its ghost, and a more intriguing one than the usual headless horseman or wailing lady: in the early days of its occupancy, a Scotch tramp came up the levee at sunset; and, stopping at the Big House, asked first for a drink of water, then for a hot meal and next, for a night's lodging. He never left the place again. He called himself Angus Holt, and he proved to be an experienced landscape architect and a classical scholar, qualified to act as tutor for the planter's children. He kept his origin secret all his life; and when he died, he was buried in the garden which was the work of his hands. It is said his spirit still haunts it. Perhaps it does. There is an eerie quality about it, especially in the moonlight. But that is true also of the great trees, draped with white wisteria and Cherokee roses, as well as waving gray moss. I never could decide whether they were more beautiful at night, or in the later afternoon, when the sun was setting and the sky all aglow with color. I used to pace up and down the long walk, bordered by scarlet amaryllis and snowy yucca, trying to decide.

Louisiana is a fascinating place to visit because of the

great variety of people you meet and places to see. Naturally, like all tourists, we visited many of the plantation man-
sions, but the two that stick most clearly in my mind were
Nottoway and Melrose. Nottoway was only a short distance
across the river, and Margaret and I drove there one afternoon as guests of the owner, Dr. W. G. Owen, and his wife
and son. Nottoway was the antebellum home of a wealthy
Virginia planter, John Hampden Randolph, built about the
middle of the nineteenth century. Though it shifted from
hand to hand over the years, it finally passed into the possession of the Owen family, who maintained it in good repair.
Dr. Owen reminded me a little of my old friend Tom Lloyd
of Antioch days. He was a tall, slender man, distinguished
in appearance with fine chiseled features, snow-white hair,
and a neatly trimmed moustache. The son shared his father's
warmth and sense of humor. Mrs. Owen was still a handsome lady and most gracious as a hostess. I must confess
that we felt quite intimidated at first by the splendor of our
surroundings, but we were soon made to feel quite at home.
We ate in a large, cypress-walled dining room that was decorated with plaster mouldings representing pink camellia blossoms with green leaves. As best as I can recall we enjoyed
a delicious dinner of chicken and rice with mushroom sauce,
a marvelous Greek salad, hot bread wrapped in napkins, deep
rich custard pie, and very dark coffee. Our glasses were re-
plenished frequently by servants, standing two deep behind
their mistress, from an ancient carafe with a wine worthy of
the gods. After dinner, over whiskey and soda, Dr. Owen
entertained us with an account of student days at Louisiana
State when it was located in the buildings of the Institute for
the Deaf and from which he graduated in 1887. In his library
was a presentation copy of Lewis Morris's poems, personally
inscribed by the disillusioned English poet who had hoped to
succeed Tennyson as poet laureate. Dr. Owen took it down
from its place on the shelves several times during the evening, which was a bit odd but rather endearing.

Melrose Plantation--which is a series of African-styled
cottages unlike the grand-mansion type--has been written about
so often that any description of the estate by me would be su-
perfluous. My interest in Melrose was stimulated by the existence of a large private library that the owner, Mrs. John
Henry ("Miss Cammie"), who was much concerned with the
state of literature in the South, had painstakingly collected
over the years. She was a modern-day patroness of the literary arts, opening her library freely to researchers in Loui-

siana history and literature and providing seclusion for a number of important writers to remain as guests on her plantation during the writing of their books. I have lost count of the number of creative writers who benefited from her patronage, but Lyle Saxon was said to have written "Fabulous New Orleans" at Melrose, and Roark Bradford, whose stories include "'Ol Man Adam an' His Children," from which the play "Green Pastures" was adapted, also worked there.

Shortly after Miss Cammie's death I spent an afternoon at Melrose with François Mignon, who spoke of himself as the librarian and who for the day at least appeared to be in charge. He was a great talker, and from his use of a cane and rather uncertain steps in moving about, I suspected him of being blind or nearly so. We divided the time that afternoon between an elegant bottle of wine and talk about books. I had hoped to gain some idea of the contents of the library and manuscript collection, but there were so many interruptions from tourists that I had very little opportunity to make more than a hurried survey of the types of material in the collection. François was gracious and recognized the purpose of my visit but was not encouraging about the likelihood of the library being sold at any time in the near future. He invited me to return to make a more leisurely inspection "when there will not be a road runner in miles and we can collapse on the gallery and compare notes in camera." The guy had a line all right. Before I left he showed me some of the paintings and murals of Clementine Hunter, who had already won fame in the Melrose kitchen for her mouth-watering recipes. She worked in the cotton fields, in the pecan orchards, and as a servant in the Henry household. Even to my untrained eye there was something exuberantly compelling about her bright colors and unconventional paintings. When I wrote François some years later thanking him for sending me a complimentary copy of the limited edition "Melrose Plantation Cookbook," he responded with one of his witty, quirky letters, which included this note about Clementine Hunter:

> Clementine goes slap ahead with her pots and at seventy-five will never live long enough to execute half the orders stacked up for her attention. She has a helper, some forty years her junior but although something of an artist in his own right with a razor, he never fiddled any with a canvas.

Next to having a brief acquaintanceship with Clementine

Hunter and François Mignon, the "Melrose Plantation Cookbook," with its pictures of persons and cottages on the estate,
and Clementine's recipes, is the best memento I have of a
very pleasant visit to Melrose.

One of the joys of the Baton Rouge era in my life was a remarkable man named Walter Watkins, one of the most engag-
ing and versatile minds it has ever been my good fortune to
know. I first knew him at the University, where he was a
visiting professor in English in 1948-49. He made his permanent home in Laurel, Mississippi, where for a short time
he served as a kind of minor-league Archibald MacLeish to
the Lauren Rogers Library and Art Museum, a unique institution for a small southern town. Walter's duties were simply to arrange the art exhibitions (the permanent collection
included Winslow Homer, Whistler, Daumier, Constable,
Corot, Inness, Bellows, and others of like stature), to advise, and to be liaison between the staff and the Trustees.
One way or another I saw quite a bit of Walter, admired his
brilliance as an art and book critic, and got to like him very
much.

A product of Princeton and Oxford (Rhodes Scholar),
and the recipient of three Guggenheim fellowships from which
emerged several scholarly books on English literary figures,
Walter appealed to me because he was always hatching out
ideas to restore America's reading habits. He was aware,
as Leonard Bacon so brilliantly expressed it, of the "dreadful
paradox concerning the times, namely that men use the fact
that there is so much to know as an excuse for knowing nothing." For example, he wrote and published a handy pocket-
sized "Guide to Current Books," selecting twelve to fourteen
titles for businessmen, professionals, and club men and wom-
en, from among the hundreds of books published each month.
His short reviews of the titles were always fresh, penetrating,
and to the point. They whet the appetite for reading the books
themselves. Alas, the "Guide" ran for only one year and
then folded. Not a single businessman, corporation, or professional in the South, I was told, subscribed, even though
the subscription fee was only seven dollars and fifty cents;
nearly all the subscriptions from individuals came from the
Northeast.

Walter was a superb popularizer. He had a knack for
clarity in exposition whether in writing or talks. In support

of the work of the Public Library of Laurel he gave free lectures on southern writers including Faulkner, Welty, and Richard Wright, demonstrating his courage and integrity in dealing frankly with such controversial problems as violence, race, and sex, which he felt had to be hurdled if people in a small southern town were to attempt modern fiction. He gave talks over the local radio station in Laurel to illustrate that there is poetry for everyone's taste. I was amused by his comment on the pioneer days of radio recording. The station wanted organ-music interludes between the poetry readings. Groaned Walter, "I finally put my foot down at that, in the end compromised with piano and harp--enough to turn your stomach." He was no dweller in the ivory tower when it came to encouraging the ordinary person to read. This got him in trouble with the trained staff of the Lauren Rogers Library, which was a subscription library open only to members. The staff did not believe in cluttering up their beautifully appointed building with just any old reader. One day he turned to them in exasperation. Pointing to a single glaring footprint, he blurted out, "Look! Man Friday has been here. One other human beside the staff."

Walter suffered from poor health throughout his short life. Once he told me, with great joy in his darkly smiling face, "Six months now of good health!" His books, his magnetic mind, and his generosity in placing his manifold talents at the disposal of his fellows are his monument. I hold a special brief for his ability to popularize and to relate literature and reading to life. I don't think it has been praised enough.

20: EMORY UNIVERSITY I: A LIBRARY PROFILE

In August of 1954 we sold our house in Baton Rouge in order to move to Atlanta, where I had accepted the position of Director of Libraries and Professor of Librarianship of Emory University. We were obliged to move quite suddenly because the purchaser of our Cherrydale home needed possession at once. There were Margaret, Jennifer, Christopher, little Ellen, and myself; Don remained at Louisiana State University to finish his studies for a degree in petroleum engineering. We were lucky to find rental quarters close to the University, but it left us squashed into a two-bedroom cottage with a dining room and small kitchen. I think we broke more china and furniture there than in all our other moves combined, but finally the younger children simmered down from a bubbling boil and the cat stopped prowling about like a caged lion. For the most part our neighbors in this cluster of Emory cottages were also newcomers. Everyone was friendly, and we enjoyed ourselves immensely--all of which helped to confirm my belief that we had made the right move.

When we left Baton Rouge, I was repeatedly asked by my colleagues and friends at Louisiana State University and elsewhere why I was resigning, particularly at a time when the Louisiana State legislature had just appropriated the funds for a new library building. A former professor who had moved from Louisiana State University to a university in another state probably gave the most truthful answer--without the details that might add a certain pungency to this memoir but that are perhaps best forgotten--when he wrote in the summer of 1954:

I hear that there was surprise that you would leave

170

just at the moment of your greatest triumph, and you can take considerable pride in bringing the University to the point of building a library. But the surprise--such as there often is when someone leaves--is itself a surprise, for it should be obvious, it seems to me, that personal relationships in one's work count as well as other things.

There were other reasons, too, of course. Emory's goal was to produce a higher standard of scholarship--"we see it as our duty to provide superior facilities for a select group of students in selected fields"--than was possible in an institution devoted to mass education. I saw the library as having an important role in a university of this character. Atlanta offered a considerable improvement in climate--certainly geographic, perhaps intellectual, although there were notable scholars and some very interesting people at Louisiana State University even after the demise of the "Southern Review" in 1942. Atlanta and environs were cosmopolitan, even in the early fifties, and one of the few book-loving sections, alas, in the South. By all accounts the faculty at Emory was outstanding. I knew only one professor personally, Bell I. Wiley, Professor of History, who spent a year at Oxford as Harmsworth professor. Formerly a member of the history faculty at Louisiana State University, he was well acquainted with both institutions. We had a long talk about Louisiana State that made me more inclined than ever to throw in my lot with Emory. We feared, all too justifiably as it turned out, that the University was succumbing once again to what one friendly critic referred to as filling head positions with "good old local boys of dependable innocuousness." Finally I was very much impressed by the top administrators at Emory during my maiden visit to the campus. The President was Goodrich C. White, a national figure in higher education with a reputation for unostentatious integrity--a president who read books. His Vice-President and Dean of Faculties, Ernest Cadman Colwell, a Greek New Testament scholar and a fine administrator, reminded me in some ways of my friend Richard J. Russell of Louisiana State University. He was widely informed on a great many subjects but always succinct, gloriously bookish, a strong supporter of libraries, and, in my particular bailiwick, shrewdly attuned to the choices that had to be made to meet the essentials of a modern university library. Also I appreciated the friendliness and helpfulness of Judson C. Ward, Jr., Dean of the College of Arts and Sciences, and Howard M. Phillips, Dean of the Graduate School, during the difficult period of negotiating a change.

171

Dr. Ward knew the University from the inside out, and Dr. Phillips was well aware of the need for a strong research library to support graduate work and research. It also appeared to me that there was very good rapport between the administration and faculty, perhaps because Emory was a relatively small university at that time. Later on, I must admit, more administrators were added and confusion set in.

When I began my duties at Emory in the fall of 1954, the library system encompassed eight units, the Asa Griggs Candler Library (the main library), the library of the junior college Emory-at-Oxford, and the libraries of the schools of Medicine, Law, Theology, Business, Dentistry, and the Division of Librarianship. As Director of Libraries I was the administrator of the Asa Griggs Candler Library and served in an advisory capacity to the deans and directors who were responsible for their school libraries. In a decentralized library system I would have preferred the title University Librarian to that of Director of Libraries--didn't like the implications of the title anyhow--but my suggestion fell on deaf ears.

Naturally my first concern was with library services to the Arts and Sciences and the Graduate School, and to what extent the Candler Library measured up or failed to measure up to meeting their needs. The University had an excellent reputation in the educational world, but this had largely been won on the basis of its undergraduate program and the high quality of the faculty. In those early days I remember several professors with whom I had professional contact who contributed much to Emory's bracing academic atmosphere: Leroy E. Loemker in Philosophy; Joseph J. Mathews and Bell I. Wiley in History; Chauncey G. Goodchild in Biology; James G. Lester in Geology; Jacob Goldstein in Chemistry; and William Beardslee in Bible and Religion. Emory's excellence in its undergraduate program was equally true of its Library. Under the direction of the former Librarian, Margaret Jemison, with substantial dependence upon the bibliographical and book selection skill of Dr. Thomas H. English, Professor in English and for many years Chairman of the Library Committee, the Candler Library had acquired a first-class book collection. Although not a major research library, it was moving in that direction. Progress had been made in building manuscript collections, as for example in Methodist history, the antebellum and Civil War periods, and southern literary history. At least one major collection in southern economic history had been acquired, but financial support for building a research collection on a broad scale had not been forthcoming.

An immediate problem was how to make the best possible use of the space that would soon be released in the Candler Library after the chief administrative offices were moved to a new building that was soon to be completed. To some parties, even though they gave lip service to library needs, the problem of making the vacated space useable for library purposes was simply a matter of knocking down a few partitions and adding lighting fixtures. It was suggestions of this kind that gave me a headache--persons offering solutions before I had time to draw up a plan. I finally decided that if we were going to arrive at a solution that would provide for growth and reasonably satisfactory service during the next five years, we would have to broaden the basis of support for remodeling to include both trustees and faculty. With Vice-President Colwell taking the lead a few administrators came together at one of his favorite breakfast meetings and agreed to ask President White to appoint a representative committee to visit a few of the modern university libraries before the plans for remodeling and renovating the Candler Library were prepared. The President appointed a committee composed of two trustees, four administrators, the Chairman of the Library Committee, and the Director of Libraries and started the committee in a joyous mood by saying that his only wish was that he were free to join the group. The committee visited Harvard's Lamont and Houghton, and new libraries at Princeton, MIT, and the University of Georgia, where they were graciously received and informed by the head librarians in each institution: Keyes D. Metcalf, William S. Dix, Vernon D. Tate, and W. Porter Kellam. These gentlemen confirmed what many of the visitors knew dimly, namely that planning a modern library was a complex matter requiring much more than a knowledge of the simple bookstack-and-reading-room combination with which they were familiar from their own college days. Not all the problems applicable to Emory's local situation were identified in these visits, but the impressions gained raised the sights of the trustees and administrators regarding the scope of our remodeling program and made them aware of the expanding role of the Library in the University.

The library tour was hard labor involving a great deal of legwork, but it also had its lighter side. Among the members of our congenial group no one could match Trustee Henry L. Bowden, attorney, whose imagination played brightly upon the events of the day when we gathered together for dinner or caucus in the evening to exchange notes on what we had seen. For a man who had spent most of his life around lawyers, university presidents, and people of consequence, he managed to take in the manners, customs, and foibles of librarians in short order. The years have slightly rotted my memory cells, but Bowden's account of a visit with the dignified, reticent Director of Harvard's library system remains one of the happiest of my recollections of the entire trip. Bowden is telling the story:

> "Mr. Metcalf, this is a magnificent Library and in it you have some rare and invaluable items, I am told. One of these, if I am informed correctly, is a copy of the Gutenberg Bible."
> To this inquiry Mr. Metcalf replied, "Yes, we do."
> I then said, "Well, the Gutenberg Bible, for instance, Mr. Metcalf, is it ever available for anyone to see?"
> To this he replied, "Yes, it is."
> I then said, "Well, is it available for just ordinary people to see?"
> He again replied, "Yes."
> Proceeding still further, I said, "Well, Mr. Metcalf, would it be available for just an ordinary citizen such as I to see it while I am here?"
> Again he replied, "Yes, and if you follow me, I shall be glad to allow you to view it now."
> We walked along the hall toward the place where the Gutenberg Bible was located, and as we did so Mr. Metcalf turned to me and said, "Mr. Bowden, I am pleased to be able to show you our copy of the Gutenberg Bible. You see, I had no idea you were interested in any of the intellectual pursuits."

On our return I prepared a plan for remodeling and renovation that was approved by the visiting committee and presented to the President. Dr. White studied the plan with some care and then called me in. "Guy," he said, with what I thought was a pained look in his eye, "do we really have to gut the building?" I think he was referring particularly to the proposal to divide the thirty-two-foot-high Reading Room, which extended almost the entire length of the building, into two rooms of equal size by installing a new floor at midpoint all the way across the room, thereby reducing the height of each room to approximately twelve feet. No sooner had this proposal reached the architect who originally designed the building, and the critics on the campus who were against all change, than they swarmed over to the President's office to suggest that this meddler was about to ruin the aesthetics of the Asa Griggs Candler Library and ought to quit. I agreed that any form of remodeling to an existing building was bound to have its defects but that the Reading Room divider gave us three-quarters of all usable new space in the building and make possible the creation of a Science Library. The Science Library in turn would take the pressure off the demands for science departmental collections, which were expensive to maintain and would further fragment the collection. It would also relieve the congestion in the bookstacks by the removal of all science material and allow for future growth. Finally I stressed the fact that we might reasonably expect a hundred percent increase in library use because the two new reading rooms would be air-conditioned and the lighting greatly improved by the reduction in ceiling heights. As it was now the students left the Library in droves when the temperature hit eighty to ninety in the large Reading Room during the late spring, summer, and fall terms.

Buttressed by the endorsement of the special building committee, the President wasted no time in approving the project, and the remodeling and renovation program got underway immediately. On November 15, 1957, the Library held an Open House to mark the completion of the remodeling project. A number of friends of Emory attended as well as a goodly sprinkling of the chief librarians of other universities in the Southeast. Dr. William Dix of Princeton made an informal address in the evening, and I expressed special thanks to President White and the nine members of the building committee.

Of immediate concern also was the enlargement and reorganization of the Library staff. I wish it were possible to acknowledge by name the good work of each member of the staff during those early days. By and large I was intensely grateful for their help and the excellence of their work. A few people must be mentioned. Marella Walker, who was already serving in more ways than would fit any known description of a librarian's duties, was made head of a new Book Order Department, where she could make best use of her remarkable memory, her amazing knowledge of library holdings, and her familiarity with the special interests of many of the faculty. Ruth Walling left Louisiana State University for Emory as Chief of the Reference Department, where she continued to apply her special talent for building one of the outstanding reference and bibliographical collections in the Southeast. In many other ways she helped clear away the manifold difficulties that constantly arise in a new administration, always managing to do this in a way that made one feel that the solution came from one's own brain.

Another person who threw his whole energies into the development of the collections at Emory was Evan Farber, who came to Emory as Serials and Binding Librarian from the librarianship of Livingston State College in Alabama. His education included an A. B. degree from the University of North Carolina, two years of graduate work at Princeton, and an M. A. from the University of North Carolina. Later he took his library degree at Carolina and worked in the University Library. Evan did a tremendous job of building the Library's files of journals, served on Library and faculty committees, edited one book and contributed to another, and helped to edit the "Southeastern Librarian." At the time he left Emory to become Head Librarian at Earlham College, in 1962, I wrote what I believe is a fair estimate of the man: "He is one of a diminishing breed of librarian who fills the highest role of bookman while serving at the same time with great competence in the administrative aspects of librarianship." One other person who helped to light up the scene at this period was Thomas Crowder, an Emory graduate with an A. B. and M. A. in English. He worked through the ranks from assistant serials librarian to the head of the Circulation Department. His strong points were his knowledge of books and his rapport with members of the faculty. Eventually he became Chief of the Special Collections Department, where he was ably assisted by Mary Davis, archivist. In the fall of 1962 Tom became Librarian of Mississippi State College and eventually gave up his profession to enter the ministry.

Finally I must mention another lady of great talent, Louise Ward, who also migrated from Baton Rouge to Emory for a short period during which she passed out some thousands of volumes to readers--and got them back. Louise, a devotee of Eudora Welty, was fine entertainment for anyone's evening. She was loved for her good cheer and wit. This quotation doesn't quite do justice to her fun-loving nature, but who except Louise Ward would end a formal library report with the note:

> My favorite moments of the past year: discovering there is a frequent library user named Etta Apple ... charging a book on prayer to a Theology student named Will Power ... the New York telephone operator requesting a connection with the person in charge of the Civil War ... finding the 1840 volume of "Gentleman's Magazine" in the Ladies' Room.

21: TO JAPAN AND BACK

Not long after the completion of the remodeling of the Asa
Griggs Candler Library I received an invitation to travel to
Japan as the first appointee to a visiting professorship in the
Japan Library School, Keio University, Tokyo, for the three-
month period beginning May 1957. The lectureship was sponsored by the Rockefeller Foundation and administered by the
American Library Association, but I owed my appointment to
my friend Robert L. Gitler. We first met during the sum-
mers of 1946 and 1947, when we were teaching at Columbia's
School of Library Service. There is nothing like the challenge
of the classroom followed by vigorous exercise and billiards
after dinner to seal a friendship, and this was pretty much
our daily schedule. Bob founded the Japan Library School and
served as its first director, and a grateful University and nation awarded him an honorary Ph.D. and the Fourth Order of
Merit with Cordon of Rising Sun. For the Japanese a nod
from Bob Gitler was as good as Jove's word.

I kept a journal during my stay in Tokyo. In rereading
a transcription of this journal I find it more revealing of the
human events that took place during my brief stay in Tokyo
than anything I can recreate today. Consequently I offer the
story, reedited in narrative form, just as it happened. At
least it has the merit of being the truth about the people and
the happenings of those days without the fallacy of recollection.

Aloa-hah-wy-ee

Aloha and welcome to the Hawaiian Islands. I'm not sorry to

178

relieve my cramped legs. Soft Hawaiian music is recorded over the loudspeaker. When do we get to Hah-na-lula? asks a passenger. The stewardess looks startled, replies in soft, separately voiced syllables, "Ho-no-lulu by 7 a.m." I figure we have been ten hours over the ocean if West Coast time is two hours ahead of Honolulu, or is it two hours behind? No matter, it is exciting to watch the descent. Gradually the clouds thin out, and there below is the beautiful calm ocean with snowy frills of foam laced between its blue and green waters. Everything is gorgeously colored as we descend over the islands, green forests, crystal-clear reef waters, fantastically beautiful rock formations--flat, spongy, brown, grey, and blue masses in the valley offsetting clusters of mountain peaks.

Landing and stepping off the plane, I'm almost blinded by the brilliance of the sun, but the breeze is refreshing, especially in the waiting room of the terminal, which is open at both ends. Tired and dirty, I head for the men's room, which seems to be inhabited by half the American army just getting ready to take off in the "Flying Tiger" for Japan. There are no towels, and I use a soiled handkerchief and then go out and sprawl pathetically on the simmering plush of a huge bamboo sofa. Hawaiian time, I am told, is the local way of saying you take your time, but there is nothing leisurely about this spot. Passengers are greeted by relatives and friends; grandfather on down to the youngest grandchild are all on hand with leis for the friend or loved one. Nowhere will you see more closely knit family groups or so many alien carved faces. I wish that beautiful Polynesian girl would put a lei on me, but no, she's saved it for her fat boyfriend, who comes in barefoot and beaming like the sunrise. The customs officials are poking through the suitcases of returning Americans. The Canadian, Japanese, and Australian airlines have long queues, and there is even jostling at the information desks of the island-hopping lines. Tourists and soldiers are shopping at the souvenir counters, which display everything from hula skirts to woodcarvings. A fellow passenger is wandering about snapping pictures of native men in flashy aloha shirts and women in muumuus, the gaily covered dress that looks good on any figure. I feel drowsy listening to the Hawaiian music, watching the slight swaying of the palm trees in the breeze.

This is what I expected to find, no real taste yet of the Far East, but different enough to know that I have left

DeKalb County, Georgia. I fall asleep and am awakened by
Shah, who is to be my seat companion on the next hop to
Wake, now announced, ready to depart.

Wake Island

"Wake Island is a coral atoll atop of an extinct underwater
volcano.... Its average height above sea level is 12 feet."
I read this bit of comforting news in the Pan American leaflet as we prepare to descend. I stare hard but see nothing.
Then great gaps open in the fleecy summer clouds, and the
view below opens up as through a skylight. The ocean is
white and it is green--a vast canvas of blue and green and
dark patches with snow-white breakers racing and sliding
through the watery depth. It is a view too sweeping to carry
wholly in mind. It is like a thousand shining window panes
flushed by the afternoon sun, swimming in empty space. But
here comes the island, or rather three islands, and together
they look very much like the wishbone of a small chicken, the
runway intersecting the joint and the two arms circling a la-
goon. It doesn't seem possible that this giant mass of quiv-
ering and straining steel can ever land there. Yet Wake was
once a battlefield of planes and ships. If you look hard you
can still see a few scars--the tailpiece of a plane, pillboxes
not wholly concealed by the tall grass, the burned end of a
half-sunken ship. Devastation yesterday, but today we glide
down in the peace of a late spring afternoon. We stagger out
of the plane and into the arms of the refreshment committee.
After a few gulps of pineapple juice I take a quick stroll
around to get the feel of my legs. The white gravel is hot,
and the shrublike magnolia and dwarf trees offer little shade.
To one side a quonset hut displays the words "Clipper Lounge"
in large black letters as unselfishly as a nightclub sign in the
Latin Quarter of New Orleans. I hurry back to the plane. I
must not get left here.

Tokyo

Darkness, rain, and clouds. There is a moon above the
clouds but no Tokyo beneath until we descend through the
bumpy mist and land on Haneda Airport. I clear the customs,
ascend the stairs to the large and nearly empty waiting room,
and am met by a smiling, pipe-smoking young man who is to
be my constant companion and interpreter for the next three

180

months. We climb into a shiny 1950 Plymouth with a feather duster on the back seat. As we drive off I feel a great sense of loneliness and dejection. It isn't just in myself; I see signs of it all around me. The streets are narrow and winding. There are few lights, and shadowy figures step out of nowhere in the heavy mist. The driver seems to trust mostly to luck and horn to keep from hitting them. This luck almost deserts him at times. Piles of rock and mire are heaped up on the streets. Road repairs often bring us to an impasse. The storefronts have meager lights, and many seem to be boarded up. Electric light poles hang at crazy and menacing angles because of their overload of wires. A stranger landing in the slum area of one of our large cities might have a first impression identical to mine. It is godforsaken, uncomfortable, and a little frightening. I scarcely pay any attention to what my companion is saying. I am thinking my own black and melancholy thoughts. I was told to avoid Western-style accommodations in order to gain a deeper insight into the mode of living of the Japanese people, but when we finally arrive at my lodging, I thank God that the room reserved for me has a shower, a comfortable bed, and a lock on the door. I lie down without taking my clothes off and fall into the deep sleep of exhaustion.

The next day I visit the Asakusa Kannon Temple, which in characteristically paradoxical Japanese fashion is located in Tokyo's famous Montmartre district. The approach to the shrine is down a narrow street arched with cherry blossoms and lined on either side by shops selling cheap clothing, shoes, magazines, jewelry, and souvenirs. Less than a block away hundreds of people are filtering in and out of movie theaters and striptease shows located in the cellars beneath. Worshippers of Kannon come and go, throw their offerings in a huge grill-covered trough in front of the shrine, clap their hands, bow, and withdraw. My companion apologizes for the fact that the shrine is a reconstruction; the original buildings, some three hundred years old, he explains, were entirely destroyed by an airraid fire in March 1945. This triggers me into that dreadful state of mind where everything you see has significance for what you would like to forget. When we leave for downtown Tokyo, I pass a street where sixty thousand people were cremated in one night's firebombing. And in the afternoon, on the campus where I am to spend most of my time for the next three months, the first sight that greets me is the skeleton of a huge building--three stark standing walls--all that remains of the main auditorium, completely gutted by bombing. The immediate area is littered with debris. This, I feel, has been left all these years for my special benefit, a kind of symbol of the fact that America is morally accountable for the devastation. I am told that the library was also partially destroyed. I turn my back on the campus and walk back toward the noisy street that leads to International House. It is cold and raining. The rocketing, rioting taxis splash mud as they horn and roar through the streets. I feel as though the people are all watching me. I read distrust and hatred in their cold, stony faces. I am pooped, low, and licked. I am glad to get back to the friendly quarters of my room.

Radio Interview

There are two Japanese instructors and myself working in a smoke-filled office about as large as a good-sized walk-in closet when a reporter from WTR Radio Station drops in for an interview. If you get far enough away from home, you're a somebody and are treated with respect and dignity. Mr. Arko, the reporter, is a slight, smiling, bowing young man with a weak back from carrying around too much tape-recording machinery. He is loaded down like a skindiver with a storage battery under each armpit and a fifty-five-pound aqualung around his neck. He says he will need a quiet place to record the interview, and since it is a lead-pipe cinch he won't find it in that building, I suggest that we go over to my room at International House. We take a taxi; it is evident that he has already walked about as far as he can go. The interview is to last about ten minutes. I doubt if it was ever broadcast, but I improve my social standing at International House when we march through the lobby and climb the stairway to my room. I ease into a comfortable chair facing the sliding doors, which open out on to a beautiful Japanese garden. The reporter squats on the floor with his apparatus. I am wondering what line of questions he will follow when, with a maximum of scratching and some ominous lead-in lines, the interview begins.

Arko: What is your first impression of Japan?

Me: Well, I haven't really formed any impressions so far. You see, I just arrived at Haneda airport a few days ago. It takes me a little while to catch on. I'm the peasant type.

Arko: Everyone says it's pleasant here, but what were your impressions of Mt. Fuji as you flew in?

Me: I'm sorry I was dozing at the time. Anyway it was nighttime and I don't suppose ...

Arko: (doggedly) Well, you must have had some impressions when you first landed.

Me: It was raining hard, I remember. Does it always rain like this in Japan?

Arko: (refusing to be diverted) You are a teacher. What are your impressions of Japanese students?

Me: I've met only three or four classes, of course, but I think the students are wonderful. They are courteous, kind, attentive. It's nice to leave home and find respect among strangers.... I wish they would ask questions.

Arko: Do they understand you?

Me: My interpreter assures me they do.

Arko: You have an inter-peeter? I thought the students came to hear you speak English.

Me: I suspect some of them do. They go for English here like our college boys go for football. They have an astonishing facility in English grammar but when it comes to spoken English, they ...

Arko: (interrupting) What do you think of Japanese women?

Me: That's easy. I would say they are God's gift to Japan. I've only really seen them in the movies, of course. I wish I knew them better.

Arko: (brightening up) Is that your purpose in coming to Japan?

Me: Holy Joe! You certainly hanker for the simple declarative, don't you? My purpose is purely academic. One of your universities made the sacrifice of asking me to come to this country to teach.

183

Arko: How long? For a month? Forever?

Me: I think something was said about three months.

Arko: Do you find the Japanese people friendly?

Me: Well, you know I have just gotten here. I have very few acquaintances among your people so far. I'm still a little confused. I wouldn't say the people are unfriendly, but Tokyo is very large compared to my home, where everybody as a matter of course sticks his nose into everybody else's affairs. Here the people seem poised for flight. Like New Yorkers during the five o'clock rush hour in Penn Station.

Arko: Are you planning trips to the other parts of Japan?

Me: I hope to--later. Perhaps Kyoto and Nikko.

Arko: Well, before you leave Japan, be sure to see Mt. Fuji!

This last, more a command than an invitation, ends the interview. I feel a little uneasy about it, having evaded most of Arko's questions because I was either not willing or ready to reply. Anxious to dispel the glum look in his eye, I invite him to join me at the bar downstairs. The beer is good Sapporo, ice-cold, and Arko sips noisily and contentedly. After a couple of glasses he seems like a changed person. He drops the quiet, somber mask, and his face shows flashes of that direct and honest friendliness that I found so appealing in my conversations with students. He is full of useful information and good advice as to what I should do and see during my stay in Japan, and he even offers to accompany me on a sightseeing trip if I wish. I ask him where he learned to speak English so well--there is little phrase-book quality about his speech--and am surprised to discover that he has never been outside Japan. It turns out that he has largely taught himself, but I think it a mark of character that he attributes his facility to the evening classes he attended, which were taught by the wife of a Fulbright scholar. He fairly smoulders with enthusiasm and goodwill for Americans and things American. He enjoys American movies, television, plays, song hits, and books. He asks a lot of intelligent questions, and he knows a lot more about us than I do about the Japanese.

"I don't mean to be probing," I say to him, "but I do want to ask you something. You get around a good bit in your job. Do your friends and acquaintances share your opinions about America?" "Oh, yes," he replies earnestly, "most of them do, I'm sure. Perhaps you are puzzled because you read the papers too much. We have our communist sympathizers, and they are permitted to say what they wish. They make a lot of noise for their number. But in sentiment most Japanese are very friendly toward America. We do not know too much about you, and we do not understand some of the things you do, but we are anxious to learn. We think Americans are friendly, and we like your friendship and conveniences."

When he rises to leave, Arko repeats his injunction about Mt. Fuji. I assure him that it was first on my list of things to do and thank him for his kind and helpful advice. The earlier interview has completely slipped my mind. I have my first real feeling of cheerfulness.

Diversions in Meiji Park

At 9 o'clock Takahisa phones to say he has the flu, and he will be unable to accompany me to the Keio-Waseda baseball game; his wife will meet me in thirty minutes at Shinanomachi station. Shinanomachi is only a two-minute walk from Meiji Ball Park. By 9:30 the station will be like an anthill. How will I ever pick out Shizuka in that crowd? I try to think back to the only time I have seen her. She was the dainty hostess then, squatting on her heels, wearing a pale blue kimono with chrysanthemums painted on it. She spoke softly, wore only light makeup, and her white skin contrasted sharply with her black olive-shaped eyes. Occasionally she would dart a glance at her husband, either a prearranged signal to refill the saki cups or an exchange of private amusement at my awkwardness in using chopsticks. She was delightful with her air of serene composure. But today she will probably be wearing Western clothes for going out, as would most of the women, so that won't help. It will be difficult to spot her. Probably she was thinking the same thing.

I am standing at the corner of the little fruit stand just outside the station when she walks, or rather floats up, with the peculiar light willowy motion of young Japanese women. She knows only a few words of English. I speak no Japanese. No husband, no interpreter. But who's complaining?

185

Not me! Even if she behaves like one of the Jukes family, she will still be awfully easy to take. We leave immediately, bumping a little in the cross-flow of the churning jam-packed crowd.

All Tokyo, it seems, is bound for the Keio-Waseda clash. It is the nearest approach to our fall gridiron scene. Students line the pathways hawking their college colors and souvenirs. I start to buy Shizuka a little pink parasol, but she reacts as though stung by a hornet. "Waseda" she hisses. I get the cue and thereafter let her take the lead.

We enter the stadium at approximately 10 o'clock and fight our way down the aisle to the wooden benches in the Keio section. By 11:30 the seats are full, sixty-five thousand people or more, and the gates close. Across the way a solid mass of pink parasols swings in unison, left to right, right to left, like rice plants swaying in the breeze. Thousands of Keio fans wave red-white-and-blue scarves while their band booms out a victory march. The main aisles are full; people are standing on the sidelines, even spilling over into the outer reaches of the field. A plane circling overhead swoops low to drop the Waseda colors; seconds later it circles and dives again to drop the Keio colors. Someone in the Keio stands hoists a bamboo cage, then another and another, and suddenly hundreds of doves are released against the sky. The crowd momentarily is hushed; all eyes stare, straining. If the doves fly one way, it is good luck for Keio; if the other, it's Waseda's lucky break. A mighty cheer rises from the fans, but I'm too busy taking pictures to see who's favored. Three and a half hours after we first entered the stadium the game gets under way. By 4:30 it is all tied up in the ninth. A two-run homer in the seventeenth clinches the game for Keio.

One kind of pain drives out another. Next morning I'm still so stiff from yesterday's sitting marathon that even the mattress feels uncomfortable. Then suddenly I notice that my camera is missing and I forget all about my stiffness. I call the front desk and the manager courteously offers to phone the ballpark. Yes, a camera of foreign make has been turned in, but I would have to come to the ballpark office to identify it. I take a cab and arrive in a few minutes, but it takes a good deal of hunting to locate the office where I am supposed to pick up the camera. The interior looks like a rundown funeral parlor. The occupants include a retinue of sad-faced male secretaries, maids, and two policemen. They invite me to sit down and kill time while they grapple with the problem. They put their heads together, gaze thoughtfully at the floor, and look as though this is a matter for international arbitration. Finally one of the policemen gets up, comes over to me and says, "What do you do?" I thought it might be difficult to explain; so I hand him my American passport, my temporary Japanese passport, a name card printed in both Japanese and English, and inadvertently a DeKalb County fishing license. This last is a mistake. They go again into a pigeon huddle and concentrate harder than ever. Occasionally they glance suspiciously at me, like a friendly mother cat whose three kittens have just been snatched. Clearly my case is getting nowhere; so I offer to identify the camera, an Argus, 35mm, encased in brown leather with a broken strap. I suggest they develop the film. There are sixteen pictures of yesterday's game. I sit down again and they continue their huddle.

Finally a policeman goes to a closet in the corner of the room, opens a drawer, and brings out my camera. I am allowed to look at it but not to keep it. A good bit of warm argument gets me nowhere. I tell them they are the damnedest unfolksy, boneheaded, shell-workers that ever operated, but I don't think they understand. One of the men who speaks a little English offers an explanation. The point seems to be that I must first go to the home of the man who found the camera and obtain a written release from him before I can have the camera. I don't argue any more; I'm boiling mad. This may be an old Japanese custom but it sounds like a phony to me. I leave with my tongue hanging out and take a fast cab to Keio. I explain to one of the interpreters that I would like my camera back that afternoon and I would decide afterward what reward to pay, and would he please get the hell over to whoever on the campus had sufficient weight to get a little action out at the Meiji Shrine Outer Garden Ball Stadium. The camera is returned within the hour. In due time I send the finder a letter of thanks and eighteen hundred yen. Two weeks later I receive the following letter:

> Dear Sirs:
> I received your letter with gift. I am glad your camera returned your hand. I shrink you care to sent gift to me. Because I have only found camera, but I will received it as you hope and I use it efficiently. I am sorry I sent this letter to you too lately.

I hope you be healthy for ever.
Yours truly
S. Nakata

Batlike Umbrella

My 8 o'clock rising is, as usual, followed almost instantane-
ously by a knock on the door, a turn of the key, and the appearance of three house maids who bow, smile charmingly,
and say in unison, "Good morning, gozaimus." I'm practically in puris naturalibus; so I don't waste much time on ceremony.   They pay no attention anyway, probably think of me
as a kind of big old skinned mule.   Come to think of it, I
probably look like one at that time of the morning.   One maid
makes the bed, another washes out the bathroom and the third
pushes a wet rag over the floor with a short stick in each
hand.   This act always fascinates me.   Once I opened my fool
mouth to ask why she didn't use a long-handled mop to spare
her back, and holy Jehosephat! you would have thought I had
invited her to spend the night.   All three giggled and shrieked
and lit out of there like a Flying Fortress with the throttle
wide open.   When they returned without the cops, I untangled
the knots in my stomach.

There is a time between the middle of March and the
first of May when the rainy season begins.   It rains continuously, and the streets are slick, dark, and dank wherever you
walk.   The Japanese prepares well for the "Bai-u" season.   He
wears a raincoat and high rubber boots, something like a
Britisher's Wellingtons, into which he tucks his trousers, and
invariably carries an umbrella.   Some wear wooden clogs in
place of boots, because of their cheapness, I'm sure, and the
memory of their clipped cadence still hangs vividly about me
as I write.

I am less well prepared to battle the unfriendly ele-
ments.   After breakfast I slip on my raincoat and hurry to
the University through tortuous streets and winding alleys,
hoping always to escape the rain-splattering traffic of taxis,
three-wheel trucks, jeeps, handcarts, bicycles, streetcars,
men, women, and schoolchildren all jostling and threading
their way through the labyrinth.   It is bad enough sloshing
through the puddles, but when a driving wind accompanies the
rain it is murderous.   I understand what they mean when they
say, "This is nasty season.   Please take care of your health."
By the time I reach the campus I am soaked from the knees

on down and not a bit disposed to use the bucket and long-handled brush which the janitors place outside each classroom building during the rainy season. The students brush off their shoes and rubbers carefully before entering. I march straight in but I still look as though I've just stepped outside of the bucket. Takahisa shakes his head. "It's time," he says, "to buy your 'kasa.'"

So at noontime, with the rain still coming down in sheets, Takahisa and I walk down the hill to the shopping district at the edge of the campus, where the streets and alleys twist and turn so much you wonder if they may not prove to be blind. Irregular rows of dismal-looking small shops stretch endlessly. Their fronts are open to the street, displaying pots and pans, footwear, confectionery in glass cases, hardware, books and magazines, and great piles of vegetables. Other shops in the street display either the short curtain ('noren') of the eating house or the cold frontage of closure. We come at last to the shop of the umbrella man and hastily crowd in under the awning out of the rain. The proprietor is squatting on a small raised platform, a few feet back from the streetfront, repairing an umbrella. Before he comes forward to greet us Takahisa points to a Japanese umbrella ('kasa') and explains that it is made of bamboo and oiled paper. The split bamboo ribs are held together at the apex of the umbrella by a circular piece of wood. It is carried with the handle downward after a rain to let the water run off. "It is cheap," he says, "and it's large enough to shelter your whole body from the rain, but I would advise you to pick out one of the western-type umbrellas. We call them 'komori-gasa' or batlike umbrellas."

The proprietor now comes forward, bows, and engages in a long conversation with Takahisa, following which he lays out an assortment of umbrellas of the "batlike" type in three shades of color: black, brown, and green. I pick out a black one, and he bows and grins happily. "You've made a hit," says Takahisa. "He thinks it is the right choice for 'sensei' (professor)." The proprietor then puts on the kind of demonstration that is ordinarily reserved in this country for the sale of a Cadillac. I ask Takahisa to tell him to quit opening and closing the damn thing before he wears it out. But the proprietor is not to be hurried. He brings out a number of varying types of handles for me to choose from. I select one of carved bamboo which triggers another flurry of honorific salutation. It is plain the proprietor is enjoying this sale, and

189

he is handling it in his own sweet way and time. He returns
to his platform, squats, greases the end of the umbrella shaft,
takes a piece of silk thread and winds it around the shaft, fits
the handle on firmly, files the edges of the bamboo where the
steel tips of the ribs come together when closed, and again
flips it open and shut several times to make sure that everything is in perfect working order. I get out my pocketbook,
but Takahisa gives me the "let's not be hasty" sign. I am
now invited to select the tape for wrapping round the umbrella
when it's closed. I delegate this detail to Takahisa. The
proprietor is at last satisfied. He presents the umbrella to
me with a low bow. I count out nine hundred yen. He is
speaking to Takahisa. Takahisa interprets: "The proprietor
says if anything goes wrong, won't you please come back and
he will be honored to fix it." I shall be glad to. The proprietor smiles and bows. We smile and bow and back out into the street.

"Well," says Takahisa, holding out his hand, "can't
imagine it. It's stopped raining at last."

Farewell

The kimono-clad girl carrying my zipper bag, the proprietor
of the "ryokan" (Japanese-style hotel), and my Japanese friends
bid Takahisa and me goodbye at the hot springs hotel as we
prepare to board the bus for the short trip down the mountain-
side to Mishima station. The train is scheduled to arrive at
Tokyo station at three. This will leave me one hour to pack
and one hour to get to Haneda airport for the homebound
flight. It is a tight schedule, but I've sworn a holy swear
that I won't leave Japan before visiting a hot springs resort.
I appear a little nervous but my companion assures me for
the ninth time that the Pigeon is never late.

The bus trip is short but harrowing, even more so going down than up. It may be an exaggeration to say there
are twenty hairpin curves on the rough gravel mountain road,
but it is a plain fact that the bus rolls senselessly from side
to side like a drunken man and that the driver takes the
curves with the throttle wide open. We sit rigidly, I more
rigidly than Takahisa, and all talking ceases. When a Japanese boy returns home from school he almost always an-
nounces his coming with a loud "Tadaima" so that the folks
at home know he is back safely. From within the house

comes a cheery "Okaeri-nasai," a sort of "Glad you're back" welcome. When we finally reach the bottom of the mountain, I mutter, "Tadaima, dammit, tadaima," and Takahisa, grinning like a monkey, repeats "Okaeri-nasai."

The train pulls into Tokyo station promptly at three. I offer a cabdriver five hundred yen to turn off his radio and get us to International House on the double, a generous impulse I regret immediately. It is possible that taxi drivers observe traffic regulations in Tokyo, but I doubt it. This fellow makes up his own. He hurtles through the narrow winding streets scattering peanut vendors, fruit peddlers, and pedestrians like ninepins. His horn sounds continuously. If a light turns against him he beats his wheel with both hands and bobs up and down on his seat like doughnuts frying in deep fat. He is a superb driver, but for my money he is trying to push a good thing too far.

Neither of us has had lunch; so, while I pack, Takahisa orders sandwiches to be sent to the room. It is evident that my belongings have multiplied prodigiously during the past three months, and that my two bags will hold only the presents that I bought and the bare necessities of travel. The rest--books, umbrella, tennis racquet and shoes, sweaters, sport coat, and other space-consuming articles--fill two cartons. It seems easier to acquire than to throw away, and this decision continually confounds me as the minutes slip by. We have numerous interruptions from the friendly servants, who want to know how we enjoyed the sandwiches, whether they can help us pack, whether they should order a cab, and so forth. Finally the University car arrives, and we pile bags, cartons, and ourselves in the back seat. We have made it so far, but the old pep is low, and I wonder how I can possibly manage to take all the stuff I have within the maximum weight limit.

This last problem is quickly settled at the airport. I put the two bags, the camera, and my raincoat on the scales, and they weigh exactly forty-four pounds. "Leave the cartons in the car," I tell Takahisa, "and send them later by surface mail." As an afterthought I add, "If this is too much trouble, give the stuff to your friends."

The information clerk, a good-looking young Japanese man, flips through my ticket folder.

"So you're on your way home to Dallas," he says without looking up.

"Not Dallas," I reply quickly, suspecting that here's where the trouble starts, "Not Dallas—Atlanta."

His head snaps up. "You're from Atlanta? I know Atlanta. I'm a graduate of the University of Georgia."

"Good Heavens!" I cry, grasping his outstretched hand. "Here I'm about to leave and I meet a Japanese who not only speaks perfect English but is a Georgia graduate to boot. Why, we're practically neighbors. I'm from Emory."

"From Emory?" His face lights up happily. "Do you know Professor Langhorne?"

"Do I know him!" I reply, "Why he's chairman of our psychology department."

The young man fairly beams and then his eye travels to the needle on the weighing scale. "Look," he says, "we've plenty of space. Is there anything else you would like to add to your baggage?"

The unexpectedness of the offer almost staggers me. "Takahisa," I practically shout, "bring in the cartons."

22: EMORY UNIVERSITY II: THE ROBERT W. WOODRUFF
LIBRARY

During the forties and fifties there was general recognition among educational leaders and foundations that the development of graduate education in the South was essential if the region was not to be drained of its research and teaching scholars. A major weakness in southern universities was lack of adequate library resources. Unfortunately graduate education and research are expensive, choices have to be made, and the library is most often low on the totem pole. As J. Douglas Brown, Provost and Dean of Faculty, Princeton University, succinctly put it: "The library, in some ways, has been the Cinderella in university administration."

The Emory University Library was no exception. For five years during the administration of President S. Walter Martin (1957-62), a good friend of libraries, the Library had exerted pressure, unsuccessfully, to secure a new library building, for which there was an obvious need. A great university library cannot stagnate. It must not stop growing, and growth means proper housing, organization of collections, and staffing. Without growth the library cannot help to create the kind of intellectual climate in which the minds of students and faculty can thrive. Good will was not enough to bring about a change. Strong administrative leadership that would recognize the vital importance of the library in Emory's future was badly needed.

It seemed to me then, as it seems to me now, that chance and circumstance, like the occurrence of harmony and discord in nature, had more to do with getting started on a new library for Emory University than all the sweat and grind of individual and committee effort. Some force beyond anything one can name was working to ensure that Emory got its new library building. Following the resignation of President Martin to rejoin the University system of Georgia as Vice-Chancellor, an Interim Committee of three, popularly known as the "Troika," was set up to operate the University until a successor to President Martin could be found. From a library point of view the key man in the Troika was Henry Lumpkin Bowden, a distinguished lawyer and graduate of the University and Chairman of the Board of Trustees of Emory University. I never met anyone who was more devoted to the interest of his alma mater than Henry Bowden, nor anyone who did not like him. He would have made a good President of Emory University following President Martin's resignation; he had educational convictions, and he spoke in an admirably straightforward manner without lawyer jargon or technicality. Certainly he had mastered the art of leaving himself a free man. Beardsley Ruml must have had him in mind when he came up with the happy aphorism, "If you find yourself doing any work, you're underorganized." Bowden loved to travel, and in the course of his travels he was at all times the keen observer and ardent learner. It was on one such journey that he discovered the glory of Princeton, the Firestone Library, and another, Harvard's triple asset, Widener, Lamont, and Houghton. He learned too that a research library can be of great service to the public as well as the world of learning.

Acting on a hunch, I prepared a short statement of Emory's library need--a building large enough to accommodate a rapidly growing collection, housed in accord with current library concepts. Incorporated in the statement was a recommendation for a joint trustee-faculty library building committee. The final version was submitted to the Troika by the Library Policy Committee of the University Senate, with Senate endorsement. About this same time I asked Vice-President Ward if he would consider making a request to the Division of Higher Education of the Methodist Church Board of Education, for which I had done considerable library consulting work, for a grant to employ preliminary architectural services.

The response came with something of the surprise and initial disbelief of a car collision. At its November 1962 meeting, acting on a motion by Trustee Charles T. Winship, the Board of Trustees of Emory University "authorized such immediate action as is practical on this matter [a new library

194

building], including the appointment of an appropriate committee to move toward perfection of architectural plans for the
building. " The Committee was composed of five trustees appointed by Mr. Bowden and four members of the faculty and
the Director of Libraries appointed by Vice-President Ward
and was chaired by Trustee Harllee Branch, Jr., with Mr.
Winship as alternate chairman. The newly appointed Committee discussed the basic capacity requirements of a new library, its relationship to the Asa Griggs Candler Library,
and possible sites; and formulated a set of principles to assist
in the selection of an architect. Shortly after the Committee's
appointment Vice-President Ward announced a grant of twenty-
five thousand dollars from the Methodist Church Board for
preliminary architectural services to plan a new building.
This proved a strong stimulus to Committee action, and after
several meetings, acting under the chairmanship of Charles T.
Winship in the absence of Mr. Harllee Branch, Jr., it recommended the New York architectural firm of Warner, Burns,
Toan, and Lunde to draw up preliminary plans and to prepare
an estimate of building cost. It so happened that Warner,
Burns, Toan, and Lunde had just recently completed the erec-
tion of a new library building for Cornell University, which
was receiving widespread attention throughout the country. By
happy coincidence Emory's newly elected President, Dr. Sanford S. Atwood, had just come from Cornell, where he last
served as Provost. Quite naturally he was well acquainted
with the New York firm, and it was not surprising that Warner et al. were commissioned to proceed with plans. For my
part I began to believe that miracles could now be counted upon as a regular thing.

The difficult task facing the architects was to create a
very large building that would accommodate a million or more
volumes and seating for fifteen hundred readers, be architecturally and structurally contemporary, meet all functional requirements, and still be in harmony with the neighboring buildings on the campus. The functional requirements set forth in
a thirty-five-page program prepared by the Director of Libraries and the heads of library departments, with critical study
by administrators, deans, and faculty members, reflected the
growing importance of graduate work and research at Emory.
For example, the tentative title of the new facility was identified in the program as the Library for Advanced Studies even
though the entire building and its resources were to be available to all students at the University. The requirements set
forth in the program in support of graduate study and instruc-

195

tion included eighty faculty research studies, a hundred and twenty-six dissertation studies where a Ph. D. student could keep all of his or her materials together in a small enclosed office space while writing a dissertation, six hundred and thirty-four carrels or small study alcoves for assignment to graduate students, and six seminars for a professor to meet regularly or informally with graduate students for the discussion of research problems. Of course all students on campus were to be encouraged to use the new library even though the required readings for undergraduates were housed in the Candler Library and the professional students had their own special libraries. In line with current concepts in library planning elaborate provision was made for the preservation of rare materials and manuscripts and their exhibition, for bringing the attention of faculty and students to new books being added to the collections, for instruction in the use of the library, and for the care, housing, and use of all forms of microtext materials. Emory scientists were to benefit by having all their book and journal resources (except in the field of chemistry) brought together on one floor, with research studies adjoining for professors writing research papers, and with a Science Librarian and staff at hand to provide reference service.

The choice of site had an important bearing on the architects' final decision. They conceived a ten-story building that satisfied the basic program requirements. By planning the two largest floors on a sloping ravine, below eye level, they were able to disguise the massiveness of the library building in comparison with the relatively modest size of the buildings on the quadrangle. Then by repeating the shape of the tall arches of reinforced concrete rising in front of the black steel panels of the outside walls, and by using a tiled roof similar to those of the other campus buildings, they provided a harmonious blending with the natural architectural surroundings. Another special concern of the architects was to avoid interposing the mass of the building as a "wall," so to speak, between the upper portion of the campus, where the women's dormitories were located, and the lower side or main quadrangle. Their solution was to place a "neutral" lobby space between the two lower floors of the library building and the book and special research facilities in the tower. This lobby was glazed to its full height in order that one might see through it from both directions. In addition, the lobby served as an arrival point from which one could go down to the major public service departments on the two lower floors or take

196

the elevators to the book tower and special research facilities. The finest view of the campus, aptly enough, is from the covered terrace surrounding the top floor of the building. Here one can get a spectacular view of Atlanta's skyline, Decatur, and the Emory campus. Looking down from that height on the surrounding buildings and grounds affords a futuristic version of a Lilliputian pedestrian campus. Even the brutal architecture of the Communicable Disease Center takes on a softer hue.

I shall forbear any description of the interior since there are guidebooks and directories of the contents of each floor, but a few aesthetically pleasing vistas that I feel should be mentioned are succinctly described by my friend and fellow-librarian Turner Cassity, who declared his preferences at the time the building was dedicated. Here is his list:

> Leading off, the main staircase, which could easily accommodate--which seems positively to call for-- a descent of Ziegfeld girls; on the main floor, the very beautiful New Book Room, which in the prose of "The Yellow Book" would have been called a symphony in yellow; also on the main floor, that troll's view of the bridge, from the Reference Department; the super-luxury conference room on stack level six; the Circulation Desk, which (43 feet) is actually the Long Bar, moved here from Shanghai after the Communist take-over; and the great flight deck in the front of the building, with its view of the new Nursing School. Before the benches were placed, the effect was that of the Maginot Line viewed from the U.S.S. "Lexington."

Whether or not one agrees with Turner's choices, he always brings to librarianship the gift of literary presentation. He is never dull, and he has a wonderfully perverse way of evoking scenes and sights from his observation of academia. I would add to his listing the handsome elegance of the Special Collections suite and the magnificent arches that surround the terrace on the top floor; also in the lobbies on all floors, and in the lounge rooms on each stack floor, the colorful array of abstract paintings and the Polish tapestry. The paintings were selected from local art galleries with the invaluable assistance of their generous donor, Elizabeth Loch.

The "super-luxury conference room" to which Turner

197

refers, is the Winship Room, the gift of Charles T. Winship in honor of his brother. It was Winship, it should be remembered, who primed the pump for the new building by his motion in the Trustees' meeting to appoint a committee to plan the new library building. No university library had a more loyal friend during my years of service at Emory.

Though the persons I have mentioned were nearest the heart of the project in getting an incredibly beautiful and well-planned library for Emory, they were by no means the only ones who helped to overcome the obstacles and lassitudes and deferred hopes that are inevitably involved in creating anything startlingly new and costly on a conservative academic campus. There was, for instance, Dean Charles T. Lester of the Graduate School, who helped to secure from federal government grants at least a million of the seven-million-dollar cost of the building. Paul Cousins, the Associate University Librarian, demonstrated what a man with a purely liberal educational background can do in applying his keen intelligence to solving highly technical problems that stumped some of the engineers and technicians. It was he also who supervised the moving of more than half a million volumes from various storage houses on the campus and the Asa Griggs Candler Library to their new home. For this purpose he designed and had the Physical Plant build special booktrucks and chose some forty sturdy lads to carry out the migration. In my mind's eye I can still see that procession of lightly clad figures under a scorching summer sun, with power in their limbs, heads down, arms stretched taut against the truck handles, crisscrossing the Sacred Bridge to move hundreds of thousands of volumes to their new library stacks. The young men became so attached to their trucks, which they called carts, that correctly, as Turner Cassity noted, "thinking that an unchristened ship is an ill omen, they gave their trucks suitable names." Turner especially liked Bank Amerikart, Cartiac Arrest, Descartes, Magna Carta, A la Carte, and Carte Blanche. There was, of course, Robert Burns, the architect chosen from the firm to head the project, a modest man of enormous architectural skill and charming personality, who, unlike too many of his successful specialized breed, was ever ready to listen to librarians who knew better than anyone else what was needed to make a great library a highly efficient and useful tool of education.

In the fifteenth century the Medici, Sforza, and other distinguished families were patrons of the arts and letters.

198

Robert W. Woodruff of Atlanta might well be called a modern-day patron of the arts and letters, if not of individual artists and writers as in Renaissance Italy or in Shakespeare's day, then of art museums and libraries and universities where in the late Dixon Wecter's fine phrase "physical beauty and intellectual achievement merge together." One year before the dedication of the new library building at Emory, October 1968, the University's Board of Trustees decided to name the library the Robert W. Woodruff Library for Advanced Studies. Their resolution read in part:

> The Library for Advanced Studies is designed as the academic heart of Emory University. It is the focal point for advanced and professional scholarship, the custodian of a vast collection of recorded knowledge. ... Now, therefore, be it RESOLVED, that the new facility of Emory University constructed as a library for advanced studies be and is hereby named the
>
> ROBERT W. WOODRUFF LIBRARY
> FOR ADVANCED STUDIES
>
> and, further, that an appropriate area within the library be set aside for such material concerning Mr. Woodruff as may be secured indicative of his life and works.

As important a single influence and force as the Robert W. Woodruff Library for Advanced Studies has been to Emory's development, it can never be to Emory what Widener is to Harvard without a major research collection of books, journals, manuscripts, and other library materials, what Larry Powell so aptly described as "a continuing stockpile of fissionable materials to spark the imagination and ideas of man." Emory's benefactors have come to the University's aid so often, however, that it is easy to see this as just another crisis that will in due course, with energy and ingenuity, be overcome.

The actual construction of the Robert W. Woodruff Library for Advanced Studies began September 10, 1967, and was completed in the fall of 1969. Two days of dedication ceremonies took place October 30 and 31, 1969. The ceremonies began with a black-tie dinner for the Friends of the Library at the Capital City Club on the evening of October 30, my birthday, a fact that passed unnoticed during the rites. A citywide array of distinguished guests and their wives or hus-

199

bands attended the dinner, which was presided over by President Sanford S. Atwood. Following remarks by Mr. Bowden and an announcement of recent gifts to the Library by Dr. Thomas H. English, Executive Secretary of the Friends' association, the principal speaker of the evening, Dr. George H. Healey, Professor of English and Curator of Rare Books at Cornell University, addressed the guests on the subject of "Scholars, Libraries and Rare Books."

The dedicatory exercises began at 10 a.m. the following day on the front plaza of the Robert W. Woodruff Library for Advanced Studies. I wanted Herb Alpert and the Tijuana Brass to lead off the ceremonies, but in view of my responsibility as host to visiting librarians, I was given a light part in the proceedings. Dr. Atwood presided over the dedication ceremonies and introduced the guests on the platform and those participating in the ceremonies. Robert Burns gracefully presented the Library in behalf of his architectural firm, and acceptance was made by Mr. Bowden as Chairman of the Board of Trustees, Charles Haynes as President of the Student Government Association, and Dr. Grant Kaiser as Chairman of the Library Policy Committee. Acceptance speeches are extremely ephemeral, and I have forgotten what was said except for Bowden's imaginative description of a library as "a catalyst which when added to the minds and morals of men serves to intensify and make more effective all the processes of man's education." At the dedication Dr. Healy spoke once again, briefly, and in his address he answered two important questions about the Robert W. Woodruff Library for Advanced Studies: "What happens in a library that is so important?" and "Why is it so important?" As I now reread what he had to say, I feel the same stirring as I did then about the library being a truly and particularly exciting place in which to work. Thus it is with special enthusiasm that I pass on what seems to me to be the essence of his remarks:

> In the flourishing years that lie ahead for this University, much that is thought, taught, studied, cherished, and written about will take its origin in this great house of books. ... The pursuit of learning as we reflect upon it, seems to be often an erratic and unpredictable enterprise, a strangely private affair, quiet, personal, even lonely. In spite of our donnish intentions, learning does not take place always and only in the class room, nor is it imparted always and only by the professor. It often just hap-

pens--that's the word--and happens most memorably and excitingly when we suddenly drop the book into our lap and sense with wonder, even awe, the inner stir that marks the advent of an idea we had never before thought of. One almost gasps at this recurrent miracle, one of those enduring and genuine joys of university life. Students readily forget their professors. No student ever forgets his library.

This library supports firmly and securely the educational program of the university, but it also provides Emory's share of those world-wide resources, available through cooperation and reciprocity, upon which the world's scholarship depends and upon which the advancement of learning is based.

But it is not just to provide material for research projects that the full, copious library is necessary. It is an indispensable asset in the daily life of studying and teaching in a busy university: the examining of a reference, the search for a date, the confirming of a fact, the quick look down an index, the sampling of a new periodical, the serendipitous discovery, the irresistible digression that may lead to a major enthusiasm, the whole moving, stimulating absorption that so often stems from encountering the odd, the rare, the out-of-the-way, the unheard-of--the unusual book or manuscript likely to be come upon only in a library for advanced study.

Scholars may soar high and wander far, but they always need to return to the sources of humane knowledge, the research libraries. It is within those walls that men of learning find refreshment at clear springs. They know, too, that the devotion and sacrifice that have produced the fine libraries have been dedicated to them and their pupils. That is why such libraries so richly deserve their high position in public esteem. It is the library that brings together the collection and the searcher, that learning may be shared. It is the library that brings together the master and the apprentice, that learning may be unbroken. One cannot doubt that this library is Emory's highest pinnacle. But it is also, and at the same time, its deepest foundation.

23: THE TESTIMONY OF FRIENDS

I must go back a bit to the spring of 1964, when on a blustery March morning I found a letter in the morning's mail from Dr. Walter J. Johns, President of the University of Alberta, my alma mater. I could not believe my eyes as I read. Out of a clear sky the President was informing me that the Senate of the University had approved the recommendation of the Committee on Honorary Degrees that I be invited to come to the Spring Convocation in May to receive the Honorary Degree of Doctor of Laws. Since brevity is the soul of wit, I telegraphed my acceptance. I was taking no chances on the Senate changing its mind. A few days later I received word again from President Johns asking me to participate in the opening of the Donald Ewing Cameron Library ceremonies on the day preceding the Convocation and also asking if I would make "a brief (8 minute) address to the graduands and their friends and relatives on the subject of the importance of university libraries in higher education." In his tolerant, sympathetic, understanding way he put this last question in a manner that I could not refuse. "Do you suppose," he wrote, "that you could take on this chore for us?" I had never made a commencement address, but this was an exercise I wasn't going to miss.

A couple of months later I gazed at the faces of fourteen hundred graduands, including twenty-four candidates for the Doctor of Philosophy, and an audience of friends and relatives numbering in all about three thousand. I had expected "O Canada" and the Invocation, but here was a brilliantly arrayed Academic Procession preceded by the Regimental Band of the Princess Patricia's Canadian Light Infantry--enough to daunt the most experienced speaker. But there was still more: the platform imperially draped; the audience rising to sing the national anthem; the President's report; and the conferring of the honorary degrees. When it finally came my turn to speak, it seemed to me a great silence fell over the auditorium. So I let it hang for a few seconds ... then I told them not to worry, President Johns had requested firmly that I confine the tempest of my oratory to eight minutes. That broke the suspense. I have forgotten precisely what I said on that occasion, but it must have been something of world-shaking importance because shortly thereafter there was an earthquake in Alaska and later another in Japan. I made use of the sermon later in a summer commencement address at Emory, which was published, and from a quick check I find that the gist of my remarks was simply that learning to discriminate--to know what to pay attention to and what to let whistle over one's shoulder--was the most important thing that can happen to any of us, in college or after college. H. L. Mencken said it all succinctly many years earlier. "If you have learned to subject popular concepts to critical scrutiny before swallowing them whole, you have learned something of great value."

My beautiful LL.D. hangs in the basement, its lovely Latin phrases overseeing the pool table. My pool partners do not seem to recognize the language they once learned as schoolboys, so I provide a translation, courtesy of my old classical friend, Kevin Guinagh, should anyone ask. Which reminds me that when I was a graduate student at Columbia University, I was rendered speechless when one of the charwomen--a character right out of Dickens--entered my room in Furnald Hall, lifted an arm and pointing to my A.B. diploma in Latin, framed and hanging on the wall, asked "Where do you come from?" I told her I was a Canadian. She said nothing but went about her business swabbing the floor, stopping several times to eye the diploma. Just as she was about to step out into the hall she turned to me and said with a dismissive frown, "A Canadian, eh! I thought you was a bloody foreigner."

The Robert W. Woodruff Library for Advanced Studies was well under construction when I received an invitation to teach in the 1968 summer session of the Graduate Library School of the University of California (Berkeley). With Ruth Walling willing to assume the extra burden of acting in place of the Director of Libraries, and with the oversight of floor, shelving, and furniture plan revisions in Paul Cousins's capable hands, I decided to accept the invitation, particularly since it involved only a short absence beyond my annual vacation from the Library. Margaret had haunting memories of an enjoyable month spent on the West Coast as a teenager and looked forward to revisiting her relatives. Ellen was in residence at Emory. Christopher, who did not take too kindly to salesmanship, was associated with Colgate in three southern states. Jennifer was busy carving out a career for herself while raising three children. Don and his college sweetheart, Pat Rushworth, had been married for some twelve years and were living in Lake Charles, Louisiana, where he was president of a wholesale plumbing and electrical company. There was really nothing to hold us back.

I was elated, of course, not only for the opportunity to visit the western United States but also to trade the role as an administrator for that of instructor, even for a short time, during the hectic days of the student demonstrations of the sixties. A precondition for running a library successfully is that the library should be occupied by students who come there to learn and not to make normal library use impossible by setting off dynamite in the building, throwing stink bombs in the stacks, pouring glue in the catalog trays, or slashing the upholstered furniture. Such wanton acts of aggression took place in academic libraries throughout the country, and Emory was not left entirely unscathed. I shall mention but two incidents, one minor with potential for chaos; the other exasperating, costly, and destructive. In the first instance a black freshman and a white coed staged a sit-in next to the wall exhibit cases in the lobby of the Asa Griggs Candler Library. By nightfall hundreds of students were rushing in and out of the reading rooms to get the latest word on what was happening below. For all practical purposes they closed down the Library for study and research. The excuse given for the sit-in tactics was a small medal in the corner of one of four large recessed wall cases, where there was displayed an exhibit for new students depicting student activities, accomplishments, and awards during the previous decade. The medal had been given to a student by a foundation for leadership in support of America's part in Vietnam during the Kennedy days. Since the medal was awarded, public opinion had taken a hundred-and-eighty-degree turn.

By nightfall more students had swelled the crowd until it was practically impossible to get in the library. In retrospect I find it very difficult to recreate in words the tensions of that long fall night, but I thought then, as I do now, that almost any incident could have provoked an explosion that would have resulted in serious injury to individuals and damage to the library. Finally, near midnight, with the assistance of a very composed young man from the office of the Dean of Men who persuaded the black student to leave the Library with him, we cleared the building and locked up for the night. Outside there were still several hundred students waiting to see what the Dean's assistant was going to do. My guess is that he persuaded the boy to go back to his room and sleep it off. The irony of the whole debacle was revealed the next morning. As soon as the library doors were open, the student returned to sit on the floor beneath the exhibit case containing the medal. I wanted no repetition of the previous day, which was a complete loss so far as library use was concerned, so I told him that I planned to have the entire exhibit on student life removed that morning and suggested that he pick up his books and go about his business or else I would be obliged to have him hauled off. I pointed out that he had made his point with his fellow students and that there was no further excuse for continuing the sit-in. He agreed, somewhat reluctantly as I remember it, picked up his books, and went upstairs to study. Half an hour later he came down to my office to ask if he could put up a sign in one of the empty exhibit cases to inform his friends that he was now located in the Science Reading Room. My answer was impolite, but there the matter ended.

The second incident resulted from an incorrect rumor that undergraduates would not be permitted to use the Library for Advanced Studies, then under construction. Some delinquents with no real injustice to fight against spray-painted an entire side of the new construction in large red letters with the message "Undergrads Read Too." This senseless act cost the University several thousand dollars to remove by sandblasting and delayed construction a week or more. A professor legitimated the act by saying that it symbolized student freedom of expression, but I doubt if this reasoning was calculated to take in any sizable portion of academics. For my part I was getting more and more fed up with academic life in the sixties. My unhappiness lay less in the academic community, no doubt, than in me. I simply had no taste for the kind of life I was leading. There was pressure on everyone to sacrifice personal convictions for the sake of campus politics. No one seemed to trust anyone else on the campus.

205

My thoughts and most of my time were occupied with everything but librarianship. I felt increasingly isolated from an
administration that seemed ready to let the sparks fly where
they may, and from those members of the faculty who seemed
all too ready to bare their liberal consciences in class in order to avoid a reactionary label among the students. Even if
I was about to enter Berkeley, the heartland of student anarchy,
I did not expect any trouble in the Graduate Library School classes. As it turned out it was not student revolt that bothered me,
but rather my feeling of insufficiency in teaching one of two
classes, a seminar, in which the students had such a wide
range of experience and specialization that it was difficult to
find common ground for lectures and discussion. What little
I saw of student anarchy might better be described as student
apathy, although there were reports of fighting at night. Each
day as I wound my way along the campus byways to the Library, I saw dozens of bodies--boys and girls, with duffle
coats, jeans, bare feet, and long dirty hair--sprawled out on
the green engaged in what might be described as a "lie-in"
or else sitting in a leaning position against the trees strum-
ming their guitars. When I returned home in the afternoon,
the guitars were still vibrating. They had no job, no classes,
no vocation. While I toiled away at my classes, they sang
"Burn, Baby, Burn." But as my friend Kevin Guinagh explained to me, "we must remember that Troy was burned to
the ground by the Greeks, and from its ashes, so goes the
myth, the seed of Rome grew."

We had a wonderful time at Berkeley and environs that
summer. In most ways Berkeley represents the last word in
climate and scenery, at least during the summer months. We
lived high on the side of a hill overlooking the campus, San
Francisco Bay, the Bay Bridge, and the Golden Gate Bridge.
By day we could see rows of houses, apartments, factories,
and other buildings, on the lower flats, shining brightly in the
sun. By late evening endless bands of electric lights ran lat-
erally across the horizon and vertically up the hill, and then,
just as suddenly as if a giant fuse had blown, they all went
out when the fog rolled in in huge waves of gray cotton wool.
If the fog remained until late morning the next day, the temperature might drop to fifty degrees, but by midday it would
climb rapidly into the seventies under a hot sun. There was
a saying around Berkeley that in the summer you got out your
overcoat and ordered a half-cord of firewood. It was that
way when we were there. The furnace turned on automatically every morning for at least an hour or so. We took won-

derful walks in the general neighborhood of our house and enjoyed the ferns and flowers and lovely gardens. Trees grew everywhere, especially oak, pine, and eucalyptus. I remember seeing a palm tree next to a Canadian spruce on the campus. We had a beautiful apricot tree in our front yard, but some varmit stole the fruit when we were absent one weekend, just when the apricots were ripe enough to eat. There were a few times when we locked our doors when motorcycles roared around the streets at night and gunshots were heard from the campus below. I suspect that our fears were wholly imaginary, fed by rumor and the press. But in any case Berkeley fascinated us even though we did not always understand it.

My class schedule was Monday, Wednesday, Friday 3 to 4 p.m. and Thursday, a seminar, 3 to 5:30 p.m. I soon felt the need to know the university library situation in California better, and fortunately I had time to look around. Accordingly, as soon as classes were over on Thursday afternoon, we rented a car and bolted for the campuses of the other seven or eight satellites of the University of California. The more I traveled the more I saw evidence of change in the thinking and practices of university librarians and libraries. In my working career, it seemed to me, we had moved from the professor-librarian stage to the professionally trained librarian-bookman and were now facing another turning point brought about by a rapidly expanding complex of knowledge communication. I began to feel that the present-day university librarian might well be a vanishing breed.

It was in this climate of rapid change that I decided it might be useful to make a record for the future, so I taped my conversations with the librarians whom I interviewed on the West Coast and recorded their observations in a small paperback entitled "The Librarian Speaking," published by the University of Georgia Press in 1970. Most of the topics covered in the talks were, naturally, familiar, but others reflected the social and technological changes that were taking place at the time. I thought of the conversations primarily as material to be used in my seminar course and hoped that they might be useful in other ways. I was delighted then when a year after the book was published I received a letter from a distinguished university librarian, whom I had met at meetings but knew largely by reputation, in which he wrote: "Your last ["The Librarian Speaking"], you will be interested to know, provoked all kinds of discussion on the part of my students. It left some of 'em in despair; others reassured, and still others, those of faint spirit, determined to go into public libraries as fast as they could!" The book had a better press than I ever dreamed of, but having said this I feel obliged to say that it received the most thorough damnation from Arthur Hamlin ("Library Journal," July 1970) of anything I ever wrote. Everything about the book was rotten, not even a good word about the photographs and the good printing job. It was "at best a potpourri of subjects, many of which could better be handled by short essays." My thought that the interviews might make for good reading missed the mark. Arthur wrote "Your reviewer certainly did not find that the 'technique of questions and answers ... makes for stimulating and pleasant reading' as promised in the preface, but something quite the opposite." I evidently showed monumental stupidity in thinking that the book might have some appeal to educators other than librarians. "It is doubtful," said the review, "that many readers outside the library profession will get beyond the first few pages, wherever the volume is opened." This was the only review of a book of mine that I ever read to my classes.

24: L'ENVOI

This is my seventy-third birthday--beyond my actuarial expectancy of life, hence the title of this book, "Beyond My Expectation," or however one may wish to interpret it. I have been without guaranteed employment for approximately eight years. When I retired in 1972, honors began falling about my graying temples like fog around the brain. Since these honors are all reported in "The Academic Library" (1974), a handsome book of essays edited by my friends Evan I. Farber and Ruth Walling, I am spared the embarrassment of mentioning them without fear of discourtesy to those who honored me. However, I would have Emory University, the American Library Association, and the Southeastern Library Association know that I am deeply grateful for their esteem. And I am of course deeply appreciative of the benefits and kindness Margaret and I received from the Library staff. When all the speeches are made, when the makeup is off, and when the press notices stop, there is still one letter among many that I received from friends at the time of my retirement that I take to a dark corner and read when my spirits are low. It was written by one of America's leading historians, Dr. Bell I. Wiley, Candler Professor of History, Emory University, a magnificent teacher and prolific researcher and author. When Bell died of a heart attack last year, a light went out. At the risk of being called an unredeemable egotist, I reprint this letter herewith. Of course, friendship rather than any merit on my part prompted the letter, but it is a fact that I have always struggled to be the kind of librarian and human being that Bell describes.

2 November 1972

Dear Guy:

Attached is a clipping from last night's "Journal"; I thought you might have use for an extra copy.

I can't realize that you've actually retired, but the fact will make itself felt in many ways as the days roll by. Since I taught my first college class 44 years ago, I have observed librarians with particular interest, because of my interest in books, and because the effectiveness and cooperation of librarians was so very essential to the work that I was trying to do. You are by far the best librarian with whom I have been associated, and I owe you a great debt for the assistance that you have given to me and to my students--and in a larger realm for the great contribution that you have made to the institutions, and the intellectual communities, with which you and I have been associated. Your professional expertness has been matched by admirable personal qualities and by a cultural appreciation that have done much to enrich the life of the campuses on which you have worked.

I know of no one who has done more than you, against considerable odds, to start Emory on the road toward greatness as a university. I shall always be proud of the fact that when Howard Phillips asked me one day in front of the history building--in 1953 I think it was--if I knew of a first-rate librarian who might be available to succeed Margaret Jemison, I immediately replied: "The best librarian I know is Guy Lyle of LSU. They are not treating him right down there, and it just might be that you could get him."

I have enjoyed immeasurably the association and friendship with you since first we met at LSU in September 1946. God bless you and give you many more years of service and happiness.

Affectionately,
Bell Wiley

After retirement it takes time to accustom oneself to the simple life--"to a definite time for rising and setting," as my friend Kevin Guinagh would say. We need a kind of decompression chamber that would permit us to habituate ourselves gradually to the routine of a new existence. And so when the opportunity presented itself to teach the winter session of 1973 at the University of Puerto Rico Graduate School of Librarianship, I jumped at the chance. It would be difficult for me to be too grateful to Dr. Frederick E. Kidder, the Director of the School, and his faculty for the opportunity to spend a delightful winter and spring in San Juan.

My first impression as a professor at the University of Puerto Rico was--why didn't I learn about this life earlier. It's a hard life. I had nine hours of classes a week; as a librarian at Emory I spent nine hours a day at the office. For Holy Week in April we were free for seven days. Some activist slugged a dean and burned off the top of the social science building; the campus was closed down for three days. In May was a three-day intervarsity track meet; classes were dismissed. This sure kept me humping.

My students in the Graduate School of Librarianship were all bilingual although hesitant about spoken English; a few had received their undergraduate education in the United States. They were very attentive in class and great note-takers. They bore down heavily on the pencil, copied down everything I said, and then memorized it. I did my best to discourage note-taking because I felt it was a kind of mental anesthetic, like TV. I handed out outlines of my lectures and used the blackboard a great deal for names and statistics, following Kevin's advice from his experience teaching at the College of Mayaguez after his first retirement. "Humor," he advised, "comes last of all."

I noticed that students seemed to have a chronic problem about getting to class on time. They would drop in at various times after the class had begun, as casually as if it were the local bar. I think I might have found this disconcerting had I taught there on a regular basis, but being merely a "prof. visitante" I thought it best to say nothing. What really bugged me, however, was my inability to arouse any satisfactory kind of unstructured class discussion. It would be easy to account for this by saying it was the students' difficulty with spoken English and my ignorance of Spanish, but this was only part of the problem. I believe the simple truth of the matter was that they were not accustomed to any kind of instruction other than lecture and note-taking. Whenever they took the bait in my class and started a discussion, it rapidly turned into a dozen or more bull sessions with each student arguing in Spanish with students on either side or im-

211

mediately in front and back. When I banged the desk to restore order, they clammed up and said nothing for the re-
mainder of the hour. In spite of my language insufficiency,
however, I had a grand time with the students in both classes
and I hope that I may have helped them in some small way.
They were very nice to me, real friendly and pleasant. One
young woman, the head librarian in a junior college in mid-
Puerto Rico, wrote a perfectly charming letter just before I
left and urged me to return.

We lived near the University on the outskirts of San
Juan, which was fortunate. Except for old San Juan, an area
seven blocks square once enclosed within the frame of the
City Wall and forts El Morro and San Cristobal, the city is
architecturally uninspiring. It is the product of the automobile age. A whole lot older than Detroit, Chicago, and Pittsburgh, the city seemed to have more automobiles per square
foot than all the other three combined. At least, after a gro-
cery shopping spree, we found it almost impossible to cross
Ponce de Leon to Barbosa Street in the late afternoon. No
matter when you left the city on the expressway to Bayamon,
the lanes were blocked with long somber lines of slow-moving
cars. They reminded me of a convoy traveling under escort
with the periscopic exhaust pipes of diesel-powered trucks
contributing their full share to the smog and dirt that hung
over the city. Even as far out as our residence, we would
wake up at 6 a.m. with the house full of exhaust fumes from
the early-morning traffic entering the city. The same was
true from 5 until 9 p.m. in the evening. However, when we
motored to the other end of the island, we learned what is
meant by good clean air. Sitting on Nina Jacobs's country
porch, about a hundred yards from a high bluff overlooking
the ocean, we felt a sense of exhilaration from the refreshing
breeze of the easterly trade winds. I sat and rocked and
watched the egrets follow the cows, and drank in great gulps
of the good air.

Another pleasant memory I have of the island is the
ocean itself, the deep blue-green ocean. As one swings
around the island by car, the ocean suddenly comes into view
with unfailing beauty and unending variety. At one point the
waves rush in to send a vast wheel of foam crashing against
the rocks. If you are standing within a hundred feet of the
rocks, you can be soaked by whirling spray. At another point
the ocean spreads out to the vast horizon like a huge blue-
green pond, and here on a clear day you can see ships like
small white shadows breaking the blue horizon.

The patio of our rented house was both a joy and, on a few occasions, a source of shock. There were few birds, but we enjoyed the lemon yellow-bellied pewees who filled the surrounding shrubs with their plaintive whistle--pee-oo-wee, pee-oo. In the evening, especially after a rain, the tiny tree frogs entertained us with their melodious call--coqui, coqui. The shrubs were all the flowering kind, and none was more beautiful than the red trinitaria and the pale blue Queen Isabella. Trees bordered the avenue in front of the house and along the street, and of these we found most striking the yellow flamboyants and the royal poincianas with their scarlet petals. Not far from our house, as was true in most suburban areas, were large blocks of public housing. Unfortunately the garbage for these places was allowed to pile high in overflowing cans at the side and rear of the housing, an open invitation to rats. I have heard the phrase "culture shock" many times without any real understanding of what it meant until I saw the children playing in the squalor of this slum. And eating breakfast on a bright sunny morning on our patio, we were revolted by seeing two large rats scurrying across the floor.

When we first landed on the enchanting island, as the natives refer to it, I hired three cars in succession from the National Rental Service before getting one in which we felt enough confidence to drive beyond the city limits. Even this one had a slow leak in the tires. The service station manager beat on the rim of each wheel with a tire iron and pronounced the tires "O. K. "--"Just keep adding air" was his advice. As a special favor he turned up the air guage from twenty-five to thirty-five pounds for our use. Our house in San Juan also presented some problems. It belonged to a doctor studying in the United States. The principal problem was the landlady in his absence--his mother. Of the three bedrooms in the house, only one was furnished. We pushed for having the mattress in this room replaced because there was grave danger of sliding off on either side when sleeping, due to a ridge in the center. There was also a short in the electric stove that gave us some nasty jolts when cooking. Our landlady would do nothing about either one. Repair work, she said, would take two months, and then the job would not last more than a month. Meanwhile we could take a chance on being electrocuted. The San Juan telephone company insisted on charging long distance telephone calls to Brooklyn against our account. When we assured them that we knew no one in Brooklyn since the mayor went to jail, they peremptorily cut off our phone. But they reckoned without our land-

213

lady, who immediately came to the rescue. A house without a phone meant a substantial loss in rent after our departure. She explained to the phone people that the ignorant Americanos didn't really understand old San Juan's boozy ways, and the phone was promptly reinstalled.

By the end of April our days in San Juan were drawing to a close. We had been royally entertained by old and new friends. We attended the Rector's ball as guests of Dr. and Mrs. Kidder, where we met members of the faculty and their wives from other departments of the University. The line was two-deep in front of the bar and the music enchanting in the lighted and flower-festooned gardens. I was a guest of one of my students at La Casa del Libro, which contained a library on the history of the book and several incunabula. The library was founded by Elmer Adler, the authority on printing and the graphic arts at Princeton before he moved to San Juan after his retirement. There were many lovely country scenes to store up in our memories as we motored around the island--the seventeenth-century Porta Coeli Church in San German, which stands high on a peak overlooking a town straight out of Old World Spain; the giant fern trees and groves of tall bamboo in the Rain Forest at El Yunge; the seine fishers at Fajardo hauling in their nets at sunset filled with the day's catch; oxen yoked to two-wheel carts carrying tobacco to the curing sheds; the sugar fields and rum factory at Arecibo; lunch at Dorado's beautiful beach and hotel; and happy hunting in old San Juan for good food, native carvings, silverwork, and other souvenirs.

I suppose we did not see enough of Puerto Ricans themselves, but that was not entirely our fault. Our Puerto Rican neighbors seemed quite reserved. There were the usual greetings and offers of assistance when we first met, but that was about all we saw of them. Yet I am sure their help in time of real need would be readily offered. A slight incident may illustrate. When we first arrived, the tire on our first rented car blew out. There were no service stations around, and I did not know quite what to do since the car apparently lacked the tools for changing a tire. At that moment a young man came out from the house across the street, took in our predicament at a glance, produced a jack and tools from his own car, and went to work immediately changing the tire. When he finished, he cautioned us to drive carefully, giving specific directions for returning to the airport where we had rented the car so that we might exchange it before the other tires gave out.   He would accept nothing for his help except our thanks.

It remained for us to visit El Commandante, which the guidebook describes as the most beautiful racetrack in the world, where "great thoroughbreds and outstanding jockeys" compete three times a week.   I knew nothing about a racetrack but liked horses very much.   We had lunch in the glass-enclosed dining room but decided to sit outside in the spectators' seating for the races themselves.   Just before they began I noticed that quite a few people were studying a yellow sheet or chart, so I thought I had better get one and left our seats to see what I could find.   By the time I discovered the person distributing the racing sheets on the lower floor, the warning bell sounded, announcing the imminent start of the first race.   I hurried back upstairs, pushed the sheet through the window slot of a betting booth and pointing my finger to number 3, said "Put five dollars on this one!"   The man gave me a strange look, somewhat disdainfully turned the sheet over and said "This is the line up for the first race."   To cover up my humiliation I pointed my finger to the same number on the side he indicated and said stubbornly "Well, put five dollars on this one then!"   The horses were already at the starting point when I got back to our seats, and in a few seconds someone behind us shouted "Come on Brandywine."   The whole row in front of us rose to their feet to join in with "Brandywine, Brandywine!" and sure enough "Brandywine" breezed in.   I looked at my ticket stub; number 3 was "Brandywine."   I collected thirty-one dollars and fifty cents.   From then on our luck deserted us.   I don't know how much the management took in that day, but we certainly contributed our share.

On our return from Puerto Rico in the summer of 1973 I devoted my spare time to preparing a complete revision of "The Administration of the College Library," consulting work, writing for the professional journals, and talks that I could not decently decline.   We exchanged visits with our children and grandchildren, coupled calls on eastern college librarians with motor trips through the New England countryside to see the gorgeous fall colors, and on our return accepted an offer from the University of Southern California School of Library Science to teach three classes during the 1974 winter semester.

In Los Angeles we were most fortunate in being able

215

to rent a comfortable and spacious furnished apartment in a complex overlooking the Pacific Ocean and located on the dividing line between Redondo Beach and Palos Verdes Estates. Old friends from Greensboro, North Carolina, Calvin and Helen Warfield, were living there and were able to rent for us an apartment that was temporarily available during the time we were there. The apartment complex was perched high on an enormous bluff overlooking the ocean, with beautiful plantings of shrubs and grass within its inner court. The buildings were almost pentagon-shaped, with one end open to the ocean side. The area around a large heated pool (eighty-two degrees) was like a mini-city park--flowers and flowering shrubs, vines, and creepers, all blooming, according to one resident "on some private schedule of their own." There were camellias and azaleas in flower from February through April; colorful beds of giant pansies, crocuses, and California poppies; terraces covered with pale-pink geraniums in flower; and hanging baskets of beautiful, flowering cacti--all interlaced among neatly clipped, bright green lawns. At one end open to the ocean there was a parking area with a low wall along the edge of the bluff. Almost every afternoon we spent a little time there watching the surf cream into the shore, young men and women in rubber suits surfing in the ocean, glider-club members flying their colorful machines in great wide circles out to the ocean and back for half an hour or longer at a time before landing gracefully on the beach, gulls following schools of fish, and literally hundreds of sailboats darting hither and yon. It was a superb seascape--gay, boisterous, youthful, and ever changing, a scene never to be forgotten. The sun touching the far horizon as day drew to a close gave us peace and rejuvenation. Blessed by ocean, soil, and climate, this was indeed an abode of happiness.

The hospitality of the Warfields was beyond praise. From the moment we arrived we were made to feel that we were part of the household. Helen took Margaret shopping, for drives along the oceanfront and past the lovely homes precariously perched on the side of the surrounding hills, to visit the Music Center and other tourist attractions in the heart of the city, to lunches and meetings of her club groups, to shop, and to attend church. This fine hospitality was as much a joy to me as it was for Margaret because it left me free to attend to my class preparation and lectures without the feeling that my wife was missing out on all the attractive things to be seen and done in this winter paradise. And on weekends there were wonderful visits together to the Huntington and its magnificent Desert and Japanese gardens, the Los Angeles County Museum and the Getty Museum, the Farmer's Market, shopping, and restaurants on the Redondo Beach wharfs. We did not make as many trips along the coastal towns as we would have liked because we had to conserve gasoline, which I got the hard way by rising at 5 a.m. to wait in line for the service station to open at 7 a.m. Even then the limit was five gallons if one were fortunate enough to get to the pumps before the gas was all gone.

There were times when I thought everybody in southern California must be on vacation. People were constantly on the move and appeared to be choosing their own time when to come and go. But amid this paradise it was not an idle one for me. I contributed to the coming and going to be sure; indeed, Kevin wrote once that he thought I must be in training for the Indianapolis 500. Five days a week I drove twenty-five miles to the University and twenty-five miles back on the Bar Harbor Freeway. I then had ten miles to go across town to reach our apartment. After exiting at Exposition Park on my way to the University, I would search for a parking space along with twenty-five thousand other students and faculty in one of several large parking areas on the boundaries of the campus. No cars were allowed inside, which made it possible to move freely on foot from building to building or anywhere on campus grounds without interruption and in safety. I loved it and frequently sat on a bench eating my lunch while listening to the University orchestra performing at a noontime concert. The Library School classes were held in a spanking-new building devoted to library science instruction. This was the product of Dean Martha Boaz's planning, administrative skill, determination, and boundless energy. Something of the Virginian spirit of superciliousness and independence of mind and action hovers over this transplanted genius, but those who know her well find her very attractive. I can never be sufficiently grateful for her inconceivable generosity to Margaret and myself. My classes were a bit larger than I was accustomed to in summer sessions, but the students were eager to learn and some had minds and personality of marked distinction. As usual I was not very successful in teaching them anything, but a guy away from home always gets credit for even the slightest manifestation of intelligence and efficiency.

After our return from Los Angeles I felt that we had been long enough in the decompression chamber and it was now

217

time to settle down and enjoy life at home. There were a
number of attractive offers, but I cast them aside. The si-
rens of consulting, teaching, and conventions could sing their
sweetest songs, but I would never hear them. Once or twice
a year thereafter I did come out of the world of infinite leisure to bring the gospel of hope to librarians who look up and
are not fed, but I remained invisible to all others who would
have designs upon my time. To give up my profession did
not mean abandoning the book. To reject the book is to reject the mind. But now for once in my life I can read without a purpose: books as ends in themselves. I can fight the
Battle of Britain with Churchill with no other reason than living through a fascinating period in British history. I can
read the mysteries of Kenneth Fearing and Cecil Day-Lewis
(much better writers of mysteries than verse) with no feeling
of guilt that I am neglecting reviews for the "Library Quarterly." I can now play tennis or squash at any hour I am able
to find a partner. I have attained what Kevin says all men
desire--"absolute control of my time." And twice a year our
lives are made brighter and more interesting by entertaining
or visiting Kevin and Marie Guinagh, who decided after re-
tiring, first from Illinois, then again from Mayaguez, to settle in Temple Terrace, Florida. Kevin and I play pool, take
walks, and browse among the bookshops. He spends much
time poring over ancient works by fifteenth-century monks on
how to make gunpowder out of cow dung and charcoal.

We are now grandparents. Grandparents usually spend
much time looking down on the present world out of oval
frames hanging on the wall, but we still manage to get around.
Both our granddaughters, Donna and Laura, are married; two
of our grandsons, Greg and Kevin, are in college; a third
grandson, David, is in school and cannot understand why we
are still about; and a fourth, two-year-old Connor, uses a
plastic lawnmower to cut our grass twice a year. Margaret
enjoys the second generation as much as she did the first.

I am a suburbanite with rural yearnings now. I maintain a locker in the Emory University gymnasium and a buck-
skin quarterhorse at a country boarding stable. I read "The
New Yorker" and the London "Spectator," the best-edited
journals of both countries, and scan the Atlanta-based "Farmers and Consumers Market Bulletin" for sales of herbs, honey, and horses. The sounds and smells of the country are
with me all day, all night, if I attend--to use Kevin's words--
"It's like the roar of the sea one hears in a large shell on

the beach, or like the cicadas that keep singing in the trees, all summer and all fall."

Hunter Ridge Farm consists of a small living quarters, barns, tack room, two small paddocks, a riding ring, trailers, tractors, and other farm equipment scattered about like the aftermath of a bombing raid. The Farm is approached by a side road bisecting white-wood-fenced pastures; gay, fussy little houses; and one fascinating Queen Anne-style residence, recently painted a dazzling white, with multiple gables and a gazebo integrated into a long balustraded veranda. There are no advertising signs there, just vast stretches of woodlands, mares with their foals running loose alongside or cavorting around the edges of the fences, cattle watering at some rusted, old discarded bathtub, and meadows full of flowering shrubs and trees. These are the kinds of things that give relief from the busyness of the city and help to fill up the blank spaces in one's sensibilities.

The scene at the Farm is dominated by a magnificent pasture spread over a great area extending at its base from the riding ring and gradually sloping upwards to a cozy-looking cabin at the hilltop. Back of the cabin, sheltered from the wind but wide open to the senses, is my harbor of repose. I love it there in every season and return time and time again like an old horse hurrying back to the barn for his feed. To me it is a place to discover one's self wholly apart from the normal requirements of everyday living, to feel intensely and satisfyingly the assurance of reality, and to catch some sense of the infinite and spiritual from nature.